SPORTS
FIRSTS_____

SPORTS FIRSTS

PATRICK CLARK

Van Nostrand Reinhold Company
New York Cincinnati Toronto London Melbourne

SPORTS

FIRSTS

First published in paperback in 1983
Copyright © 1981 by Facts On File, Inc.
Library of Congress Catalog Card Number 82-50701
ISBN 0-442-21449-9

Printed in the United States of America

Van Nostrand Reinhold Company Inc.
135 West 50th Street
New York, NY 10020

Fleet Publishers
1410 Birchmount Road
Scarborough, Ontario M1P 2E7, Canada

Cloth edition published 1981 by Facts On File, Inc.

16   15   14   13   12   11   10   9   8   7   6   5   4   3   2   1

To Mom, who always believed.

To my wife, Carol Lea, number one assistant and friend.

To Mark Clark and George Johnson, brother and friend, friend and brother.

To John Sabin, who opened the door and made it possible.

To Bill Wilson, who gave it back when it was almost gone.

CONTENTS

Marathon • First Olympic Prank • First Off-Year Games • First American to Win
an Olympic Marathon • First U.S. Athlete to Win 10 Gold Medals • First Man to
Win Both the Pentathlon and the Decathlon in One Olympiad; First American to
Have Medals Revoked • First U.S. Woman to Win an Olympic Gold Medal; First
Woman to Win Three Gold Medals in One Olympiad • First Man to Win Two
Olympic Sculling Titles on the Same Day • First Winter Olympic Games • First
Diver to Win Springboard and Highboard Diving Titles the Same Year • First
Woman to Win Gold Medals for the Same Event at Two Successive Games • First
Runner to Win Seven Gold Medals • First American to Win Gold Medals at Both
Summer and Winter Olympic Games • First Equestrian to Win an Individual Gold
Medal in Two Consecutive Olympiads; First Horse to Compete in Three Consecu-
tive Three-Day Events • First Swimmer to Win the 200-Meter Olympic Breaststroke
Event Twice • First American to Win a Gold Medal in Figure Skating • First U.S.
Skier to Win a Gold Medal • First Woman to Win Four Gold Medals in Track and
Field • First U.S. Skier to Win Two Gold Medals • First American to Play on Two
Olympic Basketball Teams • First Man to Defend the Gold Medal Successfully in the
Decathlon • First American Woman to Win a Gold Medal in Figure Skating • First
Skier to Win All Three Alpine Skiing Events in One Olympiad • First Rider to Win
Two Individual Gold Medals for Dressage • First Diver to Win Both Springboard
and Platform Diving Championships at Two Consecutive Olympiads; First Woman
to Win Four Gold Medals in Olympic Swimming Competition • First Gold Medal
Winner from Black Africa; First Man to Win the Olympic Marathon Twice • First
American Woman to Win Three Gold Medals in Track and Field • First Triple
Jumper to Surpass the 17-Meter Barrier • First Man to Win the 110-Meter Hurdles
Twice • First Athlete to Win Four Gold Medals During One Year's Winter
Olympics • First Americans to Win Medals in Men's Alpine Skiing • First Man to
Win Nine Medals in Cross-Country Skiing • First Rider to Win Two Individual
Gold Medals for Show Jumping • First Swimmer to Win Gold Medals in the Same
Event in Three Successive Olympics • First Swimmer to Win Four Gold Medals in
One Olympiad • First Middle-Distance Runner to Win Three Individual Olympic
Gold Medals • First Woman to Win Nine Gold Medals • First Woman to Carry the
Olympic Torch; First Olympic Games Held in Latin America • First American to
Win a Gold Medal in Show Jumping • First Swimmer to Win Three Gold Medals in
Individual Events in One Olympiad • First Runner to Win Two Consecutive Gold
Medals in the 100-Meter Race • First Man to Exceed 29 Feet in the Long Jump
• First Man to Win Gold Medals in Four Consecutive Olympiads • First Winter
Olympics Held in Asia • First Woman to Win Gold Medals in Both the Giant
Slalom and the Downhill • First Swimmer to Win the 1500-Meter Freestyle Event at
Two Successive Olympiads • First Female Swimmer to Win Gold Medals in Three
Individual Events While Setting New World Records in All Three at One Olympiad
• First Man to Win Seven Gold Medals in a Single Olympiad • First Man to Win
Gold Medals in Wrestling at Three Successive Olympiads • First Man to Receive a
Medal 50 Years Late • First U.S. Medalist in Cross-Country Skiing • First Gymnast
to Receive a Perfect Score in Olympic Competition • First Blacks from the United
States to Participate in the Winter Olympics • First Sisters to Qualify for the Same
Olympic Event •

LIST OF ILLUSTRATIONS

1. The 1869 Cincinnati Red Stockings
2. Moses Fleetwood Walker
3. Honus Wagner
4. Neal Ball (with Amby McConnell, Heinie Wagner and Jake Stahl)
5. Shoeless Joe Jackson
6. Ty Cobb
7. Mel Ott
8. Ernie Nevers
9. Jay Berwanger
10. George S. Halas
11. Willie Thrower
12. Harlon Hill
13. Pat Palinkas
14. Dr. James A. Naismith
15. Ann Meyers
16. Bill Smith
17. Aristides
18. Sir Barton
19. Diane Crump
20. Ray Harroun
21. Janet Guthrie
22. Kathy Whitworth
23. Richard D. Sears
24. Ellen F. Hansell (with Bertha Townsend, Margie Ballard and Louise Allerdice)
25. The America's Cup
26. Blondin
27. Anna Taylor
28. Sonja Henie
29. John L. Sullivan
30. James J. Corbett
31. Jack Johnson
32. Rocky Marciano
33. The *Gossamer Condor*

ACKNOWLEDGMENTS

I gratefully acknowledge the assistance of Facts On File editor Bob Hutchins, who helped turn *Sports Firsts* from a rambling manuscript into a book; of Penelope Edelhart, who did most of the photo research for this book, and managed to track down some wonderful pictures; of Marjorie Bank, James Johnson and K. L. Roth at Facts On File, who compiled the index; and of my wife, Carol Lea Clark, for her assistance throughout the course of this project.

INTRODUCTION

Organized athletic activity dates back almost to the dawn of human history. And sports have played an important role in virtually every human culture. But, throughout history, some cultures have placed much greater emphasis on sports than others. Today there is probably no other nation where sports constitute as important a part of the national life as in the United States. It is a rare American who has no interest, either as a participant or as an observer, in one athletic endeavor or another. One need look no farther than to the language all of us share to observe the degree to which our lives are influenced by sports: Such expressions as "Monday morning quarterback," "the ball's in your court" and "par for the course"—sports expressions all—are now widely used in contexts having nothing to do with sports.

We like to play sports, we like to watch them—and we also like to talk about them. It's a safe bet that in most gatherings, say, Monday mornings in offices, or Friday nights in bars, sports are a major topic of conversation. And our conversations about sports tend to demonstrate some other typically American characteristics: We value precision and we value success. Luckily for us, there's an easy way of taking each of these national obsessions—with sports, with precision and with success—and combining them into one neat package. It's called statistics. Statistics allow us to measure precisely an individual's success (or lack of it) in just about any sport. In fact, it would probably be fair to say that statistics have become the language of sports—a language that all sports fans understand, because it can be applied fairly and accurately to every athlete or every team. You can't argue with a win-loss record, or an earned run average, or an average speed in an auto race.

Statistics helped inspire this book. There are a lot of statistics here—but this is not a book of statistics. It's a book of firsts. After all, the baseball player who hits 60 home runs one year may hit 20 the next. The basketball player who scores 100 points in one game may only have scored 30 in the game before. But the *first* player to hit 60 home runs in a year, or to score 100 points in a game, or whatever, will always be the first.

Now, being first by no means guarantees immortality. Take, for example, Alexander Cartwright. "Who?" you may ask. Well, as it happens Alexander Cartwright, not Abner Doubleday, probably deserves to be known as the father of our national pastime.

But an account of firsts does tell us some important things about sports. There's a piece in this book, for example, on the first man to run a mile in four minutes. Fifty years from now, though, a new book called *Sports Firsts* might also include a story on the first person to run a mile in three and a half minutes. This points up two important things that characterize sports, and maybe competition in general: The first is that, over the years, levels of performance in most athletic pursuits tend to improve. The second—which may be what's responsible for the first—is that once a first has been established, it represents a standard against which every athlete can compete. Once someone has run a mile in three and a half minutes—and that will probably happen sooner than we'd think—there will be another first waiting to be established: Might a human being some day run a mile in three minutes? It hardly seems possible—but then, 100 years ago it was inconceivable that someone might one day run a mile in four minutes. Really, the only limits on athletic performance are those imposed by the human body—and the human imagination.

By no means do the firsts recounted in this book, however, all involve performance—which is why this is not a book of statistics, or of records. Many of the firsts included here cannot be surpassed, because they represent absolutes. No longer is it possible for someone to become, say, the first woman to race in the Indianapolis 500. Even there, though, the fact that one first has taken place makes another possible: A woman has yet to *win* the Indianapolis 500. And firsts of this sort tell us a lot about our history and culture—in many cases, more than we might care to know. There was a man named Moses Fleetwood Walker, for example, a black man who played major league baseball some 60 years before the world had ever heard of Jackie Robinson. That's significant for two reasons: First, it's interesting—and perhaps rather surprising—to learn that a black man was playing major league baseball in the 1880s. Second—and more importantly—for over half a century blacks were unofficially banned from the major leagues, *even after* Walker had played for a predominantly white major league team.

In other words, the *real* sports firsts are often important for what they show us has been left out of the myths we all live by. Most American schoolchildren know, for example, that Jim Thorpe, American Indian and athlete *extraordinaire*, became the first man ever to win both the pentathlon and the decathlon in the Olympics in 1912—and that his medals were subsequently revoked, an act which remains controversial to this day. But few realize that a military man named George S. Patton competed in the Olympic pentathlon that same year. And although the young "Blood and Guts" did quite creditably, his performance never threatened to overshadow Thorpe's. He finished in fifth place.

Sports firsts, then, are enlightening for what they tell us about sports, for what they tell us about our history and culture—and, ultimately, for what they tell us about ourselves. I've certainly learned a great deal in writing this book, and I hope that most of its readers do, too. But it would be misleading to say that this book was written primarily to educate—either its author or its readers. No—sports above all else are *fun*, and I hope this book conveys some of the fun we all find in sports.

It would be impossible to make a book of this sort comprehensive—the mind boggles at the thought of how many achievements *could* be chronicled here. So three factors have determined which firsts I've chosen to include: The first is significance in the development of each individual sport—that is, when a first changed the way we perceive a sport, I've tried to tell its story here. The second, since this is a book written by an American for readers who will mostly be Americans (by which, incidentally, I mean not just citizens of the United States, but also of its neighbor to the north), is whether a given first was accomplished by an American. The final factor is whether it's fun to read about the first in question. I've included, for example, the story of the first woman to ride a barrel over Niagara Falls— an event which was not terribly important but which is certainly fun to read about.

I should add here that entries on each sport are arranged chronologically, to provide an overview of each sport's historical development.

I will be pleased and gratified if readers of *Sports Firsts* find it even half as enlightening—and half as much fun—to read as I've found writing it.

—PATRICK CLARK

1/BASEBALL

ORIGINS; FIRST GAME

It's almost like learning there is no Santa Claus. But the truth is that Abner Doubleday, credited with creating the national pastime at Cooperstown, N.Y. in 1839, probably did not even play baseball, let alone create it. The Hall of Fame of Baseball at Cooperstown is just an extension of the Doubleday myth. The truth is that the Doubleday-Cooperstown fairy tale is the result of a gigantic baseball public relations effort in the 1930s.

In reality baseball grew out of the English games of cricket and rounders and was probably first played in the United States in the 1700s. In the early 1930s the owners of major league baseball teams found interest in the national sport beginning to lag. As they were looking for something to pump new life into baseball, someone discovered a dusty report from the early part of the century fixing 1839 as the birth date of baseball. It was like manna from heaven. It gave the powers of organized baseball several years to promote the "centennial" of the national pastime in 1939 and, they hoped, to bring larger throngs through the turnstiles.

In 1907 baseball's national commission (see **First Commissioner**) appointed a committee to research the history of the game. Although seven people were named to the panel, only the chairman, A.G. Mills, apparently felt any responsibility for producing a report on the origin of baseball. So at the end of 1907, on his own, Mills produced a report crediting Doubleday with designing a field much like the one in use today, with 11 players to a side rather than nine, each assigned to a position. While Mills described Doubleday as a Cooperstown schoolboy in 1839, Doubleday was actually 20 years old at the time; he had already spent two years at the United States Military Academy at West Point. Young Doubleday spent his summers as a surveyor, not as a baseball player in Cooperstown. The report was greeted with general lack of interest in baseball circles since it was known Mills had served with Doubleday in the Army and that they had remained close friends until Doubleday's death in the 1890s. There has even been speculation that Mills and Doubleday were related. Nevertheless, a quarter of a century later, the Mills report was used to mount a publicity extravaganza for the alleged 1939 centennial of the game. And thus the Doubleday myth was popularized.

Various forms of cricket-cum-baseball flourished along the eastern seaboard in the early 1800s, particularly in New York, Boston and Philadelphia. In 1841 the New York faction developed a four-base diagram of a baseball field that was put into use the following year. 1845 saw the formation of the Knickerbocker Baseball Club of New York, the first organized team for playing baseball. The rules were still somewhat vague, so the Knickerbockers named Alexander Cartwright to standardize them. And thus Alexander Cartwright—not Abner Doubleday—became the real father of modern baseball.

Cartwright rejected the four-base, square-like diagram developed in 1841. Instead he laid out a diamond-shaped playing field, with the nine playing positions that are recognized today. A committee under Cartwright's direction also developed the first set of formal rules for baseball. These rules abolished the practice of making a put-out by throwing the ball at a base-running opponent, a practice that had resulted in more than a few injuries in the early days of the game.

It was on the Cartwright-designed field, under the Cartwright rules, that the first game of baseball as we now know it took place on June 19, 1846 at Hoboken, N.J. Cartwright's Knickerbockers were defeated by a team called the New York Nine, 23-1, in four innings. Although a member of the Knickerbocker team, Cartwright did not play; instead he umpired the historic game.

Perhaps shamed by their overwhelming defeat at the hands of the New York Nine, the Knickerbockers did not play against another organized team until 1851, when they defeated another New York City ball club in the second recorded game of organized baseball. Alexander Cartwright was not present for that second game, played in Manhattan. He had been bitten by the bug when gold was discovered in California in 1849. As he trekked towards the Pacific Coast with a wagon train, he introduced baseball to others, reportedly using the same baseball that had been used in the first game between the Knickerbockers and the New York Nine.

While lionizing Doubleday in the 1939 centennial, major league baseball did add a footnote in recognition of Cartwright's contributions to the game, adding an "Alexander Cartwright Day" to the festivities scheduled at Cooperstown. But it did so only after a Cartwright descendant produced papers showing that Cartwright—not Doubleday—was indeed the founder of the national game.

EARLY EQUIPMENT

Baseball was originally played barehanded—there was no equipment designed specifically for the game. The equipment that was available in the game's early days was generally designed for cricket; it was left to the players of the new game to modify that equipment to meet their own needs.

The bases were perhaps the first piece of "equipment" to be modified. The first players had used four-foot-high stakes as bases. But so many players were injured by running into the stakes that they were replaced with rocks. The rocks, too, proved hazardous, and were replaced with bags filled with sand around 1840. The bags soon came to be known as bases, and before long the game was called baseball.

The uniforms did not appear until 1849 when the first organized baseball team, the Knickerbocker Baseball Club of New York (see also **Origins; First Game**) began wearing uniforms identical to those worn by cricket players. It's possible that they were just old cricket uniforms. It was not until 1868 that the Cincinnati Red Stockings, then an amateur team (see also **First Professional Team**), introduced uniforms similar to those worn today. The uniforms had knickerbocker pants that came to just below the knee. The new uniforms were greeted with much laughter, but went on to become the standard apparel for the game.

The first bats were flat cricket bats. At a meeting on March 9, 1859, in New York, the amateur National Association of Baseball Players adopted a rule limiting the diameter of the bat to two and a half inches. That action was prompted by pitchers' complaints that batters were using huge, flat sticks, giving them an unfair advantage. The rules were further refined in 1862 when it was decided that bats had to be round, made of wood and no more than two and half inches in diameter. No restrictions were set on length.

The first baseball glove was developed by Charles G. Waite in 1875, more than 25 years after the formation of the first organized baseball team (see **Origins; First Game**). It was an unpadded glove similar to those worn by many people in the winter, and a long way from the well-padded, bushel-basket gloves that players use today. Padded gloves for catchers were introduced in 1891.

Originally the catcher stood a couple of steps behind home plate and caught the ball on the bounce when a batter swung and missed (or did not swing). Despite his sometimes precarious position, he had no more equipment than any other fielder. The first catcher's mask was developed in 1875 by Fred W. Thayer of Harvard. Thayer had spent two years modifying a fencing mask for baseball catchers. It was first used in 1875 by Thayer's Harvard teammate James Tyng during a college game. The mask was not used by professional players, however, until 1877.

The first chest protector for catchers was introduced in 1877, but it, too, was initially rejected by the pros, who did not begin to use it until 1885.

FIRST PRINTED RULES

The first set of rules for the game of baseball printed in the United States appeared in *The Book of Sports* by Robin Carver, which was published in 1834. It also included the first printed picture of a baseball contest.

The rules were copied from an earlier English book, in which the game had been called rounders. The rules were similar to those in use today, except that the players ran clockwise; third base was thus where first base is today.

FIRST FINE

The first baseball fine was levied against a member of the New York Nine in the first game played under recognized rules, between the Nine and the Knickerbocker Baseball Club of New York in Hoboken, N.J. on June 19, 1846. (See also **Origins; First Game**.) Alexander Cartwright, baseball's "real" founder and a member of the Knickerbockers, who chose to umpire that day, levied a fine against a member of the Nine, identified only as "Davis," for cussing. The amount of the fine? Six cents.

FIRST NEWSPAPER STORY

United States Sen. William Cauldwell was the author of what was probably the first newspaper story on the game of baseball. The story, which dealt with an upcoming game between the Knickerbocker Baseball Club of New York and a team called the Gothams, appeared in April 1853 in the New York

Sunday Mercury, of which Cauldwell was editor and owner. By the way, the game Cauldwell covered was not played until the following year. The game was to be the one that is described in the next entry, **First Tie**.

FIRST TIE

The first baseball game ending in a tie was played Oct. 26, 1854 in New York City. The Knickerbocker Baseball Club and the New York Gothams played to a 12-12 tie in 12 innings. The game was called because of darkness. That was also the first game in which a record was kept of runs scored in each inning, as well as the cumulative score.

FIRST PAID ADMISSIONS

Professional baseball teams, with paid players, did not exist in 1858. (See also **First Professional Team**.) But that year two "all-star" teams, one representing New York City and the other Brooklyn (which was then a separate city), decided to play a best-out-of-three series which was to decide a champion—the champion of what, we do not know.

The two teams rented a Long Island racetrack for the championship series. Because of the rental costs and other expenses incurred by the two teams, the sponsors decided to charge admission to the series. The first game was played on July 20 before a crowd of 1,500 people, each of whom had paid fifty cents to see the game, producing a gate of $750. The New York all-stars won that game, 22-18. The second game wasn't played until Aug. 19; Brooklyn won. The final game took place on September 10. The New York all-stars won the game, and thus the "championship."

FIRST INTERCOLLEGIATE BASEBALL GAME

The first intercollegiate baseball game in the United States was an informal game between Williams College and Amherst College in Pittsfield, Mass. The game had been suggested at a meeting after chapel at Amherst, and Williams accepted the challenge. Thirteen men represented each school at the game, held on the grounds of the Pittsfield baseball club on July 1, 1859. The players wore neither gloves nor uniforms.

After taking an early lead the Amherst team won the four-hour, 26-round (or inning) match with a score of 66-32.

FIRST ROAD TRIP

The first road trip was conducted by the Excelsiors of Brooklyn, N.Y., beginning June 30, 1860. The Excelsiors played teams in Albany, Troy and

Buffalo, all in New York State, winning all three games. The Excelsiors also conducted the first road trip out of their home state, playing games in Maryland, Pennsylvania and Delaware in July 1860.

FIRST PROFESSIONAL TEAM

Baseball was originally an amateur sport, played for the good of body and soul and not, Heaven forbid, for profit. But when paid admissions were instituted in 1858 (see also **First Paid Admissions**), someone received the money—and it is generally agreed that some of it found its way into the pockets of players. As early as 1864 Al Reach, who played for a Philadelphia baseball team, called himself a professional baseball player. Nevertheless, most players maintained that they were amateur sportsmen for several more years.

Finally, in 1869, the Cincinnati Red Stockings decided to take the money from under the table and put it on top. Club officials announced that the three-year-old team would turn professional, and that players would receive salaries. Public reaction to the news was generally negative, but the Red Stockings were not to be stopped. The team soon boosted the admission price from $.25 to $.50, and team officials said that if gate receipts weren't enough to meet the payroll and other expenses, the necessary money would come out of the owners' pockets.

The top salary—$1,400—went to star shortstop and team captain George Wright. His brother, the Red Stockings' manager and centerfielder Harry Wright, received $1,200. Other players' salaries ranged from $600 to $1,000 for a season which ran from March 15 through Nov. 15.

Over those eight months, the first professional baseball team traveled from coast to coast, compiling a record of 65 wins, one tie and no defeats. The Red Stockings performed before 200,000 paying fans, making a profit of $1.39 on the season.

The success of the Red Stockings in 1869 essentially killed the National Association of Baseball Players, an organization of amateur teams. In March 1871 that group was replaced by the first professional baseball league, the National Association of Professional Baseball Players, which was founded on March 17, 1871 at Collier's Cafe at Broadway and 13th Street in New York City. James N. Kerns, the owner of the Philadelphia Athletics, was the Association's first president. Teams from Boston, Chicago, Cleveland, Fort Wayne, Ind., New York, Philadelphia and Rockford, Ill. and two teams from Washington, D.C. were the league's charter members. Each member team paid an initial membership fee of $10.

The first professional league baseball game was played May 4, 1871 at Fort Wayne between the Forest City team from Cleveland and the Kekionga team from Fort Wayne. The Kekiongas, who failed to survive that first season, won the game, 2-0. The 1871 league championship went to the Philadelphia team, which compiled a season record of 22 wins and seven losses.

FIRST UMPIRE

When baseball became organized in the early 1870s (see also **First Professional Team**), team owners decided that umpires should not be paid, lest aspersions be cast on their honesty. Umpires were chosen by the teams from a list, but the procedure was so haphazard that an umpire was frequently plucked from the fans in the stand. Only one umpire was used in a game at that time.

When the National Association of Professional Baseball Players was established in 1871, that system was still in use. But a part-time fighter named William McLean proved so outstanding as an umpire that teams were willing to pay his expenses. Ultimately they began paying him a salary of $5 per game, making him the first professional umpire.

When the National League was born in 1876 it reverted to the no-pay-for-umpires practice, but after a couple of years that proved unworkable and the League began paying umpires $5 per game.

In 1883 the American Association began paying a $140 per month salary plus traveling expenses to its umpires.

It was not until the early 1900s that a second umpire began to be used. It was another 30 years before the practice of having four umpires per game was instituted.

FIRST BI-RACIAL BASEBALL GAME

The first organized baseball game between a white team and a black team took place on July 6, 1871 in Chicago between the black Uniques and the white Alerts. The black team won, 17-16.

FIRST LEFT-HANDED CATCHER

Because it is difficult for them to throw to second base when a right-handed batter is at the plate, left-handed catchers have been a rarity throughout major league baseball history.

The first left-handed catcher was William Arthur Harbidge, who played with the Hartford Blues of the National League in 1876. He appeared behind the plate in 24 games in 1876, and also played outfield and first base that season. Harbidge played for eight years with Hartford, the Chicago White Stockings, the Troy Trojans and the Philadelphia Phillies, all of the National

League, and with a Cincinnati team in the Union League, appearing in a total of 125 games as a catcher.

Jack Clements, another left-handed catcher, broke in with Philadelphia of the Union League in 1884. He played with four National League teams through 1900, altogether appearing in 1,073 games as catcher.

FIRST EXTRA-INNING GAMES

The first major league baseball game to last more than nine innings was played on April 29, 1876 between the Hartford Blues and the Boston Red Caps of the National League. It took Hartford 10 innings to win the game 3-2.

The first extra-inning game played in the American League took place on April 30, 1901. The Boston Somersets beat the Philadelphia Athletics 8-6 in 10 innings.

FIRST NO-HITTERS; FIRST PERFECT GAMES

Through the 1980 season there have been 189 no-hitters in the National and American Leagues, including ten perfect games (but not including Don Larsen's 1956 perfect World Series game). Of these, 106 have been in the National League and 83 in the American League. Three of those no-hitters were pitched by two or more pitchers.

George Bradley of the St. Louis Reds tossed the first no-hitter in the National League on July 15, 1876 against the Hartford Blues, winning 2-0. John Lee Richmond of Worcester pitched the first perfect game in the National League on June 12, 1880 against the Cleveland Bronchos, winning 1-0.

Earl Moore, who played for Cleveland, pitched the first nine-inning no-hitter in the American League on May 9, 1901 against the Chicago White Sox, but lost the game 4-2 in 10 innings. The first complete game no-hitter in the American League was pitched by James J. Callahan of the White Sox in Chicago on Sept. 20, 1902 against Detroit. Chicago won by a score of 3-0. Baseball's winningest pitcher in history, Cy Young, threw the first perfect game in the American League on May 5, 1904 when Young's Boston Red Sox beat the Philadelphia Athletics 3-0.

FIRST MAJOR LEAGUE HOME RUN KING

George Hall of the Philadelphia team in the National League was professional baseball's first home run king. Hall hit five home runs in 1876, the first year for which complete records exist on professional baseball in the United States, to lead the league. His batting average for the season was .366.

FIRST SCANDAL IN PROFESSIONAL BASEBALL

Late in the 1877 season Louisville appeared to be well on its way to winning the National League title. The team had a 3½-game lead over its nearest rivals with only 12 games left in the season, and thus needed to win only six games to clinch the pennant. The team's star pitcher, Jim Devlin, had, however, been approached by a gambler named McLeod, who had offered Devlin a payoff if he agreed to throw some key games. Outfielder George Hall, the 1876 National League home run king (see also **First Major League Home Run King**) had received similar overtures from his own brother-in-law.

Thus it happened that, during the last road trip of the season, Louisville lost to an unimpressive Hartford team. Suspicions began to develop in some circles when it was learned that Hartford had been favored in a big Hoboken, N.J. betting pool. Louisville then lost a close game in Boston, reducing the team's lead to one game; in short order Louisville lost two more games to Cincinnati and dropped out of first place.

By Oct. 4 Louisville had lost the pennant to Boston. And Charles E. Chase, the vice president of the Louisville team, had become convinced that foul play was responsible. In particular he was suspicious of the large number of telegrams Al Nichols, a utility infielder for the team, had received. So on that date Chase confronted Nichols, Devlin, Hall and shortstop Bill Craver and accused them of conspiring to throw several games to their opponents. All four confessed, and on Oct. 30 they were expelled from the National League for life.

In 1879 Devlin crashed a National League meeting in Utica, N.Y., where he begged the league's president, William Hulbert, to reinstate him. Hulbert, not unsympathetic, handed $50 to the obviously destitute Devlin, but said that under no circumstances could he rejoin the National League. Devlin subsequently joined the Philadelphia police force, and died of tuberculosis in 1883 at the age of 34.

Craver also became a policeman, in Troy, N.Y. Hall returned to his hometown, Brooklyn, where he became an engraver; he died in 1945 at the age of 96. Nichols disappeared, but some think he played baseball with the Franklin club of Brooklyn and the Jersey City club of the Eastern League under the name of Williams.

FIRST TRIPLE CROWN WINNERS

The Triple Crown is not an award. It is instead an unofficial but generally recognized accolade for players in either league who lead their league in batting average, home runs and runs batted in, all in a single year. Only 14 players have accomplished that feat and only two players have accomplished it twice: Rogers Hornsby of the St. Louis Cardinals, in the National League, in 1922 and 1925 and Ted Williams of the Boston Red Sox, in the American League, in 1942 and 1947. The American League has had eight triple crown winners and the National League six.

The first player to take the Triple Crown was Paul Hines of the Providence Grays, in the National League, in 1878. He won the Triple Crown with four home runs, 50 runs batted in and a batting average of .358 in a season of 62 games. Napoleon Lajoie became the first American League winner in 1901 when he hit 14 home runs and had 125 runs batted in and a .422 average for the Philadelphia Athletics.

FIRST NIGHT GAME

Baseball was, of necessity, originally played only during the daylight hours. But the last years of the 20th century find baseball a game played mainly in the evening hours.

Baseball under the lights in the amateur and minor leagues dates back to 1880, when two amateur teams played a nine-inning game in an hour and a half with arc lights strung along the field at Nantasket Beach, Mass. But until 1935 night baseball was confined to the amateur and minor leagues and some exhibition games.

The first night game in major league baseball was played May 24, 1935 at Cincinnati's Crosley Field. The Reds beat the Philadelphia Phillies 2-1. Today all major league ball parks except the Chicago Cubs' Wrigley Field have lights.

The first night World Series game was played Oct. 13, 1971 at Pittsburgh as the Pirates beat the Baltimore Orioles 4-3 in game four of the Series.

FIRST BLACK COLLEGE BASEBALL PLAYER

The first black college varsity baseball player was Moses Fleetwood Walker, who played at Oberlin College in Oberlin, Ohio in 1881. The team played several intercollegiate games that year, including one with the University of Michigan, which Oberlin won on its home ground by a score of 9-2. Walker later enrolled in the University of Michigan Law School in the class of 1884, where he played on the baseball team. He did not graduate but joined a professional team in Toledo (see also **First Black Player in Major League Baseball**).

FIRST MAJOR LEAGUE GRAND SLAM HOME RUN

The first grand slam home run (a home run with men on all three bases) was hit Sept. 10, 1881 by 24-year-old Roger Connor, first baseman for the Troy Trojans in the National League. The grand slam led Troy to an 8-7 victory over a Worcester team. Connor hit only one other home run that year.

FIRST UMPIRE FIRED FOR DISHONESTY

Richard Higham, who had been an umpire in the National League for two years in 1882, was suspected of telling gamblers how to bet on the games he umpired. Handwriting experts indicated he was indeed the author of several incriminating letters and as a consequence he became the first ump fired for dishonesty.

FIRST DOUBLEHEADERS

The first major league doubleheader (two games in one day) was played in the National League on Sept. 25, 1882. Worcester and Providence split the two games; Worcester won the first, 4-3, while Providence won the second game, 8-6. The first doubleheader played in the American League took place on July 15, 1901, between Baltimore and Washington. Washington won the first game, 3-2; Baltimore won the second, 7-3.

FIRST LADIES' DAY

The first "Ladies' Day," a day when women were allowed into baseball parks either at a reduced charge or free, was staged June 16, 1883 by the New York Gothams. Ladies, either escorted or unescorted, were admitted to the Gothams' ballpark free of charge. New York defeated the Cleveland Spiders, 5-2.

FIRST BLACK IN THE MAJOR LEAGUES

Racial segregation ended in major league baseball before it did among the general population. To be sure, baseball broke no speed records in abolishing Jim Crow, as the unwritten barrier against black players was known, but it was far ahead of the court rulings and the civil rights legislation of the 1950s and 1960s. In any event, one might speculate that major league owners were perhaps more interested in drawing from the reservoir of black talent for the benefit of their own bank accounts than they were in furthering the cause of human rights.

The first black to play in the major leagues was Moses Fleetwood Walker, an above-average catcher who had also been the first black college player (see **First Black College Baseball Player**). Walker appeared in 41 or 42 games in 1884 for a Toledo team in the American Association, which was then classified as a major league. His brother, Welday Wilberforce Walker, also appeared in five or six games for Toledo that year. The two, however, quickly faded into oblivion. There were several other black players in organized baseball prior to the turn of the century, all in the minor leagues.

While blacks were not banned from organized baseball officially, some major league players refused to perform against teams which included blacks in exhibition games, strengthening the barriers encountered by black athletes. As a result, the black players formed the first professional team of their own in 1885 in Babylon, N.Y. and the first all-black league in 1920 in Kansas City.

A young man named Jack Roosevelt Robinson began his career with the Kansas City Monarchs of the Negro major leagues. Robinson had been a star football player for U.C.L.A. and had appeared in the Rose Bowl. He went on to become an outstanding infielder in the Negro major leagues.

Possessed of a deep sense of pride in himself and his race, Robinson's athletic prowess and personal integrity were just what Branch Rickey needed when he decided the time had come to bring down the color barrier in organized baseball.

Rickey, president of the Brooklyn Dodgers, signed Robinson to a major league contract, and the spring of 1946 found Robinson in Montreal playing for the Dodgers' Triple-A farm team, the Royals. After an outstanding year, Robinson was called up to the Brooklyn team in 1947 and, on July 5, became the first black to play in the major leagues in modern times. (He struck out his first time at bat.)

Robinson took his share of abuse from individuals and teams alike. The St. Louis Cardinals, playing in the nearest thing to a Southern town in the National League, threatened not to play if the Dodgers played Robinson during a May series in St. Louis. National League Pres. Ford Frick threatened suspensions if the Cardinals carried through on their strike threat. They did not.

The abuse apparently had no effect on Robinson's play. He hit 12 home runs that year, stole 29 bases and finished with a batting average of .297, winning the 1947 Rookie of the Year Award. (See also **First Rookie of the Year Award**.)

Now that the barrier was broken, Rickey also signed pitcher Don Newcombe and catcher Roy Campanella for the 1947 season. The color barrier was weakened further when Bill Veeck signed Larry Doby to the Cleveland Indians in 1947, making him the first black in the American League.

Robinson became the first black to win the Most Valuable Player Award in 1949. He went on to play 10 years in the major leagues, all with the Brooklyn Dodgers. The Dodgers traded Robinson to the New York Giants following the 1956 season, but Robinson retired before the next season began.

Robinson became the first black elected to the Hall of Fame in 1962.

FIRST SUNDAY BASEBALL GAME

Sunday baseball games were banned by blue laws in the early days of major league baseball. The National League was already more than a dozen years old when the first Sunday baseball game was played on April 17, 1892 at St. Louis. In that game the Cincinnati Reds beat the St. Louis Cardinals, 5-1.

FIRST MAN TO MAKE SEVEN HITS IN A SINGLE NINE-INNING GAME

Catcher Wilbert Robinson of the Baltimore Orioles (then a National League team) got seven hits in seven times at bat on June 10, 1892. In a routine game between the Orioles and the St. Louis Cardinals, neither of which had a chance at the pennant that year, Robinson hit six singles and one double, making him the first man to hit more than six safe hits in a single nine-inning game. Robinson's seven runs came in the first game of a doubleheader, which was held in Baltimore. In the second game he had two more hits, for a total of nine hits in one day.

FIRST MAN TO HIT FOUR HOMERS IN A GAME

On May 30, 1894, Robert L. Lowe of Boston in the National League became the first major league player to hit four home runs in one game, two of them in one inning. The New York Yankees' Lou Gehrig became the first in the American League to hit four homers in one game June 3, 1932.

FIRST MAN TO WIN THE BATTING CHAMPIONSHIPS IN BOTH LEAGUES

Edward J. Delahanty, the eldest of the five Delahanty brothers who played in major league ball, compiled a lifetime batting average of .346. But his claim to lasting fame is that he was the first man to win the batting championship in both major leagues.

In 1899, playing for the Philadelphia Phillies, he won the National League batting championship with a .408 batting average. In 1902, playing for the Washington Senators in the American League, his .376 batting average won the title for that league.

FIRST WORLD SERIES

The first modern World Series was played in 1903 between the Boston Red Sox and the Pittsburgh Pirates.

The series was arranged by the presidents of the two teams when it became apparent that Boston would take the championship in the American League and Pittsburgh in the National League. The two presidents agreed on a nine-game series. After four games the Red Sox were trailing three games to one, but rallied to win the next four games and the World Series, five games to three.

Baseball legend Cy Young pitched three complete games for Boston in the series, winning two and losing one. He also relieved in the fourth game. Another of baseball's immortals, Honus Wagner, didn't fare so well. After winning the National League batting championship with Pittsburgh that year with a .355 average, Wagner got only six hits in the eight World Series games for a series average of .222.

There was no World Series in 1904. A best-of-seven playoff was instituted in 1905 and continued until 1919, when a nine-game series was briefly reinstated. In 1922 the World Series was again a best-of-seven series and remains as such today.

FIRST WORLD SERIES WITH ONLY SHUTOUT GAMES

The first World Series in which every game was a shutout was played by the New York Giants and the Philadelphia Athletics in 1905. In the first game, held in Philadelphia on Oct. 9, Christy Mathewson pitched for the New Yorkers, clad in striking new black flannel uniforms, and won a shutout, 3-0. Then in New York the visiting Athletics were led to a shutout victory, 3-0, by Chief Bender, helped by a couple of Giant errors.

After a day's delay due to rain in Philadelphia, Mathewson held the Athletics to another scoreless game, with New York winning 9-0. Then in New York the Giants won again, 1-0, led by "Iron Man" McGinnity. In the fifth game, again played in New York, Mathewson pitched his third shutout in a row; the Giants won the game, 2-0, and the Series, four games to one.

FIRST WORLD SERIES TO BE PLAYED ENTIRELY IN THE SAME CITY

The 1906 World Series, between the American League's Chicago White Sox and the National League's Chicago Cubs, was the first to be played entirely in the same city. The Cubs had the famed double play combination of Tinkers to Evers to Chance, but the White Sox won the Series, four games to two.

FIRST STEEL STADIUM

Forbes Field, which was to be the home of the Pittsburgh Pirates for 61 years, was the first major league ball park made partially of steel, rather than wood and concrete as had been the custom. The Pirates played their first game at Forbes Field June 30, 1909, losing to the Chicago Cubs, 3-2. Forbes Field was replaced in 1970 by Three Rivers Stadium.

FIRST UNASSISTED TRIPLE PLAY

Neal Ball, playing for the Cleveland Indians, came up with the first unassisted triple play in major league history in July 1909 against the Boston Red Sox. Ball, playing shortstop, made a leaping catch of a line drive with runners on both first and second bases. He stepped on second base for the second out and then tagged the runner caught between first and second bases for the third out.

FIRST PRESIDENTS TO THROW OUT BALL

The first president to throw out a baseball at a game was William Howard Taft. On April 14, 1910 President Taft attended the season opener between the Washington Senators and the Philadelphia Athletics in Washington and threw out the first ball, signifying the start of the season and the game. Walter Johnson was the starting pitcher for the Senators against the Athletics' Eddie Plank. Johnson allowed just one hit, a single by Frank Baker, and the Senators won, 3-0.

Woodrow Wilson became the first president to throw out a ball to open a World Series game on Oct. 9, 1915. Wilson attended the second Series game, between Boston and Philadelphia, in Philadelphia. Boston won the game, 2-1. Calvin Coolidge was the first to throw out a ball to open the first game of a World Series, on Oct. 4, 1924 in Washington. The New York Giants defeated the Washington Senators, 4-3.

FIRST MOST VALUABLE PLAYER AWARDS

The Most Valuable Player award was born as the Chalmers Award following the 1911 season. The award took its name from the Chalmers automobiles that were presented to the outstanding players from both leagues. The first recipient in the National League was Frank Schulte, an outfielder for the Chicago Cubs. The first American Leaguer honored was the immortal Ty Cobb of the Detroit Tigers.

The Chalmers award died following the 1914 season. The M.V.P. award as we know it today was resurrected as an American League-only award after the 1922 season. The St. Louis Browns' George Sisler was chosen by a special committee as the recipient.

The National League got in on the act two years later in 1924, when Brooklyn pitcher Dazzy Vance was selected as the league's M.V.P. by a special committee.

In 1929 no American League M.V.P. was chosen, apparently because of a general lack of interest on the part of league officials. Rogers Hornsby, the St. Louis Cardinals' second baseman, was named the National League M.V.P. that year. No M.V.P was selected in 1930 in either league; the reason is unclear.

In 1931 responsibility for selecting the most valuable player from each league was turned over to the Baseball Writers Association of America, which has made the selections every year since. The writers' selections that first year were pitcher Robert "Lefty" Grove of the American League's Philadelphia Athletics and second baseman Frankie Frisch of the St. Louis Cardinals in the National League.

FIRST MAJOR LEAGUE PITCHER TO HAVE A 19-GAME WINNING STREAK

Richard "Rube" Marquard, who had broken into big league baseball pitching for the New York Giants in 1908, became the first major league pitcher to win 19 games in a row four years later, in 1912.

Marquard's winning streak began with the opening game of the 1912 season, but the pressure did not really begin to build until he had won his 10th game in a row, then his 11th. It was not until July 8 of that year that Marquard finally lost a game, against the Chicago Cubs, bringing to an end the longest winning streak ever recorded by a major league pitcher.

BABE RUTH'S FIRST HOME RUN

Babe Ruth hit his first home run on May 6, 1915. Ironically enough, Ruth, then with the Boston Red Sox, hit the home run off the New York Yankees' pitcher Jack Warhop. After a trade a few years later, Ruth went on to become a Yankee legend.

FIRST PINCH-HIT GRAND SLAM HOME RUN

The first pinch-hit grand slam home run was hit Sept. 24, 1916 by Marty Kavanagh of the Cleveland Indians. The ball rolled through a hole in the fence, enabling Cleveland to beat Washington 5-3.

FIRST DOUBLE NO-HIT GAME

The first game where both pitchers threw no-hit games occurred May 2, 1917, when neither Fred Toney of the Cincinnati Redlegs nor Hippo Vaughn of the Chicago Cubs allowed a hit for nine innings. Vaughn finally gave up a hit with one out in the 10th inning, while Toney held the Cubs hitless through 10 innings as the Reds beat the Cubs 1-0.

FIRST MODERN MAJOR LEAGUE SCANDAL

The most famous major professional sports scandal in the United States was the legendary "Black Sox" scandal in 1919. That year eight members of the Chicago White Sox, then the American League champions, conspired with gamblers to throw the World Series to the underdog National League champions, the Cincinnati Reds.

At that time the World Series was a best-of-nine series. The Series began in Cincinnati; Eddie Cicotte was the starting pitcher for the Sox. He gave up five runs in one inning and Cincinnati went on to win the first game, 9-1.

In the second game Chicago pitcher Lefty Williams walked three batters in one inning and then gave up a triple to one of the weaker hitters in the Cincinnati lineup. The Reds won 4-2 and Cincinnati had a two-game lead.

The third game was apparently on the level, as Chicago's Dickie Kerr threw a three-hit shutout and the White Sox won 3-0 before a Chicago crowd to take their first game of the Series.

Cicotte was back on the mound for the fourth game and made two errors. Even though Cicotte gave up only five hits, Cincinnati won 2-0 and led the Series three games to one.

The Reds won the fifth game 5-0, taking a commanding lead of four games to one in the Series, but the White Sox took the sixth and seventh games, 5-4 and 4-1, narrowing Cincinnati's margin to four games to three. However, the Reds won the eighth game in Chicago, 10-5, taking the Series five games to three.

Afterwards there were hints that the White Sox had thrown the Series, but many, including Chicago owner Charles Comiskey, defended the integrity of the games, writing off the defeat of the favored Sox as just one of those unexpected things that sometimes happen in athletic events. Comiskey even went so far as to offer a cash reward for evidence showing his team had thrown the series. But winter put a freeze on the fix allegations, and they didn't resurface for almost a year. By the following September, however, allegations of scandal had begun to proliferate in the press.

Finally, Cicotte, Williams and Shoeless Joe Jackson gave the Illinois State's Attorney signed confessions admitting the fix. But before they could come to trial, the State's Attorney's office lost the statements. When the case did come to trial at last, the three denied making the confessions and the charges were dropped.

The failure of the courts to convict the men did not stop baseball's first commissioner, Kenesaw Mountain Landis, a former federal judge, from pursuing his own course of action. Landis banned Cicotte, Williams, Jackson, Charles "Swede" Risberg, Oscar "Hap" Felsch, Arnold "Chick" Gandil, George "Buck" Weaver and Fred McMullen from baseball for life. (See also **First Commissioner.**)

Whether truth or legend, the Black Sox scandal spawned tales of disillusioned young boys trailing after Shoeless Joe Jackson on Chicago streets imploring him to "Say it ain't so, Joe."

FIRST GRAND SLAM HOME RUN IN A WORLD SERIES

The first grand slam home run in a World Series was hit by Cleveland Indians right fielder Elmer Smith in the first inning of the fifth game of the 1920 World Series, against the Brooklyn Dodgers at Cleveland. The grand slam came off Dodger pitcher Burleigh Grimes; the Indians went on to win the game, 8-1, and the World Series, five games to two.

FIRST PLAYER TO MAKE AN UNASSISTED TRIPLE PLAY IN THE WORLD SERIES

William Wambsganss of the Cleveland Indians was the first—and, to date, the only—man to execute an unassisted triple play in a World Series game. The otherwise obscure second baseman was playing in the top half of the fifth inning in the fifth game of the 1920 World Series; Otto Miller and Pete Kilduff of the Brooklyn Dodgers were on first and second, respectively. For some unknown reason Wambsganss moved out of position, more than 10 feet deeper into the field. Relief pitcher Clarence Mitchell hit a line drive more than 15 feet to the right of second base, almost nine feet above the ground. Not only did Wambsganss manage to catch the ball for one out, he also stepped on second base to put out Kilduff and then tagged Miller, who was trying to make it back to first base. (Mitchell, at his next turn at bat, hit into a double play. He was thus responsible for five outs in two times at bat.)

FIRST PITCHER TO HIT A HOME RUN IN A WORLD SERIES

The first pitcher to hit a home run in a World Series was the Cleveland Indians' Jim Bagby, in the 1920 World Series against the Brooklyn Dodgers. Bagby, a 31-game winner that year, hit his home run in the fifth game, which Cleveland won, 8-1. Cleveland also won the series, five games to two.

FIRST COMMISSIONER

Baseball was governed by a national commission from 1903, when the National League grudgingly acknowledged the three-year-old American League as a major league circuit, until 1921. The commission was composed of one team owner and the presidents of the American and National Leagues.

The 1919 "Black Sox" scandal (see First Modern Major League Scandal) severely shook the major league team owners. In seeking to restore credibility to the game, one of the steps they took was to eliminate the national commission, which they replaced with a Commissioner of Baseball. The commissioner, it was agreed, would rule over the national game with almost dictatorial authority.

The owners chose U.S. District Court Judge Kenesaw Mountain Landis. That choice was not uncontroversial. Landis had presided over a number of highly publicized trials, including the government's antitrust suit against Standard Oil in which Landis fined the company $29 million. That ruling, as well as many others Landis handed down, was overturned by higher courts, causing some to wonder about his wisdom and ability as a jurist. But many others saw him as a firm, incorruptible figure who could restore integrity to the shaken national game.

Although Landis was only earning $7,500 on the federal bench, major league owners signed Landis to a contract calling for a salary of $50,000 a year, an incredible amount in 1921. Nevertheless, Landis tried for several months to retain both his position on the bench and his job as baseball commissioner, until pressure from both legal and baseball circles forced Landis to step down from the bench.

If there had been any doubt that Landis was going to be a tough taskmaster, he quickly dispelled it. Those involved in the Black Sox scandal had ultimately gone to trial, but lack of evidence had prevented the court from convicting them. Landis, however, barred the players from organized baseball for life. If there was still any fear that the Judge would be intimidated, he put it to rest when he took on the mighty Babe Ruth. Ruth and several other players had violated a ban on post-season barnstorming after the 1921 season, despite advance warnings from the Judge. Landis retaliated by fining Ruth a month's pay and suspending him from play until May 20 of the 1922 season, 39 days after the season was to begin. Adding insult to injury, Landis confiscated Ruth's share from the 1921 World Series to ensure that the fine was paid.

Landis remained Commissioner of Major League Baseball until his death on Nov. 25, 1944.

FIRST RADIO AND TELEVISION BROADCASTS

The advent of radio and later of television helped spread the popularity of baseball, particularly in areas that did not have major league teams.

Baseball had its electronic debut on Aug. 25, 1921, when radio station KDKA in Pittsburgh broadcast a game between the Pirates and the Philadelphia Phillies. Harold Arlin called the play-by-play as Pittsburgh won, 8-5. The eight games of the 1921 New York Yankees-New York Giants World Series were the first to be broadcast on the radio by Graham McNamee (the first World Series game that year took place on Oct. 5). WMAQ in Chicago became the first radio station to carry regular season games on a regular basis in 1924, with Hal Totten calling the action.

Professional baseball made its first appearance on television on Aug. 26, 1939, when a Brooklyn Dodgers-Cincinnati Redlegs doubleheader was televised from Brooklyn's Ebbets Field over station W2XBS. (See also **First Televised College Game**.) Although there were only a handful of television sets in the metropolitan New York area at the time, famed radio broadcaster Red Barber called the play-by-play that day.

FIRST MAN TO MAKE 4000 SAFE HITS

On July 18, 1927 Ty Cobb became the first and so far the only player to make 4000 safe hits. Cobb began his career in 1905 with the Detroit Tigers. He was then a total unknown—his name wasn't even printed on the scorecard. That first season he made 36 hits, then 112 in his second season. He continued to improve.

Cobb had more than 200 hits in a single season nine times. By the time he was 34 he had made 3000 hits, the youngest player ever to have made so many. At the end of the 1928 season, when Cobb retired, he had reached the record total, which still stands, of 4191 hits.

FIRST WOMAN TO SIGN A CONTRACT

While a number of professional sports as well as most amateur, high school and collegiate sports are now open to women, no woman has ever played in a regular season major league game. But one woman did pitch for a minor league team; in fact, in an exhibition game against the New York Yankees in 1931, she struck out both Babe Ruth and Lou Gehrig.

Manager Joe Engel signed a 17-year-old woman, Jackie Mitchell (her full name was Virne Beatrice Mitchell), to pitch for his team, the Memphis Lookouts of the Southern Association. Many speculated that Miss Mitchell was hired as a publicity stunt, to draw crowds for the exhibition game. Mitchell, who claimed that she had been taught to pitch by Dazzy Vance, believed that she was of major league caliber, but said that she just wanted to stay in baseball long enough to earn enough money to buy a roadster.

Mitchell pitched in the exhibition game, striking out Babe Ruth, Lou Gehrig and Tony Lazzeri. She was then taken out of the game and greeted with cheers. The Lookouts then proceeded to lose the game, 14-4.

FIRST ALL-STAR GAME

The first All-Star game was played on July 6, 1933 at Chicago's Comisky Park. The sports editor of the Chicago *Tribune*, Arch Ward, proposed the game as a one-time-only event for Chicago's "Century of Progress" World's Fair in 1933. But the first game was so popular that the All-Star game became a permanent fixture on the major league baseball scene. Except for the period from 1959 through 1962, when two All-Star games were held each year, and 1945, when no game was played because World War II had virtually depleted the major leagues, there has been an All-Star game every summer since 1933. In the beginning, the All-Stars were chosen by the fans. However, that system was abandoned and the selections were made by baseball executives and managers until 1946. Fans resumed voting for their favorites in 1947, but that practice was again discontinued. Players, coaches and managers made the choices until 1970, when fans once more began to select the All-Star players.

More than 49,000 fans turned out for that first All-Star game as Connie Mack's American League stars hosted a National League squad led by John McGraw. The American League scored a run in the second inning to take the lead. Then, in the third inning, Babe Ruth hit the first All-Star game home run, with one man on base, putting the American League ahead 3-0. The National League scored twice in the sixth inning; one run came when Frankie Frisch hit a solo home run. But the American League scored once again in the bottom of the sixth and held on for a 4-2 victory.

FIRST MAJOR LEAGUE PLAYERS TO SCORE SIX RUNS IN ONE GAME

Baseball Hall of Famer Mel Ott was the first major leaguer to score six runs in a single game. Ott, whose career spanned 21 years with the New York Giants in the National League, first scored six runs in a game on Aug. 4, 1934. He repeated the feat nearly ten years later, on April 30, 1944. The first player in the American League to score six runs in one game was Johnny Pesky of the Boston Red Sox, on May 8, 1946.

ORIGINS OF THE HALL OF FAME

The Baseball Hall of Fame at Cooperstown, N.Y. was founded to perpetuate the myth that Abner Doubleday was the father of the American pastime (see also **Origins; First Game**). The baseball powers of the 1930s decided to use the 1907 Mills report—the same report they had used to fix 1839 as the date of baseball's birth—to justify the establishment of a baseball hall of fame at Cooperstown. A Centennial Committee was named to choose figures from baseball's past to be memorialized at the shrine. The committee members were Baseball Commissioner Kenesaw M. Landis; American League president William Harridge; National League president Ford Frick; the chairman of the board of the National League, John A. Heydler; Washington Senators owner Clark Griffith; New York Yankees owner Edward Barrow; and Philadelphia Athletics owner Connie Mack.

The Centennial Committee, working through 1936 and 1937, chose the first group of baseball old-timers to be admitted to the Hall of Fame. Those chosen were:

Abner Doubleday

Alexander Cartwright, the designer of the baseball diamond, the author of the first set of rules for the national game and thus probably the true father of American baseball

Morgan G. Bulkeley, the first National League president

Henry Chadwick, the author of the first official rule book, the chairman of the National Association Rules Committee and the inventor of the scoring system generally still in use

Ban Johnson, the first American League president

A.G. Spalding, who had been a pitcher for the Chicago White Stockings (a National League team) from 1876-78 and, later, a baseball executive

George Wright, the first manager of the Cincinnati Red Stockings, the first professional team

Connie Mack, a player for and later the manager and owner of the
   Philadelphia Athletics
Charles Comiskey, a player for and later owner of the Chicago White
   Sox
John McGraw, a player for the New York Giants from 1902-06 and the
   Giants' manager from 1907-32
William "Buck" Ewing, who had been a catcher from 1880-97 for
   teams in Troy, New York, in New York City and in Cleveland and
   Cincinnati; his lifetime batting average was .303
William "Candy" Cummings, the pitcher credited with inventing the
   curve ball in 1864
Charles "Old Hoss" Radbourn, who had pitched from 1880-91 for
   teams in Buffalo, Providence, Boston and Cincinnati. In 1884, while
   at Providence, he compiled an incredible 60-12 record and an earned
   run average of 1.38. His lifetime win-loss record was 310-192.

The Baseball Writers Association was designated to choose modern players
for admission to the shrine. In 1936 they chose Ty Cobb, Honus Wagner,
Babe Ruth, Christy Mathewson and Walter Johnson.

In 1937 the Baseball Writers chose Cy Young, Tris Speaker and Nap
Lajoie for induction, while in 1938 they chose only Grover Cleveland
Alexander. The selections by the Association in 1939 were Lou Gehrig,
Eddie Collins and Willie Keeler.

The Cooperstown Baseball Hall of Fame was officially opened in 1939 to
mark the alleged 100th anniversary of Doubleday's creation of the national
game. Since then, the Baseball Writers Association has voted annually on
candidates for the Hall of Fame. To qualify for induction into the Hall of
Fame, a candidate must have played in the major leagues for at least 10 years
and must have been retired for a minimum of five years. The player must
receive 75 percent of the votes to be inducted.

A special committee on the Negro leagues was formed in 1971 to consider
players from the now defunct Negro major leagues for admission into the
Hall of Fame.

FIRST BACK-TO-BACK NO-HITTERS

The first and so far only pitcher ever to throw two no-hitters on consecutive
appearances was Johnny VanderMeer of the Cincinnati Reds. He held the

Boston Braves hitless, 3-0, on June 11, 1938. In his next appearance, four days later on June 15, he held the Brooklyn Dodgers hitless, 6-0.

FIRST TELEVISED COLLEGE GAME

The first college baseball game to be televised was played May 17, 1939 at Columbia University's Baker Field in New York City. Famed sportswriter Bill Stern did the play-by-play announcing as Princeton defeated Columbia, 2-1, in 10 innings.

ORIGINS OF THE LITTLE LEAGUE

In the years since 1939 Little League Baseball has grown from a town league of three teams to what the Little League Organization claims is both the largest youth sports program in the world and the largest baseball organization in the world. The Little League originated in 1939 in Williamsport, Pa. It was established so that children could have a chance to play baseball without being turned away by older boys. The regular Little League age group is 8 to 12; additional leagues for older boys were formed later.

The first Little League World Series Tournament was held in Williamsport on August 21, 1947. Eleven teams from the surrounding areas of Pennsylvania and Hammonton, N.J. competed at Max M. Brown Memorial Park in what was then called the Little League National Tournament. The eleven teams played ten games, with the Maynard Midget League of Williamsport and the Lock Haven Little League playing for the championship. Twenty-five hundred fans were present at the high-scoring game, which the Maynard Midgets won, 16-7. Ed Ungard was the winning pitcher. He kept Lock Haven to eight hits, struck out seven and allowed only four bases on balls. Ingersoll and Woll were the batting stars of the final game, with seven of the team's fifteen hits. The Maynard Midgets finished the tournament with a batting average of .625.

The other teams in the tournament were the Williamsport Little League; the Lincoln League, a team from Hammonton, N.J.; the Brandon Boys; the Perry Lions; the Sunday School League, a Jersey Shore team; the Montour League; and the Milton Midgets. Lock Haven beat Hammonton 5-1 in six innings in the semi-finals, and the Maynard Midgets won over the Lincoln Boys League in ten innings in a close 10-9 game.

The center fielder of the champion Maynard Midgets, Jack Losch, became an outstanding college football star at the University of Miami and later played with the Green Bay Packers, ranking near the top of the list for punt returns in the National Football League.

The Little League World Series is now held annually at Williamsport and broadcast on national television. A World Series is also held annually for Senior League Baseball, for boys 13 to 15 years of age, in Gary, Ind.; one for Big League Baseball, for boys 16 to 18 years of age, is held at Fort Lauderdale, Fla.

FIRST OPENING DAY NO-HIT, NO-RUN GAME IN THE MAJOR LEAGUES

Bob Feller pitched the first opening day no-hit, no-run game for a big league baseball team on April 16, 1940. It was a cold day in Chicago, and only 14,000 fans watched as Feller, pitching for the Cleveland Indians against the Chicago White Sox, won the game 1-0. Twenty-one-year-old Feller had never before pitched a no-hitter or a shutout.

Feller went on to pitch two more no-hitters and twelve one-hit games in his career, but his first remained the most famous.

FIRST MAN TO HIT IN 56 GAMES IN A ROW

When Joe DiMaggio began his hitting streak on May 15, 1941 against the Chicago White Sox, nobody noticed. It wasn't unusual for DiMaggio to hit well. It wasn't until he had hit in almost 30 consecutive games that the pressure began to build. How long could he keep up the pace?

By July 16 the Yankee Clipper had hit safely in 55 consecutive games. That day he had 3 hits against the Cleveland Indians, bringing his hitting streak to 56 games in a row.

The next day it took two Indian pitchers to put an end to DiMaggio's incredible streak. In those 56 games, DiMaggio had 91 hits in 223 times at bat; he batted in 55 runs and scored 56 times.

ONLY ONE-ARMED OUTFIELDER

There has been only one one-armed outfielder in major league baseball. He was Pete Gray, born Peter Wyshner. Gray, a semi-pro standout in the New York City area who had lost his right arm in a childhood accident, wound up playing with the war-depleted St. Louis Browns in the American League in 1945.

At the plate, Gray's swing was normal, except that he held the bat with only one hand. In the outfield, Gray would catch fly balls in his glove, slip the glove under his armpit with his left hand, roll the ball across his chest to his throwing arm and then throw the ball back into the infield. Gray stopped ground balls with his glove, pushed them in front of him, took off his glove and then threw them into the infield. He was considered an adequate fielder.

Gray appeared in 77 games for the Browns in 1945, compiling a .218 average. 1945 was Gray's only year in the major leagues.

FIRST TEAM TO TRAVEL ENTIRELY BY AIRPLANE

The New York Yankees were the first major league baseball team to travel to games in other cities entirely by airplane. The Yanks took to the air for the 1946 season, signing a contract with United Airlines to provide them with transportation.

FIRST MANAGER TO BE EJECTED FROM GAMES TWICE IN ONE DAY

Baseball Hall of Famer Mel Ott holds the dubious distinction of being the first major league manager to be thrown out of a game twice in one day. Ott was ejected from the first game of a doubleheader between his New York Giants and the Pittsburgh Pirates at Pittsburgh on June 9, 1946. He was allowed to return to the bench for the second game of the twin bill, but was later thrown out of that game, too.

SPONSORS OF THE FIRST TELEVISED WORLD SERIES

The first televised world series, in 1947, was sponsored by the Gillette Safety Razor Company and the Ford Motor Company after a brewery's offer was rejected by the baseball commissioner, A.B. Chandler. The series that year was between the New York Yankees and the Brooklyn Dodgers. The Yankees won, four games to three.

FIRST ROOKIE OF THE YEAR AWARD

The Rookie of the Year Award, honoring an outstanding first-year major league player, was introduced in 1947. Initially only one player from the two leagues was chosen. The first recipient was the Brooklyn Dodgers' Jackie Robinson, who that year had become the first black to play in the major leagues in modern times. (See also **First Black Player in Major League Baseball**.)

Separate selections for each league began two years later in 1949, when Don Newcombe of the Brooklyn Dodgers was named the National League's Rookie of the Year and Roy Sievers of the St. Louis Browns, the American League's Rookie of the Year.

FIRST NIGHTTIME OPENING GAMES

After the advent of regular nighttime baseball in the major leagues in 1935 (see also **First Night Game**), it remained the custom that the opening game of each season was played in the afternoon. The St. Louis Cardinals of the National League put an end to that tradition on April 18, 1950 when they played the first nighttime season opener at Sportsman's Park (later Busch Stadium) in St. Louis. The Cardinals beat the Pittsburgh Pirates 4-2 in that game.

The first season-opening night game in the American League did not take place until a year later, on April 17, 1951, when the Philadelphia Athletics opened their season at home at night with a 6-1 loss to the Washington Senators.

FIRST RELIEF PITCHER TO WIN MVP AWARD

Jim Konstanty of the Philadelphia Phillies, in the National League, was the first relief specialist to win the Most Valuable Player Award in either league. Konstanty snared the MVP in 1950 as he posted a 16-7 record for the Phils, appearing in 74 games, more than any other National League pitcher that year. Konstanty led the Phillies to the 1950 World Series; they lost in four games to the New York Yankees.

FIRST MIDGET

Eddie Gaedel earned himself a unique page in sports history in 1951 when he became the first—and, so far, the only—midget to play major league baseball.

Bringing Eddie into the game was the brainstorm of Bill Veeck, general manager of the American League's perennial losers, the St. Louis Browns.

On Aug. 19, 1951, at St. Louis' Sportsman's Park, the 43-inch tall Eddie was sent to the plate to pinch-hit against the Detroit Tigers for Brownie centerfielder Frank Saucier, giving Saucier the ignominious distinction of being the only major leaguer ever to be taken out for a midget.

Anticipating trouble from the umpires, Veeck had manager Zack Wilson produce a legitimate major league contract for Gaedel. After a delay, Eddie thumped his bat on the plate as the Tigers' Bob Cain delivered his first pitch. It was high and away. Ball one. Three more times Cain kicked and pitched. Each time the result was the same: a ball, nowhere near the miniature strike zone. Eddie tossed down his bat and trotted to first base with a walk in his first and only time at bat in the major leagues. Jim Delsing came in to pinch-run for Eddie, who walked off the field and onto the pages of sports trivia.

FIRST PLAYER TO APPEAR IN MORE THAN 50 WORLD SERIES GAMES

On Oct. 10, 1951 Joe DiMaggio played in his 51st World Series game, making him the first baseball player ever to appear in more than 50 World Series games. It was his last baseball game before his retirement; DiMaggio and the Yankees won over the New York Giants, 4-3.

FIRST NO-HITTER IN A FIRST GAME

Alva "Bobo" Holloman of the St. Louis Browns was the first pitcher ever to toss a no-hitter in his first major league game. He did it on May 6, 1953, defeating the Philadelphia A's, 6-0. Holloman won only two other games that year and lost seven. 1953 was his only year in the major leagues.

FIRST BLACK TO PITCH A NO-HITTER

Sam Jones of the Chicago Cubs was the first black to pitch a no-hit game in the major leagues. Jones shut out the Pittsburgh Pirates 4-0 on May 12, 1955, in Chicago.

FIRST UMP TO WEAR GLASSES

Ed Rommel was the first major league baseball umpire to wear glasses while presiding over a game, during the 1956 season.

FIRST PERFECT WORLD SERIES GAME

In 1956, 27-year-old right-hander Don Larsen certainly was not a prime candidate for baseball immortality. Just two seasons before, Larsen had recorded an atrocious three win-21 loss season during the Orioles' first year in Baltimore. Baltimore then traded Larsen to the New York Yankees, where his record was 9-2 in 1955 and 11-5 in 1956.

Oct. 8, 1956 found Larsen in his pinstripes, on the mound at Yankee Stadium, pitching against the Yankees' cross-town rivals, the Brooklyn Dodgers, in the fifth game of the World Series. The Series was tied at two games apiece as more than 64,000 people gathered for the pivotal game.

In a late-season move, Larsen had done away with his windup. And on that Oct. 8 Larsen could do no wrong as he became the first—and, so far, the only—pitcher to throw a perfect game in World Series competition. He threw no more than three balls to any one batter, and that only once—in the first inning. He struck out pinch hitter Dale Mitchell on a fast ball for the last out of the game; the Yankees won, 2-0. Larsen had recorded 11 strikeouts.

The Dodgers' Sal "The Barber" Maglie didn't pitch such a bad game himself. He allowed just five hits, including a solo home run by Mickey Mantle. The other Yankee run came in the sixth inning when Andy Carey singled, Larsen sacrificed to move Carey to second and Carey came around to score on a single by Hank Bauer.

Larsen's perfect game was not only the first perfect World Series game; it was also the first perfect game that had been pitched in the major leagues in 34 years.

ORIGINS OF THE CY YOUNG AWARD

The Cy Young Award, honoring the best pitcher in baseball history, was created in 1956 because the Commissioner of Baseball, Ford Frick, thought pitchers were inadequately recongized, primarily because they didn't perform every day.

There were two good reasons for naming the award after turn-of-the-century pitcher Cy Young: with 511 victories, he was the winningest pitcher in baseball; he was also the only pitcher in the history of the game who had posted 200 victories in each league.

After originating the idea, Frick turned the selection of winners over to the Baseball Writers Association of America. Right-hander Don Newcombe, who had racked up a record of 27 wins and seven losses in 1956 with the Brooklyn Dodgers, was named as the first recipient of the Cy Young Award.

From 1956 through 1966 only one major league pitcher received the award each year. Then in 1967 the writers began to present the award to one pitcher from each league. That year the National League award went to left-hander Mike McCormick of the San Francisco Giants; right-hander Jim Lonborg of the Boston Red Sox took the American League honors.

FIRST PLAYER TO WIN ROOKIE OF THE YEAR, MVP AND CY YOUNG AWARDS

Only one major league pitcher has managed to win the Rookie of the Year Award, the Most Valuable Player Award and the Cy Young Award. Don Newcombe of the old Brooklyn Dodgers took the Rookie award in 1949 and followed it with both the MVP and Cy Young awards in 1956.

FIRST BLACK COACH

John "Buck" O'Neil was major league baseball's first black coach. He achieved that distinction in 1962 with the Chicago Cubs in the National League.

FIRST PLAYER TO STEAL OVER 100 BASES IN ONE YEAR

Maury Wills, a shortstop for the Los Angeles Dodgers, became the first man to steal more than 100 bases in a single season in 1962.

On April 13 of that year he stole his first base. By the summer the slight man had stolen so many bases that he was being called the "diamond burglar." As the end of the season approached Wills was also approaching the record for stolen bases in one season, 96. He passed the 96 mark and kept stealing until he reached 104 by the end of the season.

FIRST INDOOR GAME; FIRST GAME ON ARTIFICIAL SURFACE

The first indoor major league baseball game was played on April 12, 1965 at the Astrodome in Houston, Texas, a domed stadium which is the home of the Houston Astros of the National League.

That game also marked the first time a major league baseball game had been played on an artificial surface. The creators of the Astrodome had been unable to get grass to grow inside the domed stadium because it lacked two basic grass-making ingredients: sunshine and rain. The problem was turned over to the Monsanto Chemical Corporation in St. Louis, which came up with a green-colored, carpet-like surface called AstroTurf (registered trademark) which took care of the problem. The surface was relatively natural-looking, and required very little maintenance; it was consequently adopted by teams playing outdoors as well.

Houston lost that first indoor, artificial surface game 2-0 to the Philadelphia Phillies.

FIRST BLACK MAJOR LEAGUE UMPIRE

Emmett Ashford, a colorful, flamboyant, sometimes controversial individual, was the first black major league umpire. Ashford broke into organized baseball by umpiring in the Southwestern International League in 1951. After a long apprenticeship in the minors, Ashford became a major league umpire in 1965 in the American League. He retired in 1970.

After retirement from organized baseball, Ashford occasionally umpired Pacific 10 Conference college baseball games. Once during a college game in 1974, Ashford did a little soft-shoe dance while the organist played "Tea for Two."

Ashford had a colorful style of calling balls, strikes and outs. When he did make a call, there was usually little doubt about what Ashford had in mind. Asked how he had developed his style, Ashford once said, "I didn't go to umpiring school because they weren't taking blacks in those days, so I evolved my own system."

Like Jackie Robinson, the first black major league baseball player in modern times, Ashford ran into his share of discrimination when he broke the color barrier in the umpiring ranks. "I went through the same thing Jackie went through," Ashford said. "I had to show my authority. I think my good foundation in umpiring kept me in good stead, because they couldn't take away the job I did on the field."

After retiring as an umpire, Ashford worked for the American League and the baseball commissioner's office. He died of a heart attack March 1, 1980.

FIRST FEMALE UMPIRE

In 1969, 40-year-old Bernice Gera graduated from an umpiring school. Her goal: to umpire in professional baseball. Armed with her certificate, Gera applied to the New York-Pennsylvania Professional Baseball League for a job. But the president of the National Association of Professional Baseball Leagues, Philip Piton, ruled that Gera couldn't be signed as an umpire because she could not meet the physical requirements. Umpires were required to be at least five feet, 10 inches tall and to weigh 170 pounds. Gera stood only five feet, two inches and weighed just 129 pounds.

Gera, apparently undaunted, took her case to court in New York. Finally, on Jan. 13, 1972, three years after she had graduated from umpiring school, the court ruled in Gera's favor. The New York-Pennsylvania Baseball League then gave her a job as an umpire.

In June 1972 Gera finally made it onto the field to umpire a professional baseball game, between the Auburn Phillies and the Geneva Rangers. But it wasn't all balls and strikes for Gera. Suffering from a case of opening night jitters, perhaps partially brought on by pre-game harassment, Gera made what she herself admitted was a bad call in the fourth inning: She forgot that a runner going into second base on a ground ball did not have to be tagged, so she called an Auburn runner safe who had, in fact, been forced out. Then she realized her mistake and changed her call, making the Auburn runner out. The Auburn manager stormed onto the field but, after an argument, Gera prevailed, as umpires always do.

After the game Gera broke into tears and decided to quit umpiring, but she had at least had the satisfaction of breaking the sex barrier in professional baseball.

FIRST BLACK MANAGER

On April 8, 1975 Frank Robinson made his debut as the first black major league manager. Robinson's Cleveland Indians beat the New York Yankees that day by a score of 5-3; Robinson, who appeared in the game as a designated hitter, contributed to his team's victory by hitting a home run his first time at bat. Robinson's career as a major league player lasted from 1956 to 1976; during that time he played for five different clubs. His first year at Cleveland, which he spent as a full-time player, was 1974. Robinson's career batting average was an impressive .294. He hit a total of 586 home runs, making him fourth on the all-time list; his 2808 career games make for the eighth-highest total recorded up until now.

FIRST BROTHERS TO PITCH NO-HITTERS

On April 7, 1979 Ken Forsch of the Houston Astros pitched a no-hitter against the Atlanta Braves in Houston. No other pitcher had ever thrown a no-hitter so early in the season. Forsch's victory also marked another first: On April 16, 1978 his brother Bob, of the St. Louis Cardinals, had pitched a no-hitter against the Philadelphia Phillies in St. Louis; the Cardinals won the game 5-0. The two Forsches thus became the first brothers ever who had each pitched major league no-hitters. (Bob Forsch's no-hitter was, incidentally, the first pitched in St. Louis since 1924.)

FIRST SWITCH-HITTER TO GET 100 HITS EACH BATTING LEFT-HANDED AND RIGHT-HANDED IN THE SAME SEASON

The St. Louis Cardinals' Garry Templeton became the first major league switch-hitter to get 100 hits batting left-handed and 100 hits batting right-handed in the same season in 1979. The 24-year-old Templeton racked up 211 hits for the year to lead the National League, including 19 triples, which was also the best in the league for the season. Templeton had a .314 batting average for the season.

2/FOOTBALL

ORIGINS; FIRST INTERCOLLEGIATE GAME

American football evolved from two English games: soccer, which dates back at least to the 12th century, and rugby, which itself evolved from soccer in the 1800s, when English youths who had been playing soccer began picking up the ball and running with it as members of the other team pursued them, rather than moving the ball only by kicking it.

In the 1860s school officials at Harvard University in Cambridge, Mass. prohibited students from playing a kicking game, which they apparently did not feel was suitable for young gentlemen. In the early 1870s a group of Harvard students obtained permission to play a rugby-like game in which the players were allowed to carry the ball. A football club was formed at Harvard in 1872, but its rugby-like games were solely intramural.

In the fall of 1873 Yale invited Rutgers, Princeton, Columbia and Harvard to a meeting in New York to organize an intercollegiate football association. Harvard refused to attend because school officials felt that its rugby-like game, which had become known as "the Boston Game," was not compatible with the non-contact game the other schools were playing. Perhaps because of

Harvard's decision, football and not soccer went on to become the major intercollegiate sport.

No other school in the United States played the Boston Game on a regular basis. But in 1874 McGill University in Montreal, Canada proposed a series of games with Harvard. The two schools agreed to play a series of three games, the first two to be played at Cambridge, one under Harvard's rules and another under McGill's rules. The third game was to be played in Montreal under McGill's rules.

The two schools met for the first time on May 14, 1874 at Cambridge, playing as agreed under the rules of the Boston Game. Harvard won the game, three goals to none. Under McGill's rules the next day, the game ended in a scoreless tie.

Harvard was so taken with McGill's game that it adopted its rules, and Yale and Princeton followed shortly thereafter. Harvard and Yale met in the first American intercollegiate football game under the rugby-like rules on Nov. 13, 1875. Harvard won, 4-0.

Princeton changed to the rugby-style game in 1876 and invited Harvard, Rutgers, Yale and Columbia to a meeting in Springfield, Mass. on Nov. 23 of that year at which rules were formally worked out and the first Intercollegiate Football Association was born.

The adoption of the new game began the evolution of football as we know it today. In the 1880s the first quarterback appeared, the scrimmage line was created, the number of players was reduced from 15 to 11, and all playing positions were named. Downs and signals were also developed during the 1880s as football became a distinctly American game, less and less like its English forerunners.

FIRST USE OF GOAL POSTS; FIRST ADMISSION CHARGED

The football goal post was used for the first time in a game between McGill University of Montreal and Harvard College at Cambridge, Mass., on May 14, 1874(see also **Origins; First Intercollegiate Game)**. The game also marked the first time that admission was charged for a collegiate sporting event.

WALTER CAMP

Walter Camp is perhaps best known as the creator of the All-America selections, honoring the nation's outstanding college athletes, but he also created the line of scrimmage and the down system.

Camp was a football star at Yale in the late 1870s. As a junior, in 1880, he participated in a rules convention that decided to limit the number of players to 11 men per team and to make safeties a scoring play. But Camp also wanted to eliminate the rugby scrum and replace it with a more orderly method of putting the ball into play. Camp wanted a line of scrimmage to replace the scrum, a practice in which everybody locked arms, rugby fashion, and heeled the ball backwards, which sometimes took several minutes. Camp proposed that the ball be put on the ground; a player called the center would either snap it back with his hands or heel it back to another player. Others wanted to know what would happen when a team found itself unable to move the ball. Camp didn't have an answer.

When another rules convention was held in the fall of 1882, Camp's scrimmage proposal was adopted. Camp still had not come up with a way to prevent extended possession of the ball. He felt the players would do the right thing and punt the ball when they could no longer move it forward. Camp was wrong. In a Yale-Princeton game a short time after the scrimmage rule was adopted, Princeton took the ball after the opening kickoff and held it throughout the entire first half by clinging to it after it was snapped without any effort to move it forward.

By the time another rules convention was held, Camp had come up with a solution. He suggested that if the team with the ball failed to move it five yards in three consecutive plays, it would surrender the ball to the other team after the third down. A rules committee meeting several years later, in which Camp once again participated, extended the number of yards required for a first down to ten.

In 1885 Camp helped institute the first penalty rule, the offsides penalty— a loss of five yards for crossing the line of scrimmage before the ball is snapped.

FIRST BLACK INTERCOLLEGIATE PLAYERS

The first black intercollegiate football players were probably W.T.S. Jackson and William Henry Lewis at Amherst College in 1889, some three years before the first all-black intercollegiate football team was fielded. The Amherst College team that year played in the New England Intercollegiate Athletic Association, which included Brown, Bowdoin, Dartmouth and the Massachusetts Institute of Technology.

William Henry Lewis played in every game that year, but Jackson saw very little action after the first game, in which Amherst defeated Williston 48-6. During the entire season Amherst played twelve games, winning five and losing six, with one tie.

Lewis was elected captain of the 1891 Amherst football team. This probably made him the first black captain of a college football team. (See also **First Black All-American.**).

FIRST COLLEGE ALL-AMERICA TEAM

The first All-America college football team was chosen after the 1889 season. The selections were made by Caspar Whitney, a New York City sports expert, even though they appeared in *Harper's Weekly* under the byline of former Yale athletic star Walter Camp. Camp began making the selections himself in 1897 and his selections appeared in *Collier's* magazine every year until he died in 1925. Legendary sportswriter Grantland Rice took over the selections after Camp's death and made the choices for *Collier's* until 1947. The Football Writers Association of America joined with Rice in making the choices for *Look* magazine from 1948 until Rice's death in 1954. The Associated Press took over the All-America selection process in 1954 and continues to make them today, although All-America selections are made by a number of other news organizations and media as well. Eleven offensive and 11 defensive players are selected now, a change from the first several years, when only 11 players were named in all.

Those selected to the first All-America team in 1889 were:

Quarterback: Edgar Allen Poe, Princeton
Fullback: Knowlton Ames, Princeton
Halfback: James T. Lee, Harvard
End: Amos Alonzo Stagg, Yale
End: Arthur Cumnock, Harvard
Center: William J. George, Princeton
Guard: William W. Heffelfinger, Yale
Guard: John Cranston, Harvard
Tackle: Charles O. Gill, Yale
Tackle: Hector W. Cowan, Princeton
Halfback: Roscoe H. Channing, Jr., Princeton

FIRST BLACK INTERCOLLEGIATE FOOTBALL GAME

On Dec. 27, 1892 the first football game between two black colleges was held. Biddle University and Livingstone College met on the Livingstone University campus in Salisbury, N.C. Biddle won, 4-0.

FIRST BLACK ALL-AMERICAN

William H. Lewis, the son of former slaves who moved to New England while he was a child, played center for Amherst College from 1888-91; he then moved to Harvard for the 1892-93 seasons. (See also **First Black Intercollegiate Players.**) He was named the first black All-American in 1892, repeating in 1893. He was later to accomplish a non-athletic first: he was the first black admitted to the American Bar Association in 1911.

FIRST PROFESSIONAL GAME

The first professional football game was played Aug. 31, 1895 in Latrobe, Pa., southeast of Pittsburgh. The Latrobe football team was sponsored by the local YMCA; it was to play a team from the nearby town of Jeanette, Pa. The Latrobe team did not, however, have an experienced quarterback, so a resident of Latrobe named John Brallier, who had played quarterback in college, was offered $10 to play against Jeanette. Brallier accepted, making himself the first professional football player and the Latrobe team the first professional football team. Brallier, who later became a dentist in Latrobe, led the team to a 12-0 victory over Jeanette.

Football was growing from an amateur and collegiate sport into a professional one. Pittsburgh became the first major city to have a professional football team in the late 1890s. Other professional teams were formed in Pennsylvania, New York State, New Jersey, Michigan, Indiana, Illinois, West Virginia and Ohio. Professional football remained unorganized, however, into the 1900s. By 1919 there were a dozen professional football teams in six states, and 1920 saw the formation of the American Professional Football Association. The legendary Jim Thorpe, who played back and coached for the Canton, Ohio Bulldogs, was elected president, primarily as a public relations move to improve the image of professional football. The Akron, Ohio Pros had the best record in the first year of organized professional football with 11 wins and two scoreless ties. Amazingly enough, no one scored against the Pros in 13 games.

The American Profesional Football Association did not fare well during its inaugural season. It was reorganized in 1921 as the American Professional Football League. Joseph F. Carr, who was to rule professional football until his death in 1939, was elected as the new president, succeeding Thorpe. The reorganized league did not, however, fare much better than its immediate predecessor. During the season 23 different teams competed in the league; some teams folded before the end of the season, and new ones were formed to replace them. The Chicago Bears, which had originated as the Staley

Athletic Club in Decatur, Ill., posted the best record of the season, 10-1-1.

The A.P.F.L. became the National Football League in 1922. Initially it included 18 teams, although not all of them survived the new league's first year. The Canton, Ohio Bulldogs posted the best record that year: 10-0-2. From those beginnings professional football evolved into a sport that drew nearly 13.4 million spectators in 1980 for 448 regular season games and eight post-season contests, in addition to the Super Bowl.

FIRST COLLEGE BOWL GAME

The Rose Bowl, held in Pasadena, Calif., was the first post-season college football bowl game.

Technically, the first Rose Bowl game was played in Pasadena on New Year's Day, 1902, although it was not called by that name. The game, between Michigan and Stanford, had been set up as part of the city's annual Rose Festival. Michigan won, 49-0. There was not another January 1 game, however, until Pasadena decided once again to include a football game as part of its Rose Festival 14 years later, on New Year's Day, 1916. Washington State, which had been the outstanding team in the Pacific Coast Conference in 1915, was asked to invite an opponent for the game. The Washington State team chose Brown, which it defeated, 14-0, in "the Tournament of Roses Association Game." The game was first called the Rose Bowl in 1923, the first time it was held in Pasadena's new stadium. Harlan W. Hall of Pasadena is credited with naming the stadium, and subsequently the football game, the Rose Bowl.

The Rose Bowl has been played every year since 1916. In 1918 and 1919 the game was played between military teams—Mare Island and Camp Lewis in 1918 and Mare Island and Great Lakes in 1919—because of the war. On New Year's Day, 1942 the game was played at Duke Stadium in Durham, N.C.—this was just a few weeks after the Japanese attack on Pearl Harbor, and public gatherings on the West Coast had been curtailed. Oregon State beat Duke that year, 20-16. The Rose Bowl returned to Pasadena in 1943.

Since 1946 the Rose Bowl has been played between the Pacific Coast Conference and Western Conference champions.

The Rose Bowl proved so successful it spawned a number of similar games, most of which are played on New Year's Day.

The first East-West Shrine game was played Dec. 26, 1925 at San Francisco, pitting Eastern collegiate stars against a Western squad with the proceeds going to the charity committee of the Masonic Shrine. The first game was won by the Western team, 6-0.

A North-South Shrine all-star game for similar charitable purposes was first played in 1932 in Baltimore, Md. The Southern team won the first game, 7-0. The game was later played in Knoxville, Tenn. and Birmingham, Ala., usually in December. The series was discontinued after 1973.

The first Orange Bowl was played on New Year's Day, 1933 in Miami, Fla. The first game saw Miami of Florida defeat Manhattan College, 7-0.

The Sugar Bowl is played on New Year's Day in New Orleans, La. The first game was played in 1935; Tulane beat Temple, 20-14.

The Sun Bowl, also played on New Year's Day, was born the next year in El Paso, Texas. The first game saw Hardin-Simmons and New Mexico State play to a 14-14 tie. Hardin-Simmons became the first Sun Bowl winner when it beat the Texas School of Mines, 34-6, on New Year's Day, 1937.

The Cotton Bowl is played on New Year's Day in Dallas, Texas. At the first game, played in 1937, Texas Christian University defeated Marquette, 16-8.

The Blue-Gray game, a North-South series, was first played in 1938 in Montgomery, Ala. The Blue team beat the Gray, 7-0, that year. That game is usually played in December.

The first Gator Bowl was played on New Year's Day, 1946 in Jacksonville, Fla. Wake Forest beat South Carolina, 26-14.

The Astro-Blue Bonnet Bowl is played in December each year in Houston, Texas. Clemson won the first game in 1959, defeating Texas Christian University, 23-7.

FIRST NIGHT GAME

The first professional football game to be played at night took place in 1902 in Elmira, N.Y. The Philadelphia Athletics defeated the Kanaweola Athletic Club, 39-0.

The Athletics were owned by baseball Hall of Famer Connie Mack and was made up mostly of players from his Philadelphia Athletics baseball team. Pitcher Rube Waddell was one of the football team's star players.

FIRST FOOTBALL STADIUM

The Harvard stadium, which was dedicated on Nov. 14, 1903, was the first stadium built especially for football. It was the largest reinforced steel structure in the world at that time.

FIRST BLACK PROFESSIONAL PLAYERS

While Jackie Robinson is widely (if erroneously) known as the first black to play major league baseball in the United States, few can recall the names of the first blacks to play professional football. In fact, the first blacks were playing professional football nearly 20 years before the formation of the National Football League. It appears likely that Charles Follies, who played for the Shelby, Ohio, Blues in 1904, may well have been the first black professional football player in the United States.

A Haitian black named Henry McDonald played seven years later, in 1911, for the Rochester Jeffersons.

ORIGINS OF THE FORWARD PASS

At the turn of the century college football was a game of brute force, frequently leaving the players battered and bloody. The violence so angered Pres. Theodore Roosevelt that he threatened to abolish the game by executive order unless the violence was curtailed. The threat led the football rules committee to legalize the forward pass, beginning with the 1906 season. The forward pass did not gain instant acceptance in college football. Yale did use it in 1906 to defeat Harvard, 6-0. But it did not come into widespread use until 1913, seven years after the rules committee made it legal. And it took Notre Dame to do it.

The Irish found themselves playing against the Army in 1913. The little Catholic school in Indiana was then by no means the football powerhouse that it is now. In fact, a game between Notre Dame and the Army seemed almost as unequal as a contest between the Christians and the lions. But two of the Notre Dame players refused to give up. They were quarterback Gus Dorais and an end named Knute Rockne. The two had spent the summer working on the forward pass; when they returned to school that fall they introduced the new offensive weapon to another player, named Pliska. With Rockne and Pliska as targets, Dorais led the Irishmen to an astounding 35-13 victory over the powerful Army team. Notre Dame's upset triumph over the West Pointers legitimized the forward pass, boosting the school out of athletic obscurity and marking football's turning point from a game of brute force to a game requiring considerable finesse.

FIRST NUMBERING OF COLLEGE FOOTBALL UNIFORMS

Washington and Jefferson was the first college to number its football uniforms, in 1908. However, it discontinued the practice that same year. Numbered football uniforms reappeared at the University of Chicago when Coach Amos Alonzo Stagg used them for a November 1913 game against Wisconsin. The numbering was applauded by both spectators and the press, who had often been unable to identify individual players in the past. In spite of this favorable response, the practice did not catch on with most major colleges and universities until the 1920s.

FIRST USE OF THE DOUBLE-WING FORMATION

The double-wing formation was first used Nov. 9, 1912 by Pop Warner, coach of the Carlisle Indian School, in a game against Army. Carlisle won the game, 27-6. The legendary Jim Thorpe starred for Carlisle; a halfback named Dwight Eisenhower played for Army.

FIRST COMPLETELY ENCLOSED FOOTBALL STADIUM

The Yale Bowl at New Haven, Conn., was the first completely enclosed football stadium in the United States. It opened in 1915 with a game in which Yale defeated Princeton, 13-7.

FIRST PROFESSIONAL COMMISSIONER

Many purists in the early part of the 20th century thought football should remain a completely amateur game. But many former college football players who had enjoyed playing the game as amateurs could see nothing wrong with taking advantage of opportunities to keep playing the game while picking up a few dollars besides. Nevertheless, many college coaches and alumni mounted such a hue and cry against the professionalization of football that the crowds stayed away from professional games, giving the professional teams a bad image among the masses.

When the American Professional Football Association, the precursor of the National Football League, was formed in 1920, the game was still suffering image problems. In an effort to alleviate those problems, Jim Thorpe, the Carlisle College Indian, hero of the 1912 Olympics and back and coach for the Canton, Ohio Bulldogs, was elected the league's first president. But Thorpe proved a better athlete than administrator, and when the season was over the new professional football league was on shaky financial ground.

Thorpe was replaced in 1921 by Joseph F. Carr, and the Association was renamed the American Professional Football League. The league remained financially weak; a total of 23 teams competed during the season, as some teams folded and new ones took their places. But during his first year, Carr established the policy, still followed today, that prohibits professional teams from negotiating with a college football player before his class has graduated.

Similarly, Carr threw the Milwaukee Badgers out of the league in 1925 when it used four high school players in a game against the Chicago Cardinals. Carr also fined the owners of the Cardinals for letting their team play the game.

Under Carr's stewardship, the A.P.F.L. became the National Football League in 1922. When Carr died in 1939, Carl L. Storck became president of the league. He served until 1941, when he was succeeded by one of the legendary Four Horsemen of Notre Dame, Elmer Layden, who held the post until 1946. Layden was replaced by de Bennville "Bert" Bell, a politically well-connected member of a Philadelphia society family who owned the Philadelphia Eagles football team. Bell instituted the college player draft system and led the National Football League in its successful fight against the rival All America Football Conference. He died of a heart attack at a football game between the Eagles and Pittsburgh Steelers in 1959.

Bell was succeeded by Alvin "Pete" Rozelle, who led the NFL to a merger with the upstart American Football League in the 1960s. Rozelle still holds the post today.

FIRST COLLEGE FOOTBALL GAME BROADCAST ON RADIO

The first college football game to be broadcast on radio was played between Texas A & M and Texas on Nov. 25, 1920. The game was broadcast locally by station WTAW in College Station, Texas, home of the Aggies. Texas won the game, 7-3.

The first college football game to be broadcast coast-to-coast was played Oct. 28, 1922 in Chicago when Princeton beat the University of Chicago, 21-18. Radio station WEAF in New York City broadcast the game and provided a feed to other stations from coast to coast.

FIRST BLACK PROFESSIONAL HEAD COACH

The first—and, up to the present, last—time there was a black head coach in the National Football League, it was still known as the American Professional Football Association. Frederick "Fritz" Pollard came out of Brown University and played back from 1919-21 for the Akron Pros and in 1922 for the Milwaukee Badgers. In 1923 Pollard became head coach of the Hammond Pros while playing back for them. The team posted a 1-5-1 record in 1923. He posted his best record as coach in 1924, when the Pros were 2-2-0. He started out 1925 as the Pros' coach, but after four games, in which the team had posted a 1-3-0 record, Pollard left to join the Providence

Steamrollers, where his duties were confined to playing. Pollard's three-year record as coach of the Pros was thus 4-10-1.

There has not been a black head coach in the NFL since Pollard. A black named Willie Wood did, however, serve as head football coach for the Philadelphia Bell in the now defunct World Football League during the 1970s.

FIRST BLACK BOWL GAME

The Prairie View Bowl was the first black college football bowl game. It was played for the first time on Jan. 1, 1929 in Houston, Texas, with Prairie View College of Texas defeating Atlanta University, 6-0.

FIRST PROFESSIONAL TEAM TO GO OUT OF TOWN TO TRAINING CAMP

In 1929 the Chicago Cardinals became the first professional football team to use an out-of-town training camp. The camp was located in Coldwater, Mich.

FIRST COLLEGE FOOTBALL GAME BETWEEN U.S. AND MEXICAN SCHOOLS

At the urging of Reginald Root, a Yale graduate, the University of Mexico took up American-style football, hoping to compete with college teams in the United States. The University of Mexico thus played the first football game between colleges from the United States and Mexico in October 1929 in Mexico City against Louisiana College of Alexandria. By halftime the Americans led the inexperienced Mexican team 45-0, and the game ended at 59-0.

The University of Mexico tried again in November against Mississippi College, again losing by a score of 28-0.

Perhaps because of the University's lack of success in the sport, U.S.-style football never became very popular in Mexico.

FIRST PLAYER TO SCORE SIX TOUCHDOWNS IN A PROFESSIONAL GAME

On Nov. 28, 1929—Thanksgiving Day—the hometown Chicago Bears were favored to win over the St. Louis Cardinals, but Ernie Nevers scored six touchdowns and 40 points to bring the Cardinals to victory. Player-coach Nevers was the first man ever to score so many touchdowns, and so many points, in a major league football game. He scored three touchdowns in the first half and three in the second, as well as four conversions, accounting for all the Cardinals' points; the final score was 40-6.

FIRST INDOOR GAME IN THE NATIONAL FOOTBALL LEAGUE

The first indoor football game in NFL history was played Dec. 18, 1932 between the Chicago Bears and the Portsmouth Spartans, who later became the Detroit Lions. The two teams had finished in a tie for first place that season; a tie-breaking game was planned for the Bears' home, Wrigley Field. The day of the game, however, the temperature hovered around 30 degrees below zero and a snowstorm battered the city. The only place where the game could be played was the Chicago Stadium, an indoor arena which was used mostly for horse shows and other types of exhibitions. Both teams agreed to move the game indoors. However, the field was only 80 yards long, rather than 100, and ten yards narrower than the usual 53⅓. To compensate for this, the teams agreed to move the ball in ten yards from the sidelines and to move the goal posts from the end line to the goal line to prevent players from running into the wooden wall that surrounded the makeshift football field.

The game remained scoreless through the first three quarters. The Bears finally scored the only points of the game in the fourth quarter when fullback Bronko Nagurski passed to Red Grange for a touchdown. Portsmouth protested that Nagurski had not been the required five yards behind the line of scrimmage. But the officials rejected the protest and allowed the touchdown. The Bears later added a safety and won the game, 9-0.

ORIGINS OF THE HEISMAN TROPHY

The Heisman Memorial Trophy is presented each year by the Downtown Athletic Club in New York City to the most outstanding college football player, chosen in a nationwide poll of sports writers and broadcasters. The award originated in 1935 as the Downtown Athletic Club Trophy. Sculptor Frank Eliscu was chosen to design the trophy; he used Ed Smith, a leading player on the 1934 New York University football team, as his model. Eliscu created a bronze statue of a football player sidestepping and straight-arming his way down the field. The statue is 14 inches long and 13½ inches high and weighs 25 pounds. The original, mounted on a 17½ by 5½ inch base, is now on display in the lobby of the Downtown Athletic Club building in lower Manhattan.

The Downtown Athletic Club Trophy was presented for the first time

Dec. 9, 1935 to Jay Berwanger, a back for the University of Chicago Maroons. In 23 games over two seasons, Berwanger had gained more than a mile—1,839 yards, averaging 4.19 yards in 439 carries. He also passed for 921 yards, scored 22 touchdowns and kicked 20 extra points for a total of 152 points.

Berwanger also had the distinction of being the first player chosen in the first National Football League draft of college players in 1936 (see **First College Football Draft**); however, he chose business over professional football and went to work for a sponge rubber manufacturer in Chicago after graduation. After a stint in the Navy during World War II, primarily teaching instrument flying, Berwanger started his own manufacturing company; he and his wife now live in New Mexico.

Before the Downtown Athletic Club Trophy could be awarded a second time in 1936, it had been renamed after John W. Heisman. Heisman had been named the first athletic director of the Downtown Athletic Club in 1930. Heisman had played varsity football at Brown and Penn and then went on to a 36-year coaching career (1892-1927) at Auburn, Oberlin, Clemson, Georgia Tech, Akron, Penn, Washington and Jefferson and Rice, among other schools. Heisman is credited with helping to legalize the forward pass, instituting the center snap and creating the now-illegal hidden ball play. A Heisman team also holds the record for the highest score in a single game, when Georgia Tech shut out Cumberland by the phenomenal score of 222-0.

After seven years as athletic director of the Downtown Athletic Club, Heisman died of bronchial pneumonia Oct. 3, 1936. As a tribute to Heisman, the Downtown Athletic Club Trophy was renamed the Heisman Trophy Award. Larry Kelley, a Yale end, received the renamed award in 1936.

FIRST COLLEGE FOOTBALL DRAFT

The annual draft of graduating college football players by professional football teams was the idea of Bert Bell, the owner and coach of the Philadelphia Eagles and later the commissioner of football. In the 1930s Bell's Eagles were the perennial bridesmaids of the National Football League. Bell, hoping to improve his team, proposed in May 1935 that the NFL establish a system for drafting soon-to-graduate college football players in the inverse order of their finish in the standings—i.e., the last-place team would choose first while the first-place team would choose last. Bell's idea was adopted by the NFL in 1935 and the first draft was held in February 1936. The Eagles, who had the worst record in the NFL in 1935, made the first selection in the first draft. They chose Jay Berwanger of the University of Chicago.

If Bell thought the draft system would have immediate rewards for the Eagles, he was proven wrong. In the five years following the first draft in 1936, the Eagles won a total of just 10 games. Not until 1943, when the team merged for one season with the Pittsburgh Steelers, did the Eagles have a winning season.

FIRST PRO TO PASS FOR 1000 YARDS IN ONE SEASON

Arnold Herber was the first professional football player to pass for more than 1000 yards in a single season. He did it in 1936 for the Green Bay Packers, who went on to win the league championship that season.

FIRST COLLEGE FOOTBALL GAME TO BE TELEVISED

The first college football game to be televised took place Sept. 30, 1939 at Triboro Stadium on Randall's Island in New York City. Bill Stern called the action between Fordham and Waynesburg.

FIRST TELEVISED PROFESSIONAL GAME

The first professional football game to be televised was played Oct. 22, 1939 at Ebbets Field in Brooklyn, N.Y. Allen "Skip" Walz called the play-by-play as the Brooklyn Dodgers beat the Philadelphia Eagles, 23-14.

ORIGINS OF THE T-FORMATION

The T-formation, while not entirely unknown in 1940, had gained little popularity and was seldom used. Three standard formations were used by most football teams: the single-wing, the double-wing and the Notre Dame shift. But in 1940 the founder, owner and coach of the Chicago Bears of the National Football League, George Halas, brought the T-formation into regular use. Under the Halas system, the Bears' quarterback lined up directly behind the center, while the fullback and two halfbacks were in a line parallel to the line of scrimmage.

The 1940 season, when Halas and the Bears began using the T-formation, was a relatively successful one—they won eight games and lost just three. One reason the T-formation had such immediate success is that the opposing teams had not yet been able to develop a successful defense against it.

The T-formation became a basic part of the football play book Dec. 8, 1940, when the Bears met the Washington Redskins in the NFL championship game in Washington, D.C. The first great football passer, Sammy

Baugh, was the Redskins' quarterback; just three weeks earlier, in a regular season game, the Redskins had beaten the Bears 7-3. As a result Washington was a slight favorite to take the championship crown. But the Bears' quarterback was the brainy Sid Luckman, to whom Halas had taught more than 200 ways to run off the T-formation, more than any other coach had found possible. Halas hoped that the championship game would vindicate his faith in the T-formation and give the Bears revenge for their regular season defeat.

While 30,000 fans watched, the Bears went to the T-formation as soon as the game got underway. On the first series of plays, George McAfee moved left from the T-formation. Luckman took the snap from the center, faked a handoff, then gave the ball to Bill Osmanski, who went over to the left side, found a hole and went 68 yards for a touchdown. The Bears had the first score of the game.

On their second series of plays from scrimmage, the Bears showed the Skins another new trick. A man was put in motion to the left to draw the defense to that side. Then the ball-carrier went to the right, leading to another Chicago touchdown. After one quarter the Bears led 21-0; by halftime they were ahead 28-0.

Working off the T-formation, the Bears added humiliation to frustration in the second half, scoring time and time again. The final score: the Bears, 73; the Redskins, 0. In a championship game, no less. Operating off the T-formation, the Bears had amassed 372 yards rushing to just three for the Skins.

By the end of the decade, there wasn't a team in football that used anything but the Halas-refined T-formation.

ODD BOWL GAMES

There were a number of unusually named "bowl" football games played by members of the American armed forces overseas during World War II. Most were played only once.

Some of the more unusual "bowl games" were:

Spaghetti Bowl, Florence, Italy, 1942
Lily Bowl, 1943-45, Bermuda
Arab Bowl, Oran, Algeria, 1944
Potato Bowl, Ireland, 1944
Riviera Bowl, Marseilles, France, 1945
Tea Bowl, London, England, 1945.

The Arab Bowl was the idea of the sports editor of the *Stars and Stripes* at the time, Jim Harrigan. The game, a touch football contest, was played between Army and Navy all-star teams composed of servicemen on duty in the area at the time. Army won, 10-7.

FIRST PLAYER TO THROW SEVEN TOUCHDOWN PASSES IN A SINGLE GAME

Sid Luckman, quarterback for the Chicago Bears, was renowned for his forward pitching. He put on a showcase performance on Nov. 14, 1943, throwing seven forward touchdown passes against the New York Giants. On the day of the game the New York Polo Grounds held 57,000 New York fans, who began cheering the New York-born Luckman's incredible performance, even though he was humiliating the hometown Giants.

Luckman threw two touchdown passes in the first quarter, one a 54-yard aerial pass. He threw two more in the second quarter. Luckman hit another 50-yard-plus touchdown pass early in the third quarter, and finished up the historic game with a sixth and a seventh touchdown pass.

FIRST COACH TO TAKE TEAMS TO ALL FOUR MAJOR BOWLS

William Alexander, who spent his entire athletic career at Georgia Tech, was the first college football coach to take his team to all four major college football bowl games.

Alexander played football at Georgia Tech and then became assistant to famed head coach John Heisman. He succeeded Heisman as head coach at Georgia Tech in 1920 and held that post until 1944. He was athletic director from 1945 until his death in 1950. His 1928 team was 10-0-0; it went on to beat California, 8-7, in the Rose Bowl. His 1940 team beat Missouri in the Orange Bowl, 21-7, and his 1943 team lost to Texas in the Cotton Bowl, 14-7. In 1944 Alexander's team beat Tulsa in the Sugar Bowl, 20-18.

FIRST NETWORK TELEVISION BROADCAST OF A COLLEGE FOOTBALL GAME

The Army-Navy game in 1945 was the first college football game broadcast on network television. NBC broadcast the game to four cities: New York, Philadelphia, Washington, D.C. and Schenectady, N.Y.

Army won the game, 32-13.

ORIGINS OF THE OUTLAND TROPHY

The Outland Trophy was established in 1946 by the Football Writers of

America to honor the outstanding interior lineman on the nation's college football teams. The award was named for John Outland, a turn-of-the-century standout at the University of Pennsylvania. Outland was an All-American fullback in 1899; he played tackle on defense and was on the field for the entire 60 minutes of most games.

The Outland Trophy was presented for the first time in 1946 to Notre Dame tackle George Connor. He went on to become a pro star with the Chicago Bears.

FIRST COLLEGE ALL-STAR TEAM TO DEFEAT A CHAMPIONSHIP PRO TEAM

In 1947, for the first time in the 14-year history of the Chicago *Tribune*'s annual game pitting the college all-stars against the championship professional football team, the college all-stars won. The all-stars beat the Chicago Bears, 16-0.

FIRST PLAYER TO KICK FIVE FIELD GOALS IN A SINGLE GAME

Bob Waterfield of the Los Angeles Rams was one of the greatest quarterbacks in the history of football. In a game against the Detroit Lions on Dec. 9, 1951, he also became the first player to kick five field goals in a professional game. Waterfield kicked three goals in the first half and two in the second, the longest one a 40-yard kick, to score five times on five tries. The previous record had been four field goals in one game.

FIRST USE OF A RUBBER-COVERED BALL IN A MAJOR COLLEGE GAME

A rubber-covered football was first used in a major collegiate game on Oct. 13, 1951 in a game between Georgia Tech and Louisiana State University in Atlanta. Georgia Tech won, 25-7. Previously footballs had been covered with leather.

FIRST ALL-PRO PLAYER ON BOTH OFFENSE AND DEFENSE

In the history of the National Football League, only one man has been named All-Pro on both offense and defense—and he accomplished the feat three years in a row. Notre Dame graduate George Connor of the Chicago Bears was named All-Pro on both offense and defense in 1951, 1952 and 1953.

FIRST BLACK PRO QUARTERBACK

Willie Thrower was the first black quarterback in the National Football League. He played one season, 1953, for the Chicago Bears.

FIRST MVP

The National Football League's most valuable player award, named the Jim Thorpe Trophy after the legendary athlete and first NFL president, was established in 1955. Chicago Bears receiver Harlon Hill was the first recipient.

FIRST OVERTIME GAME

Until the National Football League adopted a sudden death overtime rule for regular season games in the 1970s, there had been only four sudden death overtime games in professional football history, all playoff games.

The first overtime football game was played Dec. 28, 1958 as the Baltimore Colts and the New York Giants played for the NFL championship in New York. The Colts led 14-3 at the half, but the Giants scored one touchdown in the third quarter and another in the fourth, while the Colts scored a field goal in the fourth quarter, and so the score stood at 17-17 at the end of regulation play. New York won the toss at the start of the sudden death overtime and chose to receive. The Giants could only move the ball nine yards on three plays and gave up possession with a punt; Baltimore took over on their own 20-yard line.

Baltimore quarterback Johnny Unitas connected on four of five passes, two to Ray Berry for a total of 33 yards, as the Colts moved the ball to the Giants' one-yard line in 12 plays. On the 13th play, Alan Ameche went through a hole on the right side to score the winning touchdown, after eight minutes and 15 seconds of overtime play. No point-after-touchdown was attempted, so Baltimore won the game 23-17 and became the 1958 NFL champion.

FIRST BLACK RECIPIENT OF THE HEISMAN TROPHY

Ernie Davis, a big left halfback with Syracuse, became the first black to win the Heisman Trophy in 1961. Davis had been the team's leading ground-gainer for three seasons. He finished 1961 with 823 yards on 150 carries, averaging 5.5 yards. He had scored 15 touchdowns and 94 points, and led Syracuse in pass receptions with 16 catches for a total of 157 yards. He broke Jim Brown's career records in rushing yardage with 2386, total yardage with 3414, scoring with 220 points and touchdowns with 35.

After graduation Davis was signed by the Cleveland Browns of the National Football League for the then-unbelievable sum of $80,000. But shortly after signing, before he could suit up for his first pro game, Davis was stricken with leukemia. He died May 18, 1963, after a 16-month struggle.

Davis was elected posthumously to the National Football Hall of Fame Dec. 4, 1979.

FIRST SUPER BOWL

The Super Bowl evolved out of the merger agreement between the National Football League and the American Football League, which had been formed in 1960.

During 1966 an agreement was reached to merge the two rival leagues beginning with the 1970 season. As part of the merger agreement, an interleague championship game between the NFL and AFL champions was established. When the leagues were merged in 1970, the championship game was to continue between the NFL's National Conference champion and its American Conference champion.

The first game was played Jan. 15, 1967 at the Los Angeles Coliseum. The National Football League's Green Bay Packers defeated the American Football League's Kansas City Chiefs, 35-10.

Although that was the first Super Bowl game, there was nothing on the game program, which called it the "World Championship Game," to indicate that it was indeed the first Super Bowl. The owner of the Kansas City Chiefs, Lamar Hunt, had suggested the name "Super Bowl," but it was not greeted with enthusiasm by others. Nevertheless, the media began using the name "Super Bowl." It gained such popularity that after several years it became the official name of the post-season game.

FIRST SUPER BOWL MVP

The first MVP in Super Bowl history, Bart Starr, quarterback of the Green Bay Packers, was also to become the only player to be named most valuable player twice. Starr was named the most valuable player in the first Super Bowl, on Jan. 15, 1967, after leading the Pack to a 35-10 victory over the Kansas City Chiefs in Los Angeles. Starr repeated as MVP in Super Bowl II, on Jan. 14, 1968, when the Packers defeated Oakland, 33-14, in Miami.

FIRST WOMAN IN PROFESSIONAL FOOTBALL

A 27-year-old weighing 122 pounds would be an unlikely candidate for professional football, regardless of sex. But Pat Palinkas wanted to hold the ball for her husband, Steve, who played for the Atlantic Coast League Orlando Panthers, and the team gave her a chance on Aug. 15, 1970.

Mrs. Palinkas went into the game just before the end of the first half to hold the ball for her husband, who was to attempt an extra point. The snap from center was bad, and Mrs. Palinkas was forced to run with the ball. She didn't get very far before she was tackled by 235-lb. Wally Florence of the Bridgeport Jets. The next two extra points that the Palinkas couple attempted were good, but despite two successful attempts out of three, she wasn't urged to sign a contract with the National Football League.

FIRST PLAYER TO RUSH MORE THAN 2000 YARDS IN A SEASON

O.J. Simpson of the Buffalo Bills was the first professional football player to rush for more than 2000 yards in a single season. Simpson piled up 2003 yards in 1973.

FIRST TWO-TIME WINNER OF THE HEISMAN TROPHY

The first and so far only two-time winner of the Heisman Memorial Trophy Award was Ohio State back Archie Griffin, who won the award as a junior in 1974 and again as a senior in 1975. As a junior he broke an all-time record for running backs in the Big Ten Conference, amassing 4064 yards. That year he led Ohio State to the Rose Bowl and a victory over UCLA. As a senior, Griffin extended his record of consecutive 100-yard-plus games to 31 and his overall yardage to 5176.

After graduation Griffin was signed by the Cincinnati Bengals of the National Football League.

3/BASKETBALL

ORIGINS

If you're looking for the roots of basketball, you may have to go back to Mexico before the birth of Christ, when a game in which a round object was passed through a ring was played. In the 16th century, the Aztecs played a game which called for putting a solid rubber ball through a stone ring.

Modern basketball, however, was born at the Training School of the International YMCA College (now Springfield College) at Springfield, Mass. in December 1891. The game was developed by Dr. James A. Naismith, an instructor at the school. Naismith's idea in developing the game was to popularize the use of gymnasiums, which at that time were regarded as boring places devoted to calisthenics and other activities aimed more at physical fitness than recreation. And that was certainly not good for building Y membership.

Dr. Naismith set out to create a game that could be played indoors. Since most games were played with a ball, it was obvious to Dr. Naismith that a ball would be used in his game, too. He decided that in order to avoid the roughness of football, the ball should not be held. He also determined that the ball should be thrown to the goal in an arc, rather than in a straight line, in order to reduce its force.

With those principles in mind, Dr. Naismith had two peach baskets attached to the balcony in the school's gymnasium, thus giving the game its name—basketball.

The first organized game was played at the Y on Jan. 20, 1892; attendance was confined to the Y's staff and members. The first public game was not played until March 11 of that year. The game remained confined to the Young Men's Christian Association for two years, until the Amateur Athletic Union joined with the Y in formalizing the rules and in playing the game. The National Collegiate Athletic Association took over rule-making for the colleges.

The game became national in scope shortly after it was taken up at the turn of the century by several Eastern schools. Yale, Columbia, Harvard, Princeton and Cornell formed the Eastern League (now the Ivy League) for basketball in the 1901-02 season. Yale became the first Eastern League champion, with a record of 6 and 2 in league play that year. The Big Ten Conference was then formed in 1906, the Missouri Valley Conference in 1908, the Southwest Conference in 1915 and the Pacific Coast Conference in 1916, making basketball an organized collegiate sport from coast to coast.

FIRST COLLEGE TO PLAY A FULL SCHEDULE

In 1894 the University of Chicago became the first college to play a full basketball schedule. Chicago played its first game against the Chicago YMCA Training School on Jan. 27, 1894. The University won the game, 19-11, and went on to compile a 6 and 1 record for the season.

FIRST GAME BETWEEN TWO COLLEGE TEAMS

Most early basketball games featured at least one YMCA team, since basketball had been devised as a form of indoor exercise for the YMCA. The first basketball game between two colleges took place on Feb. 9, 1895 in Minnesota, with the Minnesota State School of Agriculture defeating Hamline College, 9-3.

ORIGINS OF PROFESSIONAL BASKETBALL

Although college basketball began on an organized basis shortly after the turn of the century with the formation of the Eastern League (now the Ivy League), it was not for nearly 50 years that professional basketball became firmly established in the United States.

The first professional basketball league was formed in 1898. It was called the National Basketball League; member teams were located in New York City, Philadelphia, Brooklyn and New Jersey. It lasted just two seasons. The New England Basketball League was also organized in 1898. Its players received monthly salaries ranging from $150 to $225. It, too, lasted only briefly, as did several other pro loops on either side of the turn of that century.

Pro basketball took a step forward in 1925 when the American Basketball League was formed, with nine cities represented. The league remained active until the mid-1930s, when it, too, was dissolved.

One of the precursors of today's National Basketball Association was born in 1937, when another National Basketball League was organized. The N.B.L. pretty much had a lock on professional basketball until 1946, when the other forerunner of today's NBA, the Basketball Association of America, was formed. (See also **First NBA Commissioner.**)

The two leagues merged into the National Basketball Association in 1949. In the 1949-50 season there were 17 teams in the league. By the following season the league's membership had shrunk to 11 teams, and by the late 1950s to eight teams. The NBA faced another threat when the rival American Basketball Association, with 11 teams, was formed for the 1967-68 season. After years of costly competition, the ABA and NBA merged in 1976. Four ABA teams became full NBA members; players from the other ABA teams were drafted by NBA teams.

FIRST COLLEGE PLAYER TO SCORE 1000 POINTS

Christian Steinmetz, who played for the University of Wisconsin from 1903 to 1905, was the first college basketball player to score more than 1000 points in his college career. During his senior year at Wisconsin, Steinmetz scored 462 points, including 50 in one game, an exceptional feat in that era of low-scoring games.

ORIGINS OF THE HARLEM GLOBETROTTERS

There is probably no basketball team more famous throughout the world than the Harlem Globetrotters. The Globetrotters have played in more than 90 countries, performing before kings and presidents and millions upon millions of everyday people. The Globetrotters have drawn some of the largest crowds in the history of the game, including 75,000 fans in Berlin in 1951.

The Clown Princes of the Court are obviously more show than real basketball competition. Both their opponents and the referees are part of the show. When Abe Saperstein formed the first Globetrotter team in 1926, however, the 'Trotters were meant to be a serious barnstorming team. The Globetrotters played their first games in the Savoy Ballroom in Chicago, but when the dance hall fell on hard times and was turned into a skating rink, Saperstein found he had no choice but to take his team on the road. Since then, the Globetrotters have never had a home court.

Saperstein decided to call his team the Harlem Globetrotters for two reasons. The team was entirely black then, as it is now, and Saperstein thought that using "Harlem" in the team's name would make that fact clear. Saperstein said that he chose "Globetrotters" because he wanted to let people know that his team had been around.

The Globetrotters began traveling around the country, playing games wherever they could. Saperstein continued to get the best black players he could find. As a result his team was soon so good that no one wanted to play them. Saperstein then started adding comedy routines to the team's repertoire, and the clowning proved popular with the fans. The comedy routines were consequently expanded, and became a permanent part of the Globetrotters' show. The 'Trotters got another boost in 1940 when they won a world professional basketball tournament in Chicago.

Over the years the Globetrotters have signed a number of black stars. Nat "Sweetwater" Clifton, one of the first blacks in the National Basketball Association, had played for the 'Trotters; so did Wilt Chamberlain and baseball star Bob Gibson.

Abe Saperstein died in 1966, and his heirs sold the team for more than $3 million.

FIRST COLLEGE PLAYER TO SCORE 50 POINTS IN ONE GAME

Angelo "Hank" Luisetti is credited with popularizing the running one-hand jump shot in a day when the lay-up and the two-hand set shot were the backbone of basketball. Luisetti was introduced to this innovative style while playing for coach Tommy DeNike at San Francisco's Galileo High School. Luisetti and the running one-hand jump shot seemed made for each other. When he moved on to Stanford University, Luisetti took the jump shot with him. After employing it very successfully in December 1936 at Madison Square Garden in New York, where Luisetti and Stanford snapped Long Island University's 43-game winning streak, the running one-hand jumper revolutionized basketball from the playground on up.

The running one-hand jump allowed Luisetti to break the national collegiate scoring record during his four years at Stanford with a total of 1596 points. On New Year's Day, 1938, Luisetti became the first collegiate player to score 50 points in one game in a Stanford victory over Duquesne. That was a Stanford single game scoring record that stands to this day.

FIRST NATIONAL INVITATIONAL TOURNAMENT

The first National Invitational Tournament for college basketball teams was the brainstorm of the Metropolitan Basketball Writers' Association of New York. Six teams participated in the first NIT in 1938 at Madison Square Garden in New York: Bradley, Temple, Long Island University, New York University, Oklahoma A & M and Colorado.

The Temple Owls, the Eastern Intercollegiate Champions, who had finished the year with a 23 and 2 record, defeated Bradley, 53-40, in the quarter-final round, while NYU edged LIU, 39-37. Oklahoma A & M and Colorado drew byes for the quarter-finals.

In the semi-finals, powerful Temple once again came out victorious, stopping Oklahoma A & M, 54-44, while Colorado slipped by NYU, 48-47, setting the stage for a Temple-Colorado showdown in the championship game.

Paced by Don Shields' 16 points, Temple was just too much for Colorado, and the Owls scored an easy 60-36 victory. Oklahoma A & M defeated NYU in the consolation game, 37-24.

Shields, who led all players with 39 points in three games, was named the tournament's most valuable player.

FIRST NATIONAL COLLEGIATE ATHLETIC ASSOCIATION TOURNAMENT

The first National Collegiate Athletic Association (NCAA) post-season basketball tournament was played in 1939, at the conclusion of the 1938-39 season, at Northwestern University in Evanston, Ill.

In the eastern semi-finals, Villanova defeated Brown, 43-30, while the Big Ten Champion Ohio State Buckeyes, led by James Hull, stopped Wake Forest, 64-52. Ohio State then went on to an easy 53-36 victory over Villanova for the eastern regional championship.

In the western semi-finals, Oklahoma defeated Utah State, 50-39, while the Oregon Webfoots, the Pacific Coast champions, scored an easy 56-41 victory over Texas. In the championship game Oregon notched an easy 55-37 victory over Oklahoma to take the western regional crown, setting the stage for an Oregon-Ohio State showdown in the championship game. The

Webfoots proved too much for the Buckeyes, winning the first NCAA championship with a 46-33 victory. Webfoot John Dick led all scorers with 15 points per game.

FIRST TELEVISED COLLEGE GAME

The first college basketball game to be televised was played Feb. 28, 1940 at Madison Square Garden in New York. Viewers saw Pittsburgh beat Fordham, 50-37.

FIRST MAJOR COLLEGE SCANDAL

After remaining relatively scandal-free for more than 50 years, college basketball was struck by its first major scandal in 1945. And the scandal was discovered by accident.

New York police had staked out the home of 29-year-old Henry Rosen, who was suspected of being a fence for stolen garments. One day in January two police officers were watching Rosen's home when they spotted Larry Pearlstein and Bernard Barnett going inside. When the two left they were picked up for questioning in connection with the garment fencing investigation. But they panicked and confessed they had received $1,000 from Rosen to split among the five members of the Brooklyn College basketball team for which they played. Pearlstein and Barnett said there were plans to meet with Rosen in Boston before Brooklyn's game with Akron to receive instructions. There were also plans for Brooklyn to throw a game to St. Francis College on Feb. 10.

Because of the scandal, the Akron University team arrived in Boston, after traveling several hundred miles, to find that its game had been canceled.

Three other members of the Brooklyn team subsequently confessed to taking money from gamblers and, along with Barnett, were expelled from the school. It was later learned that although Pearlstein had played on the college's basketball team, he had never been registered as a student.

Rosen and another gambler named Harvey Stemmer were ultimately convicted of conspiracy to cheat and defraud in connection with the Brooklyn College fix. Each was sentenced to a year in prison and fined $500.

FIRST NBA COMMISSIONER

Modern professional basketball was born in June 1946 when a group of arena owners, led by Boston Gardens president Walter Brown and Cleveland Arena owner Al Sutphin, formed the Basketball Association of America. Teams were planned for 11 cities stretching from Boston to St. Louis. The owners chose Maurice Podoloff, a New Haven, Conn. lawyer, as president of the new league. Podoloff, a Russian immigrant who had graduated from Yale Law School, was then serving as president of the American Hockey League.

Podoloff is credited with holding the BAA together during its early days. When the BAA merged with the National Basketball League in 1949 to form the National Basketball Association, Podoloff was chosen as the first NBA commissioner. He shepherded the NBA through its infant days and negotiated the first NBA television contract in 1954, a move that gave the game new national prominence.

Podoloff served as NBA commissioner for 17 years before retiring in 1963.

FIRST BLACK ALL-AMERICAN

UCLA center Don Barksdale was the first black basketball All-American. He received this honor in 1947.

FIRST TEAM TO WIN THE NCAA TOURNAMENT AND THE NIT THE SAME YEAR

Only one college basketball team has ever won both the NCAA and NIT tournaments in the same year. City College of New York did it in 1950. After posting a 17 and 5 regular season record, CCNY went on to defeat the nation's first, second, third, fifth, sixth and 12th ranked teams in the two tournaments, defeating number one ranked Bradley in the finals of both tourneys. The members of the CCNY team were Al "Fats" Roth, Ed Warner, Floyd Lane, Irwin Dambrot and Ed Roman.

FIRST BLACKS IN THE NBA

Today some 65 percent of the members of the National Basketball Association are blacks, making basketball the only major professional sport in which blacks constitute a majority. That fact is amazing considering that there were no blacks at all in the NBA in its first season, 1949-50. The first blacks to play in the league were Nat "Sweetwater" Clifton and Chuck Cooper, who both made their debuts during the 1950-51 season.

The New York Knicks acquired Clifton from the Harlem Globetrotters. Clifton, from Xavier College, played seven seasons for the Knicks before winding up his NBA career with the Detroit Pistons in the 1957-58 season. He appeared in over 500 games, compiling a career scoring average of 10 points per game.

The Boston Celtics drafted Chuck Cooper from Duquesne. Cooper played six years in the NBA—four with the Celtics before moving on to Milwaukee, then to St. Louis-Fort Wayne, where he wound up his NBA career during the 1955-56 season. Cooper appeared in slightly more than 400 NBA games, posting a 6.7-point career scoring average.

FIRST NBA ALL-STAR GAME

The first National Basketball Association All-Star Game was played March 2, 1951 at the Boston Garden in Boston, Mass. A crowd of 10,094 turned out to watch the squad from the East defeat the West, 111-94. Playing before a home town crowd, the Boston Celtics' "Easy" Ed Macauley paced the eastern team's attack, leading all scorers with 20 points. Macauley was voted the game's most valuable player. The West's George Mikan, who had won the NBA scoring title for the season, was held to just four field goals in the first All-Star Game.

FIRST MAN TO SCORE 100 POINTS IN A MAJOR COLLEGE GAME

Frank Selvy of Furman College became the first major college basketball player to score 100 points in one game as he led the Furman Paladins to a 149-95 victory over Newberry College on Feb. 13, 1954 on Furman's home court at Greenville, S.C.

The six-foot, three-inch Furman senior was the nation's leading college basketball scorer when he took the court for the Newberry game. As his parents, visiting from his hometown of Corbin, Ky., looked on, Selvy scored 24 points in the first quarter and 13 in the second. After three periods Selvy had racked up 62 points; his Paladin teammates were by that time feeding him the ball at every opportunity.

Midway through the fourth quarter he had broken the NCAA record of 73 points in one game, set by Bill Mlkvy of Temple in 1951. By the time the final buzzer had sounded, Selvy had scored 38 points in the fourth quarter, giving him a nice round 100-point total for the game.

FIRST PLAYER TO SCORE 100 POINTS IN A PROFESSIONAL GAME

Wilt Chamberlain of Philadelphia was the first and, so far, the only player to score 100 points in one game in the National Basketball Association. He did it against the New York Knicks on March 2, 1962 at Hershey, Pa. Philadelphia won the game by a score of 169-147. Chamberlain never repeated the feat.

FIRST PLAYER TO MAKE ALL-AMERICAN TEAMS THREE YEARS IN HIGH SCHOOL AND THREE YEARS IN COLLEGE

Jerry Lucas was the only basketball player ever to be named an All-American every year he was eligible both in high school and in college. After being named a high school All-American from Middletown High School in Middletown, Ohio in 1956, 1957 and 1958, Lucas attended Ohio State and made the college All-American team in 1960, 1961 and 1962. Lucas also starred on the 1960 U.S. Olympic basketball team.

FIRST BLACK COACH IN THE NBA

Bill Russell was named player-coach for the Boston Celtics on April 18, 1966, becoming the first black coach in National Basketball Association history. At the same time he became the first black named head coach for any major professional sports team.

FIRST GUARD TO SCORE 1000 FIELD GOALS

Nate Archibald was the first guard in the National Basketball Association to score 1000 field goals in one season. Archibald, who played for Kansas City-Omaha, scored 1028 field goals during the 1972-73 season. He scored a total of 2719 points that year, for an average of 34 points per game.

FIRST GAME OF THE WOMAN'S PROFESSIONAL BASKETBALL LEAGUE

The first game of the Woman's Professional Basketball League took place between the Chicago Hustle and the Milwaukee Does on Dec. 9, 1978. The Hustle won by a score of 92-87, with high scorer Debra Waddy-Rossow scoring 30 points.

FIRST WOMAN TO SIGN A PRO CONTRACT

Ann Meyers, a former Olympian and star on the women's basketball team at UCLA, became the first woman to sign a contract to play in the National Basketball Association on Aug. 30, 1979. The 24-year-old Meyers signed a one-year contract with the Indiana Pacers, guaranteeing her $50,000 whether she made the team or not. She was to remain with the team in a front office job if she did not make the team. Meyers did not make the team; she subsequently left the Pacers' organization altogether.

The five-foot, nine-inch tall, 135-pound Meyers, the first woman to receive a full athletic scholarship to attend UCLA, was a four-time All-American. She also played on the American basketball team which won a silver medal in the 1976 Olympics at Montreal.

Dave Meyers, a forward with the Milwaukee Bucks of the National Basketball Association, is Meyers' brother.

FIRST COLLEGE TEAM TO WIN THE NAIA, NIT AND NCAA TOURNAMENTS

The University of Louisville in Louisville, Kentucky was the first college to win the National Association of Intercollegiate Athletics tournament, the National Invitational Tournament and the National Collegiate Athletic Association tournament. Louisville won the NAIA in 1948, the NIT in 1956 and the NCAA in 1980.

4/HOCKEY (FIELD AND ICE)

ORIGINS OF FIELD HOCKEY

Field hockey is probably the oldest stick and ball game—it originated in Persia around 200 B.C. It was played in Europe during the Middle Ages, but was outlawed in England because it interfered with archery training, which was the basis of the national defense.

Modern field hockey was developed in England around 1850 and soon spread around the world, although it has never found great popularity in the United States. Field hockey has been an Olympic sport since 1908; India has consistently dominated the Olympic competition.

Field hockey had been played only informally in the U.S. prior to 1926. That year Henry K. Greer headed a group in New York City and West-chester County that tried to arrange regular matches between men's teams. They had been introduced to hockey by Miss Louise Roberts, an English coach at a girl's school in Greenwich, Conn., who later became Mrs. Henry K. Greer. The first organized men's field hockey match in the U.S. probably took place on Oct. 28, 1928 at the Germantown Cricket Club in Philadelphia. The teams were the Westchester Field Hockey Club of Rye,

N.Y. and the Germantown Cricket Club. Westchester won, 2-1.

The U.S. Olympic committee was interested in having an American field hockey team appear in the 1932 Olympics, so it asked the men's hockey teams to organize. They formed the Field Hockey Association of America in 1930 and sent a team to the Olympics. Outside of Olympic competition, however, the game has generally been considered a women's game in this country.

Constance M.K. Applebee of the British College of Physical Education introduced field hockey to women in the U.S., teaching the game first to women at Vassar and later at other colleges, including Wellesley, Smith, Mount Holyoke and Bryn Mawr. In 1922 she opened her famous Mount Pocono Hockey Camp for women.

Women formed a field hockey association in 1922, the United States Field Hockey Association, with Edward B. Krumbhaar of Philadelphia as the first president. The game has increased in popularity over the years among women and is played at many colleges and universities, with a national competition each year since 1975. The first national champion was West Chester (Pa.) State College.

ORIGINS OF ICE HOCKEY

Ice hockey was first played in eastern Canada sometime in the middle part of the 19th century. Members of Her Majesty's Royal Canadian Rifles are known to have played a game similar to hockey in Kingston, Ontario around 1855. (It is possible, in fact, that hockey—or "shinny," a game which may have been a precursor of hockey—was played in the Kingston area in the 1830s.) In any event, students at McGill University in Montreal first began to establish formal rules for hockey around 1875. By the mid-1880s the sport was fairly well established in Canada.

Ice hockey appears to have been introduced to the United States by way of Yale University in New Haven, Conn. Two Yale tennis players, Malcolm G. Chace and Arthur E. Foote, had discovered hockey in Canada and brought it back to New Haven. By the late 1890s the game was being played throughout the northeastern United States. Since then hockey has continued to grow in popularity in the United States; Canada is still universally recognized, however, as the stronghold of ice hockey.

ORIGINS OF THE STANLEY CUP

The Stanley Cup is awarded each year to the team that wins the National Hockey League's best-of-seven final playoff round. It symbolizes the world hockey championship, even though only NHL teams, which represent cities in the United States and Canada, participate in the playoffs.

The system for determining the winner of the Stanley Cup has been changed for the 1981-82 season. Under the new system, the top four teams in each of the four divisions of the NHL will qualify for the playoffs, rather than the 16 teams with the best overall records. Two best-of-five series will be played in each division, followed by a best-of-seven series which will determine the division championship. A best-of-seven series in each conference will determine the two conference championships; then another best-of-seven series will determine the winner of the Stanley Cup.

The Stanley Cup is the oldest trophy for which professional athletes compete in North America. It was donated by Frederick Arthur, Lord Stanley of Preston, the son of the Earl of Derby, in 1893. Lord Stanley bought the trophy for the equivalent of about $50 for presentation to the amateur hockey champions of Canada. Since 1926, however, the cup has been awarded solely to NHL teams.

An amateur team in Montreal won the first Stanley Cup at the conclusion of the 1892-93 season. Between 1892 and 1917 only amateur teams participated in the Stanley Cup competition. From 1917 to 1926 teams from the NHL (formed in 1917) and teams from other leagues competed for the trophy.

FIRST U.S. TEAMS IN THE NHL

The National Hockey league was formed on Nov. 22, 1917, but it consisted solely of teams from Canadian cities. It was not until 1924 that the Boston Bruins, the first U.S. team, were admitted. Two years later teams from Detroit and New York were added.

FIRST NHL SCORING CHAMPION

Joe Malone of the Montreal Canadiens was the National Hockey League's first season scoring champion. He had 44 goals in 20 games in the 1917-18 season.

ORIGINS OF THE HART MEMORIAL TROPHY

The Hart Memorial Trophy is presented each year to the National Hockey League player named most valuable to his team. The recipient is chosen by a vote of the Professional Hockey Writers' Association in the 21 cities with NHL teams.

The original Hart Trophy was donated in 1923 by Dr. David A. Hart, father of Cecil Hart, one-time manager and coach of the Montreal Canadiens.

The original Hart Trophy was retired to the Hockey Hall of Fame in 1960 and replaced with another trophy by the NHL.

The Hart Trophy was presented for the first time after the 1923-24 season to Frank Nighbor of the Ottawa Senators.

The man chosen most valuable player now receives $1,500 in addition to the Hart Trophy, while the runner-up in the voting receives $750.

ORIGINS OF THE PRINCE OF WALES TROPHY

His Royal Highness Edward, Prince of Wales, presented what is known as the Prince of Wales trophy to the National Hockey League in 1924. In 1925, 1926 and 1927 the trophy was presented to the National Hockey League champions. The Montreal Canadiens, champions for the 1924-25 season, were the first team to win the trophy. From 1928 through 1938 the trophy was presented to the team finishing first in the NHL's U.S. division. The Boston Bruins were the first to win the trophy under those rules for the 1927-28 season.

From 1939 through 1967, when the NHL reverted to one section, the trophy went to the team winning the league championship. The Boston Bruins won it for the 1938-39 season. When the NHL expanded for the 1967-68 season, the trophy once again became a divisional award and Montreal won it for the 1967-68 season. Beginning with the 1974-75 season, the trophy was awarded to the top team in the Prince of Wales Conference. The Buffalo Sabres won it for the 1974-75 season.

ORIGINS OF THE LADY BYNG MEMORIAL TROPHY

Lady Byng, the wife of Canada's governor-general at that time, contributed a trophy after the 1924-25 season to be presented for sportsmanship and gentlemanly conduct. The Lady Byng trophy was first awarded to Frank Nighbor of Ottawa. After Lady Byng died in 1949, the National Hockey League continued to present the award as the Lady Byng Memorial Trophy.

ORIGINS OF THE VEZINA TROPHY

The Vezina Trophy is awarded each year to the National Hockey League goalkeeper with the best record for the season. The trophy was contributed by Leo Dandurand, Louis Letourneau and Joe Cattarinich, former owners of the Montreal Canadiens, in honor of Canadiens' goalie George Vezina, who collapsed during a 1925 game and died a few months later.

The Vezina trophy was awarded for the first time after the 1926-27 season to George Hainsworth of the Montreal Canadiens.

FIRST GOALIE TO WEAR A FACE MASK

The first National Hockey League goalie to wear a face mask for protection was the Montreal Maroons' Clint Benedict, during the 1929-30 season. Benedict began wearing the mask after the Montreal Canadiens' Howie Morenz broke his nose with a shot. Benedict stopped wearing the mask after a short time, however, and it was another 30 years before face masks gained wide acceptance among NHL goalies.

FIRST ROOKIE OF THE YEAR

The first National Hockey League Rookie of the Year was chosen after the 1932-33 season. The honor went to Carl Voss of Detroit; Voss, however, received nothing for the honor. After the 1936-37 season, National Hockey League president Frank Calder began giving the Rookie of the Year a trophy. Syl Apps of Toronto, Rookie of the Year for the 1936-37 season, was the first to receive the trophy. After Calder died the award was named the Calder Memorial Trophy. Gaye Stewart of Toronto was the first to receive the Calder Trophy, for the 1942-43 season.

FIRST U.S. HOCKEY GAME TO BE TELEVISED

The first hockey game to be televised in the United States was played between the New York Rangers and the Montreal Canadiens at Madison Square Garden in New York City on Feb. 25, 1940. The game was televised by station W2XBS in New York.

FIRST PLAYER TO SCORE A GOAL A GAME

The fans loved him enough to stage the worst sports riot in North American history in 1955 when he was suspended for hitting an official. He played hockey only one way: as hard as possible. He was Maurice "Rocket" Richard of the Montreal Canadiens.

The Canadiens signed the 20-year-old Richard in 1942. Halfway through his first season in the pros, he suffered a broken ankle. Early the next season (1943-44) he suffered a shoulder injury, but nevertheless managed to score 32 goals.

Fully recovered by the beginning of the 1944-45 season, the Rocket took off. He got his first goal in the third game of the season. In the fifth game Richard got his first hat trick of the season with three goals. A week later he got another hat trick, running his scoring streak to 12 goals in 13 games. Since the National Hockey League had taken on its present shape in 1926, no one had managed to average a goal per game for an entire season. Furthermore, no one had scored more than 43 goals in a single season. But Richard, playing only his third NHL season, was well on his way to breaking both records.

Richard, who shot left-handed but played right wing anyway, got his 44th goal in the 40th game of the season, setting a new NHL mark and bringing him within six goals of the 50 goals in 50 games mark. He scored five goals over the next nine games.

Finally, in the 50th and last game of the season, Richard scored his 50th goal in a 4-1 victory over the Boston Bruins, becoming the first player in NHL history to average a goal per game for an entire season.

FIRST ALL-STAR GAME

The National Hockey League All-Star Game has been an annual event since 1947. Prior to 1947, there had been three benefit games in which teams composed of all-stars opposed a regular NHL team. The first such benefit game was the Ace Bailey Benefit Game, held Feb. 14, 1934 at the Maple Leafs Garden in Toronto. The Maple Leafs defeated a team of stars from the other seven NHL teams, 7-3. The game was for the benefit of Toronto's Ace Bailey, who had suffered a fractured skull during the 1932-33 season as a result of a check by Boston defenseman Eddie Shore; the injury ended Bailey's career.

The second benefit all-star game was played Nov. 3, 1937 at the Montreal Forum in memory of Howie Morenz, one of the game's all-time great players. Morenz died March 8, 1937 from complications arising from a broken leg suffered during a game between Montreal and Chicago on Jan. 28, 1937. In that game, the all-stars defeated a team of players from the Montreal Canadiens and the Montreal Maroons by a score of 6-5.

The third benefit game was played Oct. 29, 1939, again at the Montreal Forum, in memory of Albert "Babe" Siebert of the Canadiens, who had drowned in Lake Huron on Aug. 26 of that year. In that game the all-stars beat the Canadiens, 5-2.

The first annual All-Star Game was played Oct. 13, 1947 at Toronto. The original format for the game pitted the men from the official first and second All-Star teams, plus stars from the other five teams, against the defending Stanley Cup champions on the champions' home ice. The first game saw the All-Stars defeat the Toronto Maple Leafs, 4-3, before a crowd of 14,169.

The game has been revised over the years. It now pits the All-Stars from the Clarence Campbell conference against those of the Prince of Wales Conference. The location is now rotated among the NHL cities.

ORIGINS OF THE ART ROSS TROPHY

The Art Ross Trophy is awarded each year to the National Hockey League player who leads the league in scoring points. The trophy was presented to the NHL in 1947 by Arthur Howie Ross, one-time manager and coach of the Boston Bruins. The trophy was presented for the first time after the 1947-48 season to Elmer Lach of the Montreal Canadiens, who led the league in scoring that year with an overall total of 61 points (30 goals and 31 assists).

The National Hockey League's first season scoring leader prior to the inception of the Ross Trophy was Joe Malone of the Montreal Canadiens, who scored 44 goals during the 1917-18 season.

In addition to the Ross Trophy, the NHL's leading scorer also receives $1000, while the runner-up receives $500. The leading scorer after the first half and the leader after the second half also each receive $500, while the runners-up in both halves each receive $250.

ORIGINS OF THE JAMES NORRIS MEMORIAL TROPHY

The James Norris Memorial Trophy was presented by Norris's four children in memory of their father, who at one time was the owner and president of the Detroit Red Wings. The trophy was presented for the first time after the 1953-54 season to the best defenseman in the National Hockey League. Red Kelly of Detroit was the first recipient of the Norris Trophy.

FIRST BLACK IN THE NATIONAL HOCKEY LEAGUE

Boston Bruins left wing Willie O'Ree became the first black to play in the National Hockey League on Jan. 18, 1958. O'Ree was called up from the Bruins' Canadian Aces farm team and did not score in his first game against the Montreal Canadiens. But the Bruins won the game, 3-0.

FIRST PLAYER TO WIN THE NATIONAL HOCKEY LEAGUE SCORING CHAMPIONSHIP SIX TIMES IN A ROW

Gordie Howe of the Detroit Red Wings became the first man to win the National Hockey League scoring championship six years in a row in 1962.

The 35-year-old Howe was in his 17th big league season and was already the first hockey player to have scored more than 1000 points in regular season play. No other hockey player had ever won the scoring championship more than twice.

FIRST DEATH AS A RESULT OF A GAME INJURY

Bill Masterton of the Minnesota North Stars died Jan. 15, 1968 of brain injuries suffered in a game against the Oakland Seals two days earlier. It was the first death as a result of a game injury in National Hockey League history.

ORIGINS OF THE CLARENCE S. CAMPBELL BOWL

The Clarence S. Campbell Bowl is presented each year to the team scoring the most points in the Clarence S. Campbell Conference of the National Hockey League. From 1968 through 1974 the bowl was awarded to the West Division champions. The bowl, made by a British silversmith in 1867, was placed into competition in 1968 by NHL member clubs in recognition of the service of Clarence S. Campbell, president of the National Hockey League from 1946 to 1977.

The bowl was presented for the first time in 1968 to the Philadelphia Flyers, Campbell Conference champions for the 1967-68 season.

FIRST GOALIE TO GET 100 SHUTOUTS

Terry Sawchuk was the first, and so far the only, goalie in National Hockey League history to notch more than 100 shutouts in a career. Sawchuk's career spanned 20 seasons, from 1949 through 1970, mostly with the Detroit Red Wings, although he also played for the Boston Bruins, Toronto Maple Leafs, Los Angeles Kings and New York Rangers. He had 103 shutouts in 955 games. In three seasons he had an even dozen shutouts and finished his career with a 2.50 goals against average.

FIRST GOALIE TO SCORE A GOAL

Goaltender Bill Smith of the New York Islanders is the only goaltender in the 62-year-history of the National Hockey League who has scored a goal in a game in which he was playing goalie. Smith got his goal in an unusual sequence of events in the third period of a game against the Colorado Rockies on Nov. 28, 1979 at the Nassau Coliseum in Uniondale, N.Y.

The Rockies were ahead, 4-3, when referee Bryan Lewis called a delayed hooking penalty against Islander center Mike Kaszycki. That enabled the Rockies' goalie, Bill McKenzie, to go to the bench so that Colorado could add an extra forward. Islander goalie Smith then stopped a shot; the rebound went behind the net, where it was picked up by Colorado forward Rob Ramage. Ramage tried to get the puck back to the blue line, but it went past the pointmen all the way down the ice into the open net.

The goal was first credited to Islander defenseman Dave Lewis, but videotape replays later showed that Smith had been the last Islander to touch the puck; he was thus credited with the goal. Despite Smith's unique goal, the Islanders lost the game, 7-4.

5/RACING:

HORSES, DOGS, BICYCLES, AUTOS, MOTORCYCLES, MISCELLANEA

HORSE RACING

ORIGINS

Thoroughbred horse racing, called the sport of kings, dates back to the days of Richard II and Henry IV of England. The owners of purebred horses naturally wanted to know whose horse was fastest, so they marked out four-mile tracks and began racing their horses. Four miles became the standard for races because that had been the length of chariot races in the ancient Olympic Games.

The first public race track was the Smithfield Track in London, built in 1174. Horse racing flourished, however, on a less formal basis in various locations throughout England.

Until the early 16th century, no prizes were given to the winners of horse races. But in 1512, at the fair in Chester, a wooden ball with flowers—the first horse racing trophy—was given to the winner of a race. The wooden ball was replaced by a silver one in 1540. The custom of awarding three prizes in a horse race—win, place and show—also began in Chester, in 1609. Chester Sheriff Robert Ambrye, who was responsible for securing the prize for the race, ordered a silver ball from a silversmith. But when Ambrye received the ball he didn't like it and demanded another. The second ball was no more to his liking, and Ambrye demanded still another ball, which he finally found satisfactory. So when, on the day of the race, he found himself with three silver balls, he decided to give the best ball to the winner, the next best to the second place finisher and the third best ball to the third place finisher.

It was Queen Anne, who reigned from 1702-14, who originated the practice of racing for money. She donated a gold cup to be awarded to the winner of a race in 1714 at Doncaster. But she also insisted that each horse owner put up a sum of money as well; the winner would take both the cup and the money. Queen Anne's own horse, Star, proceeded to win the race, becoming the first horse ever to win a race for money.

Those races were all four miles—the length that had been established by the first English horse racers. That distance, however, could not be covered by a horse until it was five to seven years old. That led horse breeder Col. St. Leger, in 1776, to propose a two-mile race for three-year-old colts. The race, held near Doncaster, drew six entries; St. Leger's own horse, Sampson, won. The race became an annual event, and was soon known as St. Leger's Race. Later it officially became the St. Leger Race; it is the oldest stakes in the world today.

In 1779 the 12th Earl of Derby proposed a race for three-year-old fillies, which were ineligible for the St. Leger race. The first race, a mile and a half long, was won by the Earl's horse, Bridget. The race became known as the Epsom Oaks in honor of the Earl's estate, and it retains that name to this day. The Earl also established the Epsom Derby for three-year-old horses of either sex in 1780. Although that name is still used in England, the race is the English Derby to the rest of the world.

Col. Richard Nicolls, the first English governor of New York, brought horse racing to America. Nicolls called a public meeting in February 1665 on Long Island, N.Y., to propose a series of horse races, primarily to encourage the improvement of horse breeding. Shortly after the meeting, a race course was laid out near what is now Hempstead, N.Y. The track was named the Newmarket Course. There are no records of any races at the course in 1665, 1666 or 1667, although it is assumed that races did take place there during those years. It is definitely known that a race took place in 1668, however; there is a silver porringer in the Yale University collection, engraved "1668, wunn att hanstead planes." It is thought to be the oldest piece of silver made in America that is still in existence. The porringer also bears the initials P.V.B., which may stand for Peter Van Brough, a well-known silversmith of that time from Albany, N.Y. The porringer does not indicate who won the 1668 race, but it may have been a horse owned by English Army Capt. Sylvester Salisbury.

In 1669 Nicolls' successor, Gov. Frank Lovelace, proposed a race at Newmarket for two silver cups; the entrants were required to pay one crown or its equivalent in wheat. This was the first sweepstakes race in America.

During the hundred years after horse racing became established in New York, it spread to Virginia, Maryland and Kentucky. The first race track in Kentucky, the Williams Race Track, was built outside Lexington in 1797. It was rebuilt as a larger facility in 1828 and continued to operate until 1935.

Former prize fighter John Morrissey, who had found politics and wealth after his youth, established a race track in Saratoga Springs, N.Y. in 1864. Saratoga, noted for its water, was a gathering place for the well-to-do, including the Travers family from New York City. Morrissey, who was nobody's fool, named his first stakes the "Travers." The race, the oldest of its type in America, is still being run today.

Betting on horse races in the United States took place just among owners or spectators until bookmakers started operating on race tracks in about 1873. Bookmakers from England monopolized the business at first, but Americans later took over. Pari-mutuel wagering was also introduced in the United States around 1873, but it was not very popular at first. In fact, it was not until about 1940, when bookmaking was made illegal, that pari-mutuels became widespread.

The reform movement around 1906 greatly cut down on racing in the United States, closing down racetracks except in Kentucky and Maryland. Track operators in those states escaped by using pari-mutuel machines, which later became standard in other states.

OLDEST CONTINUOUS HORSE RACING EVENT

The oldest continuous horse racing event is the Newmarket Town Four Mile Race in England. The race was originated in 1665 by England's King Charles II.

The first woman jockey to win the race was Eileen Joel, on Oct. 8, 1925. Joel, aboard Hogier, defeated four other women and three men.

FIRST WOMEN JOCKEYS

The first woman jockey may well have been an English woman named Alicia Meynell. She rode against Capt. William Flint in a four-mile race in York, England Aug. 25, 1804. She won two races at York in August 1805. It should be noted that she was the mistress of the horse's owner.

An English woman, Judy Johnson, rode Lone Gallant to a 10th place finish in a field of 11 horses in a steeplechase event at the Pimlico Racetrack at Baltimore, Md. on April 27, 1943.

The first licensed woman jockey in the United States was Kathy Kusner, who received her license in 1968. On Feb. 7, 1969, however, Diane Crump became the first American woman to ride at a pari-mutuel track. Barbara Jo Rubin was the first winning woman jockey, riding Cohesian to victory by a neck at the Charles Town, W. Va., track on Feb. 22, 1969.

American Robyn Smith was the first woman to score a victory in a major stakes race. She guided North Sea to a win in the $27,450 Paumanauk Handicap at the Aqueduct Raceway in New York City on March 1, 1973. It was Smith's first year as a professional jockey.

FIRST LARGE CROWD AT A SPORTING EVENT IN THE UNITED STATES

May 1823 saw the first large crowd ever to attend a sporting event in the United States. Some 100,000 people came to watch a match race between Eclipse, the Northern horse racing champion, and Sir Henry, the fastest thoroughbred in the South. The race was a matter of pride for people from both sections of the country, and people came from hundreds of miles around to watch one of the horses win two out of three four-mile heats over a mile-long course for a prize of $20,000.

Sir Henry won the first heat, but Eclipse won the last two and all the money.

FIRST INTERNATIONAL HORSE RACE

The first international horse race took place on April 25, 1829 over a 10-mile course between Cambridge and Godmanchester, England. The American horse, Rattler, defeated the Welsh mare, Miss Turner, by 60 yards.

FIRST AMERICAN HORSE TO WIN A MAJOR RACE ABROAD

Prioress won the Cesarewitch Handicap race in Newmarket, England on Oct. 13, 1857, thus becoming the first American-born racehorse to win a major race in Europe.

ORIGINS OF THE BELMONT STAKES

The Belmont Stakes is the oldest of the three jewels that make up thoroughbred racing's Triple Crown for three-year-olds. It was first run at Jerome Park, in the Bronx, N.Y., in 1867 over a distance of one and a half miles. A filly, Ruthless, ridden by jockey J. Gilpatrick, was the first winner.

The Belmont is named for August Belmont, Sr., a co-founder of Jerome Park and of Monmouth Park Race Track in Oceanport, N.J. In 1905 the Stakes was moved to Belmont Park, built by August Belmont, Jr., founder and first president of the New York Jockey Club. The younger Belmont was also the breeder of the legendary thoroughbred Man O'War.

ORIGINS OF THE PREAKNESS

The Preakness Stakes, held at Pimlico Race Track in Baltimore, Md., is the second oldest of the three jewels of thoroughbred racing's Triple Crown for three-year-olds.

Pimlico opened in 1870, and the first Preakness Stakes was run in 1873. The race, run over a mile and three-sixteenths, was first won by Survivor, ridden by G. Barbee.

ORIGINS OF THE KENTUCKY DERBY

It's called the Run for the Roses, and is probably the single most famous thoroughbred horse race in the United States. It is the Kentucky Derby, and is run each year at Churchill Downs at Louisville, Ky.

The Derby is the youngest of the three races making up thoroughbred racing's Triple Crown for three-year-olds. The Kentucky Derby was run for the first time in 1875, the same year that Churchill Downs was opened.

There were 15 horses entered in the first Derby in 1875, 14 of which were ridden by black jockeys. The winner that first year was Aristides, ridden by black jockey Oliver Lewis.

The Derby was originally run over a mile and a half, but has been shortened to a mile and a quarter.

FIRST PACER TO COVER A MILE IN LESS THAN TWO MINUTES

Star Pointer became the first pacer to cover a mile in better than two minutes, on Aug. 28, 1887. He was clocked in a one-mile race at Readville, Mass., at one minute, 59¼ seconds.

FIRST JOCKEY TO WIN THE KENTUCKY DERBY THREE TIMES

Famed black jockey Isaac Murphy was the first jockey to win the Kentucky Derby three times and the first to win it back-to-back. Murphy rode his first

Kentucky Derby winner, Buchanan, in 1884. He repeated in 1890 riding Riley and again in 1891 riding Kingman.

ORIGINS OF THE HARNESS RACING TRIPLE CROWN

Just like thoroughbred racing, harness racing has a Triple Crown for three-year-old trotters: the Kentucky Futurity, the Hambletonian and the Yonkers Trot.

The Kentucky Futurity is the oldest event of the three. It is run each fall as part of the Lexington Trots meeting at Lexington, Ky. The Futurity has been run annually since 1893, except for four years (1942-45) during World War II. Oro Wilkes, driven by J.A. Goldsmith, won the first Kentucky Futurity in 1893.

The Hambletonian is probably the best known of the three jewels, even though it is not the oldest. The Hambletonian began in Syracuse, N.Y. in 1926 and is now run each year as part of the Du Quoin, Ill., State Fair, on a best two out of three heat plan. Guy McKinney, driven by Nat Ray, won the first Hambletonian in Syracuse in 1926.

The baby of the trotting Triple Crown events is the Yonkers Trot, run each year at the Yonkers Raceway in Yonkers, N.Y. The Trot is a one-dash event and was first run in 1955. Scott Frost, driven by Hall of Famer Joe O'Brien, won the first Yonkers Trot, covering the mile and one-sixteenths distance in two minutes and 12 seconds. With that win Scott Frost also became trotting's first Triple Crown winner; he had also taken the Hambletonian and the Kentucky Futurity that year.

FIRST $50,000 HARNESS RACE

The first $50,000 harness race was the American Trotting Derby, held in 1908 in Readville, Mass. A trotter named Allen Winter won the race and the money.

FIRST $2 WAGER

From 1878 to 1911 the standard pari-mutuel wager in horse racing was $5. But in 1911 Col. Matt Winn introduced the $2 wager at Churchill Downs in Louisville, Ky., the home of the Kentucky Derby. The $2 bet was an instant success. William Riggs of the Pimlico racetrack in Baltimore, Md., brought the $2 wager home to his track after a visit to Churchill Downs, and the idea soon spread throughout the North.

The term "pari-mutuel" is a corruption of the term "Paris Mutual," a system invented by Pierre Oller and used at Longchamps beginning in 1872.

FIRST MUTUEL TICKET PAYING OVER $1000

The first mutuel tickets paying over $1000 were sold June 17, 1912 at a race track in Latonia, Ohio. Four tickets were sold on 900-to-1 long shot Wishing Ring; the horse won the race, and paid $1885.50 to win, $744.40 to place and $172.40 to show.

FIRST FILLY TO WIN THE KENTUCKY DERBY

Regret, ridden by Joe Notter, became the first filly to win the Kentucky Derby in 1915. It was not until 1980 that another filly won the Kentucky Derby.

FIRST TRIPLE CROWN WINNER

The Triple Crown is a mythical award for three-year-old thoroughbreds that win victories in three races—the Kentucky Derby, the Belmont Stakes and the Preakness—in the same year. Since 1875, when the Kentucky Derby, the youngest of the three Triple Crown races, began, there have been only ten Triple Crown winners. Not until 44 years after the first Kentucky Derby did a horse take the first Triple Crown. That horse was Sir Barton, in 1919. Jockey J. Loftus was aboard Sir Barton for all three victories.

FIRST HORSE TO WIN OVER $100,000 IN ONE RACE

Whichone was the first horse to win more than $100,000 in one race. He won the Belmont Futurity—and the winner's purse of $105,730—at Belmont Park in New York on Sept. 14, 1929.

FIRST JOCKEY TO WIN 400 RACES IN A SINGLE YEAR

In 1935 Willie Shoemaker of Texas became the first jockey to win 400 races in a single year. He broke the old record of 390 victories, winning 485 races.

FIRST ELECTRIC EYE PHOTO FINISH CAMERA

The first electric eye photo finish camera at a race track was installed at the Hialeah race track in Hialeah, Fla. on Jan. 16, 1936.

FIRST ANNUAL MOTION PICTURES HANDICAP

The first annual Motion Pictures Handicap, a race for horses belonging to people directly connected with the motion picture industry, was run at Del Mar race track in Del Mar, Calif. on July 9, 1937. Best Bid, owned by Columbia Pictures mogul Harry Cohn, won the race.

FIRST DAILY DOUBLE TO PAY MORE THAN $10,000

The first daily double to pay more than $10,000 took place on Aug. 14, 1939 at the Washington Park Race Track in Chicago. Joy Bet and Merry Caroline combined to pay $10,772.40. One ticket was sold for the combination long shots; Claude Elkins of Anna, Ill. walked off with the bundle.

FIRST HARNESS RACING DRIVER TO WIN FOUR HAMBLETONIANS

Harness Hall of Fame driver Benjamin White was the first driver to win four Hambletonians (see also **Origins of the Harness Racing Triple Crown**). White won his first in 1933, and repeated in 1936, 1942 and 1943.

ORIGINS OF THE PACING TRIPLE CROWN

Just as thoroughbred racing and trotting have three major events comprising a "Triple Crown" for three-year-old horses, so does pacing: the Little Brown Jug Classic, the William H. Cane Futurity and the Messenger Stakes.

The first leg of the pacing Triple Crown is the Cane Futurity, run in late June or early July each year at the Yonkers Raceway in Yonkers, N.Y. The race is named for a man who served the racetrack for more than 30 years, as harness racing administrator, as president and general manager and as a booster. He also helped form the United States Trotting Association; his Good Times Stables in Goshen, N.Y. produced two Hambletonian winners.

The Cane Futurity was first run in 1955. Quick Chief, driven by William Haughton, won the inaugural race.

The Little Brown Jug Classic is the most famous of all races for three-year-old pacers and the second jewel of the pacing Triple Crown. The Classic is held each September in Delaware, Ohio. The race was first held in 1946 as a result of the efforts of two Delaware natives, Joseph A. Neville, attorney and racing supporter, and H.C. Thompson, the publisher of the *Delaware Gazette*. The race is named for Little Brown Jug, one of the legends of the high-wheeled sulky days of racing. The first Little Brown Jug Classic was won by Ensign Hanover, driven by Wayne Smart.

The last leg of pacing's Triple Crown is also the newest, the Messenger Stakes. The Stakes is named for the patriarch of the harness horse in the United States. While Messenger was never hitched to a harness or raced under a saddle, most of the great pacing and trotting horses in the U.S. can trace their heritage to this late 18th century animal, which produced a new breed of horse that became known as the American trotter. The Messenger Stakes is run each year in the early fall at Roosevelt Raceway at Westbury, N.Y. The Messenger Stakes was first run in 1956; Belle Acton, driven by William Haughton, was the winner.

Adios Butler, driven by Clint Hodgins, was the first horse to win pacing's Triple Crown in 1959.

FIRST JOCKEY TO RIDE TWO TRIPLE CROWN WINNERS

Eddie Arcaro was the first and so far the only jockey to ride two Triple Crown winners. Arcaro guided Whirlaway to the Triple Crown in 1941 and then repeated the feat in 1948 with Citation.

FIRST JOCKEY TO WIN FIVE KENTUCKY DERBIES

Eddie Arcaro was the first jockey to win five Kentucky Derbies. Arcaro rode Lawrin for his first Derby win in 1938. He won again with Whirlaway in 1941, with Hoop Jr. in 1945, with Citation in 1948 and with Hill Gail in 1952.

FIRST PACER TO WIN THE TRIPLE CROWN OF HARNESS RACING

The first pacer to win the Triple Crown of harness racing was Adios Butler, in 1959. The Cane Stakes, the Messenger Stakes and the Little Brown Jug Classic are the harness racing Triple Crown races. (See also **Origins of the Pacing Triple Crown.**)

FIRST LEGALIZED HORSE RACING LOTTERY SINCE THE CIVIL WAR

The nation's first legalized horse racing lottery since the Civil War was held on Sept. 12, 1964 in New Hampshire. Roman Brother won the New Hampshire Sweepstakes Classic, run at Rockingham Park race track at Salem, N.H.

FIRST HORSE VOTED HORSE OF THE YEAR FIVE YEARS IN A ROW

The thoroughbred Kelso was the first horse to be voted Horse of the Year five consecutive years, 1960-64. Kelso set a record for lifetime earnings in 1964 with a total of $1,893,362.

FIRST ALL-AMERICAN FUTURITY RACE

The first All-American Futurity race was held at Ruidoso Downs in New Mexico on Sept. 4, 1967, with a purse which was (and still is) the richest in horse racing. Laico Bird won the race for quarter horses, capturing the winner's purse of $225,000 out of a total purse of $486,593.

FIRST HORSE TO WIN THE TRIPLE CROWN FOR FILLIES

Dark Mirage became the first horse to win the Triple Crown for fillies on June 22, 1968 when she won the Coaching Club American Oaks at Belmont Park in New York.

FIRST WOMAN JOCKEY TO BE SUSPENDED

Mrs. Tuesdee Testa has the dubious distinction of being the first woman jockey to be suspended. On Aug. 27, 1969 she was suspended for 10 days for careless riding.

FIRST WOMAN JOCKEY TO RIDE IN THE KENTUCKY DERBY

Jockey Diane Crump became the first woman to ride in the Kentucky Derby on May 2, 1970. Crump was aboard Fathom, which finished 15th.

FIRST LEGAL OFF-TRACK BETTING

The first legal off-track betting system in the United States was established in New York City. It began operation on April 7, 1971.

FIRST BLACK WOMAN JOCKEY

Seventeen-year-old Cheryl White was the first black woman jockey. She rode Ace Reward, which finished last in a field of seven horses at the Thistledown Race Track in Cleveland, Ohio on June 15, 1971.

On Sept. 17, 1971 White became the first black woman in American thoroughbred racing history to win a race. She won at the Waterford Park Race Track in Chester, W. Va., riding a horse named Jetolara. The horse was owned and trained by White's father.

FIRST WOMAN JOCKEY TO RIDE 100 WINNERS

Mary Bacon was the first woman jockey to ride 100 winners. She posted her 100th victory on June 30, 1971 at the Thistledown Race Track in Cleveland, Ohio aboard California Lassie.

FIRST UNDEFEATED TRIPLE CROWN WINNER

With his victory in the Belmont Stakes in 1977, Seattle Slew became not only the 10th Triple Crown winner, but also the only undefeated one.

The Belmont Stakes, with jockey Jean Cruguet aboard, was Slew's ninth consecutive victory, and helped put to rest criticism of the famed three-year-old for his less than noble blood lines. He had also been criticized for his looks, his less than remarkable margins of victory (four lengths over Run Dusty Run in the Belmont) and the unimpressive quality of his opposition. He was the only Triple Crown Winner ever to have been sold at a public auction, bought by Karen and Mickey Taylor and Jim and Sally Hill for $17,500.

Despite the criticism, however, Seattle Slew was named Horse of the Year for 1977.

FIRST INTERNATIONAL WOMEN'S DRIVING TOURNAMENT

The first International Women's Driving Tournament for harness racers was held in the United States in 1978. Women from eight countries participated in a total of 16 races on five American harness racing tracks. Bea Farber, an American, won the first international tournament with 367 points, finishing far ahead of Italy's Agnese Palagi, who had 246 points.

Farber, one of the nation's outstanding harness racing drivers, was also the first woman ever to cover half a mile in two minutes. In 1978 she became the first woman harness racing driver to make the harness racing top ten list.

FIRST $3 MINIMUM WAGER

Inflation is taking its toll on the harness racing bettor. In February 1980, Louisville Downs, a harness racing track in Louisville, Ky., became the first track in the country to raise the minimum wager to $3. A track official said at the time that while the $2 wager had once been the backbone of racing, that was no longer true, at least at Louisville Downs. He said that more and more people were betting at the $10 and gimmick windows (i.e., on daily doubles, perfectas, etc.). According to this official, the track's share of a $2 bet was $.13, less than the cost of handling and processing the bet.

DOG RACING

ORIGINS

Today's greyhound racing derives from the ancient game of coursing—the pursuit of game animals by dogs relying upon sight rather than scent. Such dogs, which sometimes possess tremendous speed, were used for hunting wild game in 5000 B.C., perhaps even earlier.

The first formal coursing organization recorded was the "Swaffham Club" in Norfolk, England, started by Lord Orford in 1776. At that time the sport was increasing in popularity among the English nobility. In 1836 the Waterloo Cup for coursing was established; it soon became the most widely attended coursing event in the world.

The National Coursing Organization was formed in the United States in 1897. Coursing in the U.S. was at first confined mainly to the West and the Midwest; antelope were commonly used for the hunt, rather than rabbits, as was the usual practice in England.

Because of public sentiment against the killing of rabbits and other game, mechanical rabbits or lures were eventually introduced. Greyhound racing has grown in popularity since the 1930s with the legalization of pari-mutuel betting on greyhound races in several states. The American Greyhound Track Operators Association was formed in 1960 in an effort to maintain high standards in the sport.

FIRST MECHANICAL RABBIT; FIRST LIGHTED TRACK

At the turn of the century dog racing was banned in many parts of the United States because the dogs chased a live rabbit and the winner caught and killed the animal. Owen P. Smith, realizing that the racing greyhounds had nearly no sense of smell and responded mostly to the sight of the live rabbit, designed a mechanical rabbit that traveled around the course on an electrical track. He opened a dog racing track at Emeryville, Calif. in 1919, using his electric rabbit, which proved successful. Smith also opened the first dog racing track with electric lights in Tulsa, Okla. in 1920.

BICYCLING

ORIGINS

Competitive bicycling is primarily an amateur sport in the United States; in Europe, on the other hand, bicycling competitions are held at both the amateur and professional levels.

Like the automobile, the bicycle was originally intended as a form of transportation; only later did it turn into a recreational and competitive vehicle. A Frenchman, M. de Sivrac, developed a two-wheeled vehicle in 1690. But it had one flaw that led to its eventual extinction: it had no pedals. That meant that the rider had to push himself along with his feet. Not very convenient. Another Frenchman developed a similar device in 1795 that also suffered from the absence of pedals. But it did, nonetheless, represent an advance over de Sivrac's early bicycle: the designer placed the front wheel on a pivot. That at least permitted the rider to steer the contraption as he pushed himself along. The French remained dubious, however, that riders would be able to balance themselves on the vehicle after they had developed enough speed to coast awhile or during downhill stints. That led, four years later, to the creation of a three-wheeled vehicle by two other Frenchmen. The two-wheel device soon became known as the bicycle, and the three-wheeler as the tricycle. The names were coined by a French newspaper, *Journal de Paris*, which reported on the development of the two vehicles on July 27, 1789. To distinguish the two in its story, the newspaper took the astronomical term "cycle," meaning circle, and added the prefixes "bi-," for "two," and "tri-," for "three."

The tricycle, like the bicycle, was handicapped by the problem of propulsion: it also had to be pushed along with the feet. It fared little better than its two-wheeled predecessors, although tricycles, produced by a British inventor, did turn up in England by 1818.

1818 also saw the development of the high-wheeled bicycle. A Frenchman, Baron de Saverbrum, designed a bicycle with a 64-inch front wheel and a 12-inch rear wheel. The rider pulled a rope attached to a gear. Despite the refinement this represented over the push-along method, the Baron's bicycle did not gain popularity because the motions needed to pull the rope and steer oneself along were rather awkward.

The forefather of today's bicycle chain was developed in 1821 by an

Englishman; then in 1834 rope and pedals were developed by a Scottish blacksmith who attached them to a wheel with connecting rods. That same Scottish blacksmith later built a tricycle equipped not only with pedals but with a gear shift, too. All the early bicycles and tricycles had wooden wheels until in 1865 a Frenchman built a high-wheeler with iron-covered wheels, giving birth to the expression "bone-shaker." The iron-wheeled bone-shaker died a quick death. The bicycle took its next steps forward with the introduction, in 1868, of hard rubber tires, and of wire spokes (in place of wood) in 1869.

By the end of the 1880s, after further refinements, the high-wheel bicycle was fairly common throughout both the United States and Europe. That set the scene for the first bicycling records. In 1883 one H.L. Cortis set one of the first bicycling records. He rode his high-wheeler continuously for 24 hours, covering a distance of 200 miles and 300 yards. That's an average of less than 9 miles per hour.

Perhaps the first bicycle race in the U.S. took place in September 1883. G.M. Hendrie of Springfield, Mass. competed against W.G. Rowe in a road race that was advertised as a battle "for the championship"; the championship of *what*, it is not exactly clear. Hendrie won the race and was thus, officially, the top bicyclist in the U.S. Hendrie went on to gain fame as a builder of automobiles and motorcycles.

An Englishman, J.K. Starley, designed a bicycle in 1885 whose front wheel was only slightly larger than its rear wheel. This innovation made the bicycle faster and easier to ride. The bicycle took its next step forward in 1888 when J.B. Dunlop, a veterinary surgeon in Belfast, Ireland, invented inflatable pneumatic tires, which smoothed the bicycle's ride and thus contributed considerably to its popularity. The pneumatic tires also increased the bicycle's speed, spawning road races throughout the U.S. as the bicycle was transformed from a curiosity into a form of transportation and, in turn, a vehicle for recreation and competition.

FIRST AMERICAN LEAGUE OF BICYCLERS MEET

In 1881 bicyclists had to be careful where they rode. Many communities would not let them use parks or public roads. Riders found safety in numbers, however, in the first meet sponsored by the American League of Bicyclers, held in Boston in the first week of June that year.

It was not just a riding event—races were held as well. Lewis Frye of Marlboro, Mass. won a quarter-mile dash. He also won a half-mile race. The third race, a one-mile dash, featured a three-man pileup; Frye was one of the three. They picked themselves up and finished the race, but lost to William Woodside of Waltham. Woodside also won the final race, a two-miler.

FIRST TRIP AROUND THE WORLD BY BICYCLE

The first person to bicycle around the world was an American named Thomas Stevens. He left San Francisco, Calif. on April 22, 1884 and returned to San Francisco on Jan. 4, 1887.

FIRST WOMEN'S SIX-DAY MARATHON

Six-day marathon bicycle races were a popular fad throughout the United States and Canada at the turn of the century. The first marathon for women was held Jan. 6-11, 1896 at Madison Square Garden in New York. Frankie Nelson traveled 418 miles over the six days to win the race.

FIRST MAN TO PEDAL A MILE A MINUTE

In 1899 many people believed that it was impossible for a man to pedal a bicycle a mile a minute. Charles Murphy persuaded the Long Island Railroad to build a three-mile wooden track between its rails near Hempstead, N.Y. On June 30, 1899, with a train pacing him at 60 miles an hour, Murphy pedaled a measured mile in 57 and 4/5 seconds—better than a mile a minute.

Murphy's feat made him famous. He was thereafter called "Mile-a-Minute" Murphy.

FIRST TOUR DE FRANCE

The Tour de France is the premier event in competitive bicycling. Each year some 100 cyclists cover a course of 2500 to 3000 miles in France and neighboring Belgium, Spain, Switzerland and Italy in 25 to 30 days. The course, different each year, runs through hundreds of communities which compete fiercely to have the race pass through. The course typically crosses mountains almost 7000 feet high. The scores of cyclists are accompanied by mechanics, officials and reporters in dozens of vans, trucks, cars and motorcycles.

The Tour de France began in 1903 when bicycle enthusiast Henri Desgrange organized the race at the suggestion of a colleague. A Frenchman, M. Garin, won the first Tour de France. The race has been held annually since then (except during the two World Wars); no American has ever won the Tour de France.

FIRST U.S. WOMEN'S BICYCLING CHAMPIONSHIP

The first United States women's bicycling championship under the auspices of the National Amateur Bicycling Association was held in Buffalo, N.Y. on Sept. 4, 1937. Doris Kopsky of Belleville, N.J. won the one-mile race, covering the distance in four minutes, 22.4 seconds.

AUTO RACING

ORIGINS

There is probably no other country in the world where auto racing is followed by so many millions of people as the United States. Each week thousands of people gather at tracks in virtually every state, from the dirt tracks in the South and Midwest to the salt flats in Utah, to watch every type of automobile, from midget racers to jet-propelled rocket cars, strive for one single goal: speed.

If you ask where the automobile was really invented, you'll get different answers in the U.S., England, Italy and France; the claim may, however, rightfully belong to Germany. Steam-powered vehicles were developed in the U.S., England, Italy and France during the early and mid-19th century. But because heavy equipment—typically a boiler—was required to generate steam, the steam-powered vehicle was probably doomed from its very beginnings.

The automobile as we know it today was probably born in 1885 when a German, Gottlieb Daimler, perfected an internal combustion engine which burned kerosene. He attached his internal combustion engine to a bicycle, thus creating the first motorcycle; later he attached it to a rowboat, giving birth to the first motorboat.

A Frenchman, Emile Levassor, took Daimler's internal combustion engine one step further. He built an automobile body into which he placed an internal combustion engine in 1887 or 1888, thereby becoming the father of the modern internal combustion-powered automobile.

Although there are other claims, Charles and J. Frank Duryea are generally considered to have developed the first internal combustion-powered automobile in the U.S. in 1892 in Springfield, Mass. Across the ocean, meanwhile, the French began to cash in on Levassor's idea by building self-propelled automobiles in the early 1890s. There were several manufacturers; this naturally led to the question: Whose car was the best? That gave birth to the first automobile race, on June 22, 1894, from Paris to Rouen. There is no formal account of the race, but it seems likely that the original program called for the automobiles to race from Paris to Rouen, a distance of 78 miles, and back. The winner of the race is not known.

Probably the first organized automobile race in the United States took place on Nov. 28, 1895. The race was sponsored by the Chicago *Times Herald*; the route stretched a little more than 54 miles, from Chicago to a suburb and back. Automotive pioneer J. Frank Duryea, driving a Duryea car, won the race. His average speed: seven and a half miles per hour.

Both the Paris-Rouen and Chicago races were aimed at showing the durability of the new automobiles as much, or more than, their speed. But by 1898 there was considerable speculation as to just how fast a car could really go. A man named Chasseloup-Laubat in France responded to the speculation by driving an automobile over a one-kilometer course and having its speed measured. Chasseloup-Laubat covered the distance at an average speed of 39.24 miles per hour. (See also **First Recorded Land Speed Record**.)

FIRST RECORDED LAND SPEED RECORD

The pioneer motoring journal *La France Automobile* held the first competition for a land speed record in 1898. The *concours de vitesse* was held in Acheres Park north of Paris; timekeepers holding stopwatches stood at the beginning and at the end of a measured kilometer. A Jeantaud electric car, driven by Comte Gaston de Chasseloup-Laubat, covered the distance in 57 seconds, setting the world's first land speed record of 39.24 mph (63.16 kph).

FIRST WOMAN AUTO RACER

The first automobile race in which a woman participated, a two-day race from Marseilles, France to Nice, was held in 1898. A woman named Laumaille finished fourth; her husband finished sixth.

FIRST SUCCESSFUL WOMAN AUTO RACER

A French woman, Camille du Gast, was the first female auto racer of any distinction. Du Gast, driving a Panhard, competed in a 1901 race from Paris to Berlin. She finished an acceptable 33rd. In 1904, however, du Gast switched to motor boat racing when the organizers of that year's Paris-Berlin race refused to let her enter the competition as a member of the Benz team.

FIRST PERSON TO DRIVE A MILE A MINUTE

Barney Oldfield was a professional bicycle rider when Henry Ford needed a test driver for his first racing car in 1902. Oldfield had never driven a car before, but learned how in two weeks, and then became Ford's test driver. In 1903, driving Ford's "999" automobile, Oldfield became the first man to drive a mile a minute—60 miles per hour.

ORIGINS OF THE VANDERBILT CUP RACE

The first annual automobile race in the United States was probably the Vanderbilt Cup race on Long Island, N.Y. As the number of cars increased after the turn of the century, the interest in their competitive abilities also rose. As a result of that interest, William K. Vanderbilt donated a cup for an annual auto racing competition on Long Island.

The first Vanderbilt Cup race was held Oct. 8, 1904 on a 28.4 mile course. Eighteen cars started the 10-lap race before more than 25,000 spectators. The winner, A.L. Campbell, who drove a Mercedes, won a cup more than 30 inches high which weighed an incredible 500 pounds. Campbell's average speed was about 30 miles per hour.

The Vanderbilt Cup races were held annually through 1908. Because accidents, injuries and even deaths had occurred during the races, and because foreign cars had usually won the races, Vanderbilt withdrew the cup from competition in 1908. It now rests in the Washington offices of the American Automobile Association.

FIRST NEW YORK TO PARIS AUTO RACE

The year was 1906. The automobile was still a novelty. Paved roads were the exception, not the rule. But that didn't stop the normally staid New York *Times* from sponsoring the first New York to Paris automobile race. A band played as the six entrants left New York City on the first leg of the journey, bound for San Francisco. From San Francisco the cars were shipped to Valdez, Alaska; they were then driven across the icy tundra to Nome, then across the ice of the Bering Strait and on to Moscow, Berlin and Paris. The total distance from Alaska to Paris was about 8000 miles.

Each car was driven by a crew of three, wearing heavy clothing to protect them from the Arctic cold. Each vehicle also carried a large supply of spare parts. The cars traveled over roads that were literally cow paths and were forced to plow their way through miles and miles of mud. The cars even traveled for a while on the tracks of the Trans-Siberian Railroad; the American entrant was at one point forced to back up when the car ran into a train in a tunnel.

While there was only one American entry in the race, there were three from France, one from Italy and one from Germany. The race came down to a battle between the American and German cars. The Germans came into

Paris four days ahead of the American car. Because the Americans had been given a 30-day allowance, however, they were proclaimed the winners by 26 days.

FIRST TRANSCONTINENTAL CAR RACE

The first transcontinental car race, from Peking to Paris, was held in 1907 as a result of a challenge of the French newspaper *Le Matin.* Several prominent motorcar enthusiasts, including Prince Scipione Borghese, agreed to take part in the race.

Luigi Barzini, who covered the race for the *Daily Telegraph* and the *Corriere della Sera,* wrote that the competition was as unreal as a dream, with modern motorcars in Peking, an ancient town which had never before witnessed such a sight.

There were no roads over much of the terrain the cars covered. The cars had to be maneuvered over mountain ranges and rivers; pickaxes were sometimes used to clear a path wide enough for the cars. They drove on the track of the Trans-Siberian railroad through Russia to Moscow.

By the time Prince Borghese's crew reached Moscow, the other competitors were still in Siberia. The Prince made a detour up to St. Petersburg to receive the enthusiastic welcome of the Russians; the remainder of his trip to Paris was a triumphal procession. The race ended on Aug. 10, two months after it had begun, when the Prince drew his Italia up in front of the offices of *Le Matin* in Paris.

FIRST AMERICAN WINNER OF THE VANDERBILT CUP RACES

The Vanderbilt Cup Races were first held in 1904 on Long Island when William K. Vanderbilt put up a cup for the winner of the 284 mile auto race. (See also **Origins of the Vanderbilt Cup Race.**) It was not until 1908 that an American, George Robertson, won the race, driving a Locomobile and averaging 64 mph.

The race was really the first major road race in the U.S. At that time foreign-made cars were generally the best, and Vanderbilt wanted to stimulate interest in American racing. The Vanderbilt races were very popular with the American people. Crowds of up to 500,000 people attended the races, which attracted the fastest cars in the world. Robertson's win against the best European cars and drivers gave a tremendous boost to the American auto industry.

FIRST INDIANAPOLIS 500

It is perhaps the greatest single sports event on earth: The Indianapolis 500 auto race. The race, held each Memorial Day weekend at the two and a half mile Motor Speedway in Indianapolis, Ind., draws more than 300,000 spectators each year. They come to watch cars approaching the 200 mile per hour mark, and drivers competing for prize money totaling more than $1 million, of which the winner receives more than $200,000.

The Speedway was built in 1909 by four prominent Indianapolis businessmen, all affiliated with the nascent U.S. automobile industry: Carl G. Fisher, James A. Allison, Arthur C. Newby and Frank H. Wheeler. The track was designed as an outdoor laboratory for the young American auto industry. It rapidly gained recognition as a proving ground for such automotive advancements as high compression engines, four-wheel brakes, front-wheel and four-wheel drive systems, tires and hydraulic shock absorbers.

The original course was a combination of crushed stone and tar, but it began to disintegrate after the first two days of races in August 1909. The track was rebuilt with 3,200,000 paving bricks grouted in cement and reopened for racing in December 1909. Races were held sporadically in 1910, but the decision was soon made to concentrate efforts on a single major event each year. May 30, 1911 was selected as the date for the inaugural event; the distance was set at 500 miles because a race of that length would give spectators about the same six or seven hours of track action that most of the 1910 racing programs had offered.

The Speedway management put up $25,000 in prize money. Forty teams, most of them representing factories, entered the inaugural race. Ray Harroun won the first race at the wheel of a six-cylinder Marmon Wasp in six hours, 42 minutes and eight seconds, for an average speed of 74.59 miles per hour. Harroun, along with Cyrus Patschke, his replacement driver for several laps near the halfway point, circled the course steadily at about 75.5 miles per hour, thereby reducing tire wear. Harroun and Patschke were the only drivers to compete in the first 500 without the aid of a riding mechanic to operate the fuel pressure pump and perform other chores, as was the custom in that era, because Harroun believed weight was an important factor in tire wear on the turns. As a result, they ran the full distance with only three stops for tire changes; several of the other outstanding drivers, trying to maintain speeds of 80 miles per hour or more, were forced to make as many as 12 or 13 stops to change tires.

Harroun's Marmon Wasp was the first of only two six-cylinder automobiles ever to win the Indianapolis 500.

MULTIPLE WINNERS OF THE INDY 500

It took only a dozen years, even including two years off for World War I, for the Indianapolis 500 to produce its first two-time winner. Tommy Milton, driving an eight-cylinder Frontenac, won the 1921 race in five hours, 34 minutes and 44.65 seconds for an average speed of 89.62 miles per hour. That was the first time an eight-cylinder car had won the 500.

Milton repeated his triumph in the 11th Indianapolis 500 in 1923. That year he won in five hours, 29 minutes and 50.17 seconds, driving an H.C.S. Special at an average speed of 90.95 miles per hour.

It took 25 years—until 1936—for the Indy to produce its first three-time winner. Louis Meyer won his first race in 1928, driving a Miller Special. He won the 1933 race in a Tydol Special, and gained his third victory three years later, winning the 1936 Indy in a Ring Free Special.

A.J. Foyt, Jr., was the first four-time Indy victor; it took him nearly two decades to accomplish the feat. Foyt won his first 500 in 1961, driving a Bowes Seal Fast Special. He took his second Indy in 1964 behind the wheel of a Sheraton-Thompson Special, and his third in 1967, again in a Sheraton-Thompson Special. It took Foyt another decade to win again in Indianapolis. He took his fourth 500 in 1977, driving a Gilmore Racing Team car.

FIRST INDY 500 BROADCAST ON RADIO

The 1924 Indianapolis 500 was the first to be broadcast over the radio. The race was carried by WGN in Chicago, with Quin Ryan describing the race. L.L. Corum and Joe Boyer won that year in a Duesenberg Special.

FIRST INDY 500 WINNER TO EXCEED 100 MPH

The 13th Indianapolis 500 race in 1925 (there had been no races in 1917 and 1918 because of World War I) marked the first time the winning car finished with an average speed in excess of 100 miles per hour. Peter DePaolo, driving an eight-cylinder Duesenberg Special, won the 1925 race in four hours, 56 minutes and 39.46 seconds, for an average speed of 101.13 miles per hour. Not until 1930 did the winner's average speed again exceed 100 miles per hour. That year Billy Arnold, driving a Miller-Hartz Special, just barely topped the 100 mile per hour mark, with an average speed of 100.44 miles per hour. The winning car in 1931 again slipped below the century mark, but since 1932 the average speed of every Indianapolis 500 winner has exceeded 100 miles per hour.

FIRST WOMAN TO DRIVE AROUND THE WORLD

Violet Cordery was the first woman to drive around the world. She traveled 10,266 miles across five continents in 1927. Her average speed was a little better than 24 miles per hour. She was driving a three-liter Invicta.

FIRST MAN TO DRIVE MORE THAN 300 MPH

Sir Malcolm Campbell was the first man to drive an automobile more than 300 miles an hour, in his "Bluebird Special," on Sept. 3, 1935. Campbell reached 301.13 miles per hour in a timed trial at the Bonneville Salt Flats in Utah.

FIRST WORLD CHAMPION

Italian Nin Farina was the first driver named World Champion in 1950. Farina raced from 1930 until 1955. He was killed in an ordinary automobile accident in 1966.

FIRST BACK-TO-BACK WORLD DRIVING CHAMPIONSHIPS

An Italian, Alberto Ascari, was the first driver to win back-to-back World Driving Championships, copping the honor in 1952 and again in 1953. Ascari, the son of a Grand Prix driver, was killed while testing a sports car in 1955.

FIRST MAN TO WIN THE AUTO DRIVING CHAMPIONSHIP OF THE WORLD FIVE YEARS IN A ROW

Argentine racing driver Juan Manuel Fangio was 46 when he won his fifth consecutive world driving championship in 1957. Fangio was the first, and so far the only, man to win so many championships in a row. On Aug. 4, 1957 Fangio won the German Grand Prix with his Maserati to take the world title. He had covered the 312.4 mile course in three hours, 30 minutes and 38.3 seconds.

FIRST WOMAN TO RACE IN A EUROPEAN GRAND PRIX

An Italian, Maria-Teresa de Filippis, was the first woman to compete in a modern European Grand Prix race in 1958. She competed in three Grand Prix races overall. Her best finish, 10th place, came in the 1958 Belgian Grand Prix; she drove a Maserati.

FIRST U.S. WORLD DRIVING CHAMPION

American Phil Hill was the first U.S. citizen to be named World Driving Champion, taking the honor in 1961. Hill had won at LeMans, Daytona, Sebring and Nurburing, among others. Hill has retired as an active driver.

FIRST WOMAN TO WIN A SPORTS CAR OF AMERICA CHAMPIONSHIP

Donna Mae Mins became the first woman to win the Sports Car Club of America championship in 1964, in competition with 31 men in the Class H production category for imported two-seaters. The striking platinum blonde had her motto written on her car: "Think Pink."

FIRST 600 MPH LAND SPEED RECORD

Craig Breedlove set the first land speed record of over 600 miles per hour in his car "Spirit of America" on Nov. 15, 1965. Breedlove attained a speed of 600.601 miles per hour at the Bonneville Salt Flats in Utah.

FIRST WOMAN DRAG RACER

Shirley "Cha-Cha" Muldowney was the first woman licensed in the United States to drive top fuel dragsters. She qualified in 1975 at the age of 35. Muldowney, who at one time held the quarter-mile speed record in drag racing, was the first woman to drive a quarter mile in under six seconds. She was also the first woman to win the National Hot Rod Association Spring Nationals, taking the honor in 1976. She repeated her victory in 1977.

FIRST WOMAN TO DRIVE IN THE INDIANAPOLIS 500

The Indianapolis 500 auto race has had only one woman driver to date: Janet Guthrie. Guthrie passed her rookie test at Indianapolis in 1976, driving the prescribed 50 miles at speeds of over 170 miles per hour, in a car built by Rolla Vollstedt. But a rash of mechanical problems prevented Guthrie from achieving competitive speeds. A.J. Foyt, Jr., offered Guthrie the use of his backup car, and within a dozen laps Guthrie was running at 181 miles per hour. Foyt, however, decided against letting Guthrie make a qualifying attempt with the backup car.

On May 7, 1977 Guthrie was back for the opening day of time trials for the 1977 race. Driving a Lightning-Offenhauser, she posted the fastest speed of the day—185.6 miles per hour. On May 10 she reached 191 miles per hour before spinning out of control and into a wall. She suffered only minor injuries, but her Lightning-Offenhauser was badly damaged, and she had no backup car. The entire right front suspension had to be fabricated from scratch; the steering was also shot. The repairs were made, but when the car returned to the track on May 13, there were still problems. The car was unpredictable in the turns, and Guthrie could not reach her earlier speeds. Skeptics claimed that Guthrie had lost her nerve.

On May 17 Dick Simon, driving a Vollstedt-Offenhauser, also crashed, nearly wiping out his car. While it was being repaired, Simon turned his attentions to Guthrie's car. In two days Simon, a chassis expert, had straightened out Guthrie's Lightning-Offenhauser, renewing her chances of qualifying for the race.

On May 22, 1977, the last weekend of qualifying, Janet Guthrie became the first woman ever to qualify for the Indianapolis 500, posting a four-lap average of 188.404, the fastest speed of the entire second weekend of qualifying. She was also the only driver to increase her speed on each consecutive lap.

Said Guthrie afterwards, "It was certainly the most significant accomplishment of my career. I think a lot of drivers will tell you that making the show here (at Indianapolis) is such an achievement that the race itself is almost an anticlimax."

Shades of prophecy, for the race was indeed an anticlimax for Guthrie. After a clean start, Guthrie had just begun to improve her position when the engine in the Lightning-Offenhauser sputtered. Efforts to repair the car failed. What had sounded like an ignition problem was actually a broken valve seal that couldn't be repaired except by taking the entire engine apart.

The race was over for Guthrie after only 27 laps, but she had earned her place in history as the first woman to drive in the Indianapolis 500.

FIRST DRIVER TO WIN THREE CONSECUTIVE GRAND NATIONAL TITLES

The only man in the history of NASCAR, the National Association for Stock Car Racing, to win three consecutive Grand National titles is South Carolina's Cale Yarborough. He won the Grand National crown in 1976, 1977 and 1978. The award is presented each year to the driver who has accumulated the most points in 30 NASCAR-sanctioned races.

FIRST AUTO TO BREAK THE SOUND BARRIER

Hollywood stunt man Stan Barrett became the first man to break the sound barrier on land in December 1979. Barrett drove his car to a speed of 739.666 miles per hour on a dry lake bed at California's Edwards Air Force. His car was not exactly your usual family sedan. The three-wheeled vehicle was powered by a rocket engine as well as a Sidewinder missile to give it that little extra shove.

MOTORCYCLING

ORIGINS

After Gottlieb Daimler of Germany perfected internal combustion in 1885, using kerosene, he built an engine, only to realize that he didn't have a carriage to test it on. So Daimler attached the engine to his bicycle. While the engine-equipped bicycle wasn't a great success, it did prove that the engine could be used to propel a bicycle, thus giving birth to the first crude motorcycle.

The first real motorcycle in the U.S. was built by George Hendee of Springfield, Mass. in 1901-02. Hendee called it "The Indian Motorcycle." Not long after Hendee's invention appeared, the Davidson brothers of Milwaukee, Wis. produced the first of the legendary Harley-Davidson motorcycles.

Hendee set the first known distance record for a motorcycle, traveling from New York City to Boston on July 4, 1902. The first major motorcycle race was held in Brooklyn in 1903, and was won by George Holden, who covered 10 miles in 14 minutes, 57 and one-fifth seconds, for an average speed of about 40 mph.

The first man to ride a motorcycle at a speed of 100 miles per hour was Lee Humiston. He accomplished the feat in 1912 on an Excelsior motorcycle.

FIRST WOMEN TO MAKE A TRANSCONTINENTAL TRIP BY MOTORCYCLE

Sisters Adelina and Augusta Van Buren were the first women to travel across the continent on motorcycles. They left New York City on July 5, 1916 and arrived safe and well in San Diego, Calif. on Sept. 12.

ORIGINS OF DIRT TRACK MOTORCYCLE RACING

Dirt track motorcycle racing (or motorcycle speedway racing) was invented to fill an unexpected gap in an agriculture show in Australia. In 1925 Johnny S. Hoskins was presenting various attractions as part of an agricultural show in Maitland, New South Wales. When a scheduled number fell through, Hoskins asked a couple of local motorcyclists to race around the grassy track of the Agricultural Society's grounds. They found on a trial run that the grassy surface was too slippery, so they covered the track with a coat of cinders from a nearby slagheap. The race was a big success. Dirt track races were soon included as novelty events at Sydney's Speedway Royal. The first permanent dirt racing track was laid in 1926 at the Sydney Show Grounds.

Hoskins and A.J. Hunting took the sport to England in 1928. The first world dirt track championship was held at Wembley, in London, in 1936. The winner was Lionel Van Pragg from Australia.

FIRST MAN TO RIDE A MOTORCYCLE MORE THAN 200 MPH

Wilhelm Hertz was the first man to ride a motorcycle at more than 200 miles per hour. He set the record in timed trials at Wendover, Utah, over the salt flats.

MISCELLANEA

FIRST CAMEL RACE IN THE UNITED STATES

The first recorded U.S. camel race took place on April 7, 1864 at the Agricultural Park in Sacramento, Calif. There's no record of who the winner was.

6 / GOLF

ORIGINS

Golf is about 500 years old. Similar longevity is claimed by very few other athletic pursuits. It is an extremely successful commercial sport played around the world by kings and presidents and plain old weekend duffers who delight in breaking 100 strokes for 18 holes as much as touring pros delight in posting sub-par scores in tournaments in which thousands of dollars are at stake.

King James II of Scotland was playing golf as early as the 15th century. Mary, Queen of Scots, learned to play golf at a young age, continuing a tradition that led to the creation of the St. Andrews Golf Club in Scotland in 1552. St. Andrews is recognized as the birthplace of golf as we know it today. It was some 200 years later, in 1754, that the Society of St. Andrews Golfers, later renamed the Honourable Company of the Royal and Ancient Club, was founded. The members drafted the 13 articles of basic rules that still govern golf today.

The game spread from Scotland into Ireland and then into England. Ships traveling to North America in the mid-1800s took golfers to the United States and Canada. But golf was not an instant success in the United States.

Those 19th-century settlers more often became enamored of two newly-born games, baseball and football. Golf's detractors looked upon it as a sport played only by slackers afraid of real exertion.

Sports historians credit a Scotsman, John Reid, with laying out the first golf course in the United States, in Yonkers, N.Y. Play began there Feb. 22, 1888. The Amateur Golf Association of the United States (later the United States Golf Association) was formed in 1894. The first U.S. and Amateur Championship tournaments were held in Newport, R.I. in 1895.

But nearly 20 years passed before golf began to gain real popularity in the United States, and then it was thanks mostly to the performance of Francis Ouimet. The 20-year-old son of a gardener lived near the Brookline Country Club in Massachusetts. When the club was chosen as the site of the 1913 U.S. Open, Ouimet, an ex-caddy, entered the match.

Ouimet's score stood at 151 after 36 holes, four strokes off the pace. As the final round began, Ouimet was nervous, but he soon settled down and moved past the early leaders. Finally, on the 18th hole, Ouimet sank a four-foot putt for a par round and took the title. News of Ouimet's upset victory over the best golfers in the world brought the sport into the limelight and contributed enormously to its popularity.

FIRST BRITISH OPEN TOURNAMENT

The first British Open golf tournament was played in just one day, on Oct. 17, 1860. The golfers made three circuits around the 12-hole course at the Prestwick Golf Club at Ayrshire, Scotland. Eight professionals made up the field. Willie Park, using the gutta percha ball, shot a 174 for the 36 holes to win the tournament. Tom Morris Sr. was runner-up.

FIRST USGA MEN'S AMATEUR CHAMPIONSHIP

The United States Golf Association's Men's Amateur Championship has been held annually since 1895, with the exception of two years during World War I and three years during World War II.

The first USGA Men's Amateur Championship game was held Oct. 3, 1895 at the Newport Golf Club, Newport, R.I. Charles B. MacDonald, a founder of the Chicago Golf Club, won the tournament, defeating Charles Sands in match play, 12 and 11. There were 32 entries in the first tournament; matches were determined by draw.

Match play continued through 1964, but the tournament was changed to stroke play in 1965. Bob Murphy won the first tournament under stroke play at the Southern Hills Country Club, Tulsa, Okla. with a 72-hole total of

291. Bob Dickson finished second, one stroke behind Murphy.

FIRST USGA WOMEN'S AMATEUR CHAMPIONSHIP

The United States Golf Association's Women's Amateur Championship game, like the Men's Amateur Championship game, has been played every year since 1895, with two years off during World War I and three years during World War II. The tournament is one of the few major golfing events still determined by match play, although the first tournament was conducted under stroke play. Thirteen women participated in the first tournament at the Meadowbrook Country Club in Westbury, N.Y. in 1895. Nine holes were played in the morning and nine in the afternoon. Mrs. C.S. Brown won the tournament.

FIRST AMERICAN TO WIN THE BRITISH AMATEUR TOURNAMENT

Walter Travis was the first American to win the British Amateur Golf Tournament. He took the title in 1904. Travis attributed his victory to the "Schenectady putter" he had invented. The British subsequently banned Travis' putter.

FIRST FOUR-TIME U.S. OPEN WINNER

Fifteen-year-old Willie Anderson arrived in the United States in 1895 from North Berwick, Scotland. Just two years later he was runner-up in the U.S. Open Golf Tournament at the Chicago Golf Club, finishing behind Joe Lloyd. Four years after that, at the age of 21, Anderson won the 1901 U.S. Open at the Myopia Hunt Club in South Hamilton, Mass., with a 72-hole score of 331. He became the Open's first two-time winner with another victory in 1903, with a score of 307, the first three-time winner in 1904, with a score of 303 and the first four-time winner in 1905, with a score of 314. Anderson was also the first to win two U.S. Open titles consecutively, in 1903 and 1904, and the first to win three titles consecutively, in 1903, 1904 and 1905.

Anderson, who holds a place in professional golf's Hall of Fame, died in 1910 of arteriosclerosis. He was only 30 years old.

FIRST MAN TO WIN FOUR U.S. AMATEUR TITLES

Jerome D. Travers was the first golfer to win four U.S. amateur titles. Travers won his first in 1907, repeated in 1908, won again in 1912 and repeated once more in 1913.

FIRST PROFESSIONAL GOLF ASSOCIATION CHAMPIONSHIP

The first Professional Golfers Association Championship tournament was played in 1916 at the Siwanoy Country Club in Bronxville, N.Y., under match play rules. Thirty-year-old James M. Barnes of England won the first tournament. He first gained the lead on the 25th hole, lost it on the 31st hole, but regained it on the 33rd and went on to edge out 32-year-old Jock Hutchinson Sr. of Scotland, one up.

Match play continued through 1957, after which stroke play was instituted for the 1958 tournament. Dow Finsterwald was the first to win the tournament under stroke play with a four-round total of 276, two strokes better than runner-up Billy Casper, at the Llanerch Country Club at Havertown, Pa.

The PGA championship has been played annually since 1916 except for two years (1917-18) during World War I and one year (1943) during World War II.

Walter Hagen was the first American-born golfer to win the PGA championship in 1921, 3 and 2, over runner-up James M. Barnes. Hagen also won the tournaments from 1924 through 1927, inclusive, for a total of five PGA championships.

The winner of the PGA championship wins a cash prize and the Rodman Wanamaker Trophy.

FIRST WALKER CUP MATCHES

The Walker Cup was originated by George H. Walker, who was president of the United States Golf Association in 1920. Informal matches between U.S. and British amateurs were held in 1919, 1920 and 1921. The Walker Cup competition was formalized in 1922, and the first match was held at the National Golf Links of America in Southampton, N.Y. that year. The original competition consisted of foursome matches and eight individual matches to be played over 36 holes in two days. The United States won the first Walker Cup matches, 8-4.

Walker Cup matches were held annually in 1922, 1923 and 1924 and since then have been played biennially.

FIRST RYDER CUP TOURNAMENT

In 1926 a wealthy British seed merchant, Samuel A. Ryder, proposed a golf match between the United States and England and contributed a trophy, which has become known as the Ryder Cup, to be awarded to the winning team. The first Ryder Cup matches were played in 1927 at the Worcester Country Club in Worcester, Mass. The United States won by a score of 9½-2½. Ryder Cup matches are held every two years.

FIRST CURTIS CUP MATCHES

In 1927 sisters Harriot and Margaret Curtis, both former winners of the women's U.S. Amateur title, contributed a cup to be presented to the winner of women's match play between the United States and Great Britain. Although some informal matches were held in the 1920s, it was not until 1932 that the first Curtis Cup matches were played. The first competition took place at the Wentworth Golf Club in Wentworth, England. The United States team won, 5½-3½. Since then the Curtis Cup matches have been played every two years.

Since 1964 the competition has consisted of three 18-hole foursomes in the morning and six 18-hole singles in the afternoon of each day. One point is awarded for each match. When there is a tie, there is no playoff, and a half-point is awarded to each team.

FIRST MASTERS TOURNAMENT

The Masters Tournament is the youngest of golf's big four tournaments. It was first played in 1934.

The Masters was born when golfing legend Bobby Jones and architect Allister Mackenzie developed the Augusta, Ga., National Golf Course on a 365-acre site that had been a nursery. After the course was completed, Jones invited the best golfers to test it, and so the first Masters Tournament was played in 1934. For a while it appeared that Craig Wood would win the first tournament, but in the fourth round Horton Smith sank a 20-foot putt on the 17th hole for a birdie and went on to a par four on the 18th, winning by one stroke over Wood with a 72-hole score of 284.

The tournament has been held annually since 1934 except for the years from 1943 through 1945, when it was canceled because of World War II. Horton Smith became the Masters' first two-time winner when he won again in 1936. Jimmy Demaret was the first three-time winner, taking first place in 1940, 1947 and 1950. Arnold Palmer was the first four-time winner, finishing first in 1958, 1960, 1962 and 1964.

Participants in the Masters include past winners, specially invited foreign golfers and amateurs. The opening round field includes 80 to 90 golfers, but is cut in half after 36 holes.

The Masters winner receives a cash prize, a plaque and a green jacket, the symbol of a Masters winner.

FIRST VARDON TROPHY

The Vardon Trophy is awarded each year to the golfer with the best average in the Professional Golfers Association. The award originated in 1937 as the successor to the Harry E. Radix trophy and is named for famed British golfer Harry Vardon, who died in 1937. Vardon was among the first great modern golfers, winning the British Open an unequaled six times. In the three times he played in the U.S. Open, he won once and finished second twice.

The Vardon trophy was awarded for the first time in 1937 to Harry Cooper. Cooper was a hard-luck golfer—although at one time he held 20 course records, he never won a major championship.

The Vardon trophy is a bronze-colored plaque measuring 27 by 39 inches. It has been awarded annually since 1937 except for the years from 1942 through 1946, when it was canceled because of World War II.

FIRST WOMAN TO SCORE TWO HOLES IN ONE IN ONE ROUND

Mrs. W. Driver was the first woman to score two holes in one in one round. She got aces on the third and eighth holes at the Balgowlah Club in New South Wales, Australia, May 19, 1942. Apparently no man has ever accomplished this feat.

FIRST USGA WOMEN'S OPEN CHAMPIONSHIP

The Women's Open Championship has been played annually since 1946. The tournament was sponsored from 1946 through 1949 by the Women's Professional Golfers Association. From 1950 through 1952 the Ladies Professional Golf Association sponsored the tournament, and since 1953 the United States Golf Association has sponsored it.

The first Women's Open Championship was a match play competition at the Spokane Country Club in Spokane, Wash., in 1946. Patty Berg won the qualifying match with a two-round total of 145, then defeated Betty Jameson of San Antonio, Texas, 5 and 4, in the match play. Berg received $5600 in bonds for her victory.

The Women's Open was changed to stroke play in 1947. Betty Jameson won the first tournament under stroke play at the Starmount Forest Country Club, Greensboro, N.C., with a four-round total of 295. The tournament has been played under stroke play ever since.

FIRST AMERICAN TO WIN THE BRITISH WOMEN'S CHAMPIONSHIP

The first American to win the British Women's Championship was Babe Didrikson Zaharias, in 1947.

ORIGINS OF THE LPGA

Twelve women golfers formed the Ladies Professional Golf Association in 1950 to provide organized professional tournament golf for women.

The 12 founding members were Alice Bauer, Marlene Bauer Hagge, Patty Berg, Bettye Danoff, Helen Dettweiler, Betty Jameson, Betsy Rawls, Sally Sessions, Marilynn Smith, Shirley Spork, Louise Suggs and Babe Zaharias. The LPGA was chartered in 1951. Patty Berg was chosen as the organization's first president and Betty Rawls as its secretary.

In its early years the LPGA was run entirely by its players, with the exception of Fred Corcoran, who served as the first tournament director. Corcoran was responsible for the scheduling and operation of tour events.

FIRST AMERICAN ELECTED CAPTAIN OF THE ROYAL AND ANCIENT GOLF CLUB IN SCOTLAND

The first American to win the highest English honor for a golfer, election as Captain of the Royal and Ancient Golf Club at St. Andrews, Scotland, was Francis Ouimet in 1951. Ouimet had won the favor of the English golfers during the many years he had been a member or the non-playing captain of the U.S.Walker Cup team, from 1913 to 1949.

FIRST MAN TO WIN THE U.S. OPEN, THE MASTERS AND THE BRITISH OPEN IN ONE YEAR

In 1953 Ben Hogan became the first man to win the triple sweep of golf—the U.S. Open, the Masters and the British Open—all in one year. Hogan won the U.S. Open with a 72-hole score of 283, the Masters with a score of 274 and the British Open with a score of 282.

The little Texan had already won every golf championship in the U.S. He had also made a remarkable recovery from an automobile accident that had left him so injured it had seemed likely he would never again walk normally, much less play golf.

ORIGINS OF THE LPGA VARE TROPHY

The Vare Trophy was presented to the Ladies Professional Golf Association by Hall of Fame golfer Betty Jameson in 1952 in honor of the pioneering American woman golfer Glenna Collett Vare. Jameson requested that the trophy be awarded to the player with the lowest scoring average at the end of each year.

Vare Trophy scoring averages are figured on the basis of a player's total yearly score in official LPGA tournaments divided by the number of official rounds she has played during that year. It is now also required that a player must compete in 70 official rounds of tournament competition during the LPGA tour year to be eligible for the Vare trophy.

Patty Berg was the first to receive the trophy in 1953 after compiling an average of 75 in 65 official rounds.

FIRST MOST IMPROVED GOLFER AWARD

The Most Improved Golfer award is presented each year by *Golf Digest* magazine. It was presented for the first time in 1953, to golfer Doug Ford. The award is presented to the golfer whose performance in PGA-sanctioned tournaments has improved the most over the preceding year.

FIRST ROOKIE OF THE YEAR AWARD

The Rookie of the Year award is presented each year to the outstanding first-year professional golfer in the U.S. by *Golf Digest*. The award was presented for the first time in 1957, to Ken Venturi.

FIRST FOREIGNER TO WIN THE MASTERS TOURNAMENT

Gary Player became the first foreign golfer to win the Masters Tournament at the Augusta, Ga., National Golf Course. The South African won the 1961 tournament at the age of 25, with a 72-hole score of 280.

FIRST LPGA ROOKIE OF THE YEAR AWARD

The Ladies Professional Golf Association established its Rookie of the Year Award in 1962. The award is presented each year to a first-year player on the basis of her tournament performance and playing ability. Mary Mills was the first recipient of the Rookie of the Year Award in 1962.

FIRST MAN TO WIN OVER $100,000 IN ONE SEASON

Arnold Palmer was the first male golfer to win over $100,000 in a single season. He won $128,230 in 1963.

FIRST LPGA PLAYER OF THE YEAR AWARD

The Ladies Professional Golf Association established its Player of the Year Award in 1966 to honor the player who, during the current tour year, had the most consistent and outstanding record. Points are awarded only to those players who have finished in the first five positions in official LPGA co-sponsored or approved events.

Kathy Whitworth was the first to receive the award in 1966. She repeated in 1967, 1968 and 1969. After Sandra Haynie won the award in 1970, Whitworth regained it in 1971 and held on to it in 1972 and 1973.

ORIGINS OF THE WORLD CUP

The World Cup golf tournament was born in 1953 as the Canada Cup, fathered by Canadian industrialist John Jay Hopkins. It was renamed the World Cup in 1967. Cup matches are played every year, with two-member professional teams representing each participating country. It is customary for the host country to choose which two pros it would like to have compete. The two United States representatives are the reigning U.S. Open and PGA champions.

The first Canada Cup matches were played in 1953 at the Beaconsfield Golf Club in Montreal, Canada. Antonio Cerda and Roberto de Vicenzo, representing Argentina, won the first tournament with a combined 36-hole score of 287. The Canadian team of Stan Leonard and Bill Kerr finished second with a combined score of 297.

The United States duo of Arnold Palmer and Jack Nicklaus won the Cup in 1967, the first year of the World Cup. Palmer and Nicklaus combined for a 72-hole score of 557, while New Zealand's team of Bob Charles and Walter Godfrey finished second with a score of 570. That tournament was played at the Club de Golf Mexico in Mexico City.

FIRST INTERNATIONAL TROPHY WINNER

The International Trophy is awarded to the golfer with the lowest individual score in the World Cup matches. Antonio Cerda of Argentina won the first International Trophy at the Canada Cup matches in 1953 with a 36-hole score of 140. When the Canada Cup was renamed the World Cup in 1967 (see also **Origins of the World Cup**), American Arnold Palmer won the International Trophy with a 72-hole score of 276.

FIRST WOMAN TO WIN OVER $100,000 IN ONE SEASON

Judy Rankin was the first professional female golfer to win more than $100,000 in a single season. She won $150,734 in 1976.

FIRST WOMAN TO SHOOT CONSECUTIVE HOLES IN ONE

Sue Press was the first woman to shoot holes in one on two consecutive holes. She got aces on the 13th and 14th holes at the Chatswood Golf Club in Sydney, Australia May 29, 1977. There is no record of any man's ever having accomplished this feat.

FIRST WOMAN TO WIN ROOKIE OF THE YEAR AND PLAYER OF THE YEAR AWARDS IN THE SAME YEAR

Nancy Lopez was the first female golfer to win Rookie of the Year and Player of the Year honors in the same year. She took both in 1978.

FIRST FEMALE CADDIES IN THE U.S. OPEN

Female caddies were allowed for the first time in the U.S. Open in June 1980 at the Baltusrol Golf Club in Springfield, N.J. Pamela Shuttleworth of Santa Monica, Calif. was one of the first, caddying for Jim Dent. Another was Jane Betley, who carried clubs for her husband, Bob Betley.

FIRST MAN TO WIN THE U.S. OPEN TWICE ON THE SAME COURSE

On June 15, 1980 Jack Nicklaus became the first man to win the U.S. Open twice on the same course, with a record 272 at the Baltusrol Golf Club. With this win, Nicklaus also tied Willie Anderson, Ben Hogan and Bobby Jones as the only four-time winners of the U.S. Open. Nicklaus had first won at Baltusrol in 1967 as an upstart, dethroning Arnold Palmer. In 1980 he was a 40-year-old sporting idol trying to reestablish his supremacy.

7/RACQUET SPORTS:

TENNIS (COURT AND LAWN), BADMINTON, SQUASH, TABLE TENNIS AND PADDLE TENNIS

TENNIS (COURT AND LAWN)

ORIGINS OF COURT TENNIS

Court tennis is the ancestor of all racquet and paddle games played against walls and across nets. The game which is called royal tennis in England, real tennis in Australia and *jeu de paume* in France may or may not be descended from a game played in Greece about 2500 years ago and described by the Greek historian Herodotus. But there's no question that the origins of court tennis can be traced to a game played in the 12th century, first outdoors, and later in an enclosed space. The ball was hit by hand against any type of obstruction. Many members of the French royalty were devoted court tennis players from the 15th through the 18th centuries. Under the Tudors the sport was the royal game in England throughout the 16th century. The tennis court built at Hampton Court Palace during the Tudors' reign is, in fact, still in use. Nor was the game's popularity confined to the ruling classes—in the 17th century there may have been as many as 1,800 courts in Paris alone.

Gloves were sometimes used to protect the hand with which players hit the ball; later wooden paddles were introduced. Around 1500 there appeared a paddle with an extended handle and a hitting surface strung with sheep's gut. At first the racquets were laced diagonally in the frame, but by 1875 the lacing was strung at right angles.

Court tennis declined in popularity in France during the French Revolution. By the end of the 18th century there were only 50 tennis courts still in use in the entire country. At the same time the British were losing interest in the game, although it did experience a slight revival in England during the 19th century. Indoor courts had become too expensive to build or maintain.

There is some evidence that court tennis had been played in the U.S. as early as 1659. The governor of New York, Peter Stuyvesant, had signed a proclamation that year prohibiting the playing of tennis during church services. It is certain, in any event, that a court was built in 1876 in Boston's Back Bay, when Americans Hollis Hunnewell and Nathaniel Thayer sponsored a trip to America for Ted Hunt, a well-known English tennis player from Oxford. Eighteen courts were built in the U.S. between 1876 and 1923, but the sport never caught on as lawn tennis did.

WIMBLEDON; ORIGINS OF LAWN TENNIS

Wimbledon, perhaps the ultimate in world tennis competition, was born undramatically in England in 1877, an after-effect of the formation of a croquet club. The London home of J.W. Walsh, the editor of an English journal, was the scene of frequent weekend gatherings of the young ladies and gentlemen of London society for the purpose of playing croquet. At one of these gatherings Henry Jones, a writer, aide and friend of Walsh's, pointed out that the group was wreaking havoc on Walsh's flowers and lawn. Jones suggested that another site should be found for the get-togethers, and Walsh agreed. Walsh then dispatched a man who found a four-acre meadow for rent at 120 pounds per year in the Wimbledon area of London. The land was seeded and surveyed and, by June 1870, the All-England Croquet Club was ready for its first croquet tournament.

In December 1874 Walsh's journal received a letter from court tennis champion John Moyer Heathcote, expressing his satisfaction with a new flannel-covered tennis ball which was more elastic and more easily controlled, particularly on grass, than those commonly used at the time. Jones apparently shared the letter with others at the All-England Croquet Club; this ultimately led to the playing of lawn tennis among the club members. In 1875 the club's management appropriated 25 pounds to prepare a special area for lawn tennis and badminton. As a result, the name of the club was changed in 1877 to the All-England Croquet and Lawn Tennis Club. Jones soon persuaded Walsh's journal to offer a trophy and 25 guineas as prizes for a lawn tennis tournament. This led in turn to the formation of a subcommittee that formalized a set of rules for lawn tennis much the same as those in use today. Finally a notice appeared in Walsh's journal in 1877: "The All-England Croquet and Tennis Club at Wimbledon proposes the organization of a tennis tournament open to all amateur players on Monday, 9 July and successive days . . ."

The entrance fee was one pound and one shilling; a first prize in gold was offered, along with a second prize in silver. Entrants were told that they had to provide their own shoes, without heels, and racquets, but that the gardener would provide balls for practice.

The start of the tournament was later postponed until July 19 in order to permit participants to attend a cricket match between Harrow and Eton.

Two hundred spectators, who had paid an admission fee of one shilling each, were on hand for the opening matches. Twenty-two men entered the first Wimbledon competition, with Henry Jones, who had participated in the drafting of the rules, serving as referee.

Spencer Gore, a racquets player who had expressed a distaste for the new lawn tennis rules, persevered through round after round of competition to win the first Wimbledon tournament and the challenge cup. Maud Watson was the first women's singles champion in that inaugural tournament.

Wimbledon was expanded to include a men's doubles competition in 1879 and a women's doubles competition in 1913.

FIRST U.S. OPEN

The United States Open tennis tournament was first held in 1881 as the National Lawn Tennis Tournament at Newport, R.I. The national championship was played at Newport through 1914; it was moved to Forest Hills, N.Y. in 1915 and was held there for many years. The site of the tournament has recently been moved to Flushing Meadow, N.Y.

Richard D. Sears won the first national championship tournament in 1881, and went on to win every subsequent year through 1887. Men's doubles matches were also held for the first time in 1881. Clarence M. Clark and F.W. Taylor were the first men's doubles champions.

A national championship women's singles match was not held until 1887. Ellen F. Hansell was the first women's singles champion. National championship women's doubles matches were held beginning in 1890. The team of Ellen C. Roosevelt and Grace W. Roosevelt won the first women's doubles crown.

Mixed doubles matches for the national championship started in 1892. Mabel E. Cahill and Clarence Hobart won the first mixed doubles title.

FIRST AMERICAN WORLD CHAMPION IN COURT TENNIS

Thomas Pettit, who was born in England but later became a citizen of the U.S., was the first American to win the world championship in court tennis. Pettit challenged George Lambert of Great Britain in 1885. At one point Pettit was behind five sets to one, but he rallied to win six in a row and the match. He defended the title successfully in 1890 against Charles Saunders, but then resigned the title. Pettit challenged the reigning champion in 1898, only to lose.

FIRST NATIVE U.S. CITIZEN TO WIN THE WORLD TITLE IN COURT TENNIS

Jay Gould, son of railroad financier George Gould, became the U.S. amateur champion in court tennis in 1899. He trained on one of the only 18 court tennis courts ever built in the U.S.; this one had been built by the elder Gould on his estate in Lakewood, N.J. In 1914 Jay Gould won the world championship in court tennis from G.F. Covey, an English pro, in a one-on-one challenge, becoming the first native U.S. citizen to gain the title. (See also **First American World Champion in Court Tennis.**)

ORIGINS OF THE DAVIS CUP

Dwight Davis was a tennis player from St. Louis. He attended Harvard University, where he paired up for tennis with a frail, color-blind young man named Holcombe Ward. Thanks to Ward's ferocious serve and Davis' net assault, they won the university doubles championship. Then, in 1899, they took the men's doubles title at the U.S. Open at Forest Hills, N.Y. The two were not, however, satisfied with that distinction. They wanted to play tennis against foreign players as well as Americans.

The next year Davis ordered a 217-ounce sterling silver cup with the inscription "International Lawn Tennis Challenge Trophy." Not surprisingly, the trophy became known as the Davis Cup. Davis invited the British Lawn Tennis Association to compete against American players for the trophy. The group responded by sending three of its members: Arthur W. "Baby" Gore, Herbert Roper Barrett and Scotsman Ernest Black. The matches began on Aug. 7, 1900, one day later than scheduled, due to rain, at the Longview Cricket Club in Boston, Mass. There was really no contest. Davis defeated Black while American Malcolm Whitman stopped Gore in singles matches. In the doubles competition the British team of Barrett and Black found Davis and Ward too much to handle. The U.S. team went on to shut out the British team 5-0 in four singles matches and one doubles match.

Although originally intended as a competition between U.S. and British players, the Davis Cup was later expanded to include all countries. The challenge round matches are hosted each year by the country which is the defending champion.

FIRST AMERICAN WOMAN TO WIN
AT WIMBLEDON

May Sutton Bundy was the first American woman to win the women's singles championship at Wimbledon, in 1904 and again in 1907. But perhaps her most interesting accomplishment came at the U.S. Open at Forest Hills in 1930, where she became probably the only player in the tournament's history to finish a match while using a crutch. Bundy had slipped while playing, fracturing her left leg. Rather than conceding, she got hold of a crutch and finished the match.

FIRST BLACK CHAMPIONS

In the early days of American tennis, blacks were usually excluded from major tennis tournaments. Black tennis players thus began to hold their own tournaments at the Monumental Tennis Club in Baltimore, Md. Participants generally came from major eastern cities: New York, Philadelphia, Baltimore, Boston, Washington and others. Lucy Slowe thus became the first black woman tennis champion in the U.S., winning the women's singles title at the Baltimore tournament in 1917.

Tally Holmes was the first black man in the U.S. to become a tennis champion. He won singles championships at the tournament in Baltimore in 1918, 1921 and 1924.

FIRST AMERICAN TO WIN MEN'S
SINGLES CHAMPIONSHIP AT WIMBLEDON

William T. Tilden II, or, as he was popularly known, "Big Bill," dominated the U.S. tennis scene, amateur and then professional, from 1920 until the 1940s.

Tilden started out as a less than sparkling performer on the tennis court, but in 1913 he teamed with Mary K. Browne to win the mixed doubles outdoor title at the U.S. Open. They repeated as champions in 1914. By 1920, when Tilden was 27 years old, he had reached his peak. He took the men's singles titles that year both at the U.S. Open and at Wimbledon, where he met defending champion Gerald L. Patterson of Australia in the finals. Tilden easily controlled Patterson's serves and then, playing to Patterson's weak backhand, wiped him out with drop shots. The victory made Tilden the first American to win the Wimbledon men's singles title.

Tilden repeated as the men's singles champion at Wimbledon in 1921 and 1930.

FIRST WIGHTMAN CUP COMPETITION

In 1923 Mrs. Hazel Hotchkiss Wightman, who had been an outstanding tennis player in the early years of the 20th century, donated the trophy that became known as the Wightman Cup, to be awarded to the country whose team won a competition among women's teams from all over the world. Only the United States and England, however, have participated in the matches; the site of the matches now alternates annually between the two countries.

The United States won the first Wightman Cup matches in 1923 at Forest Hills, N.Y. by a score of 7-0. The reigning queen of tennis in the United States, Helen Wills Moody, was the star of the show. Moody conquered Kathleen McKane in the first match, 6-2, 7-5, and scored a singles victory. She then teamed up with Molla Mallory for a doubles victory.

FIRST PRO TOUR

Famed promoter C.C. Pyle (many said his initials stood for "cash and carry") organized the first professional tennis tour in 1926. He signed French tennis star Suzanne Lenglen and guaranteed her $50,000. Lenglen's career up to that point had been rather impressive: She had won the women's singles championship at Wimbledon an unprecedented six times, every year from 1919 through 1923 and again in 1925. She had also won the women's doubles championship at Wimbledon those same six years, as well as the mixed doubles championship in 1920, 1922 and 1925. And in 1925 and 1926 she had won the women's singles title in the French national championship tournament, which was then considered a major tournament. Other players Pyle signed for the tour included Mary Browne, Vincent Richards, Harvey Snodgrass, Howard Kinsey and Paul Peret. Pyle turned an $80,000 profit, then gave Lenglen a $25,000 bonus. Pyle's success with the pro tour led to the formation of the U.S. Professional Lawn Tennis Association in 1927. Pyle also helped popularize endorsements by the athletes (see Chapter 18, "Other Firsts," **First Commercial Endorsement by an Athlete**).

FIRST WOMAN TO WEAR SHORTS AT WIMBLEDON

Lili de Alvarez was the first woman ever to wear short trousers at Wimbledon. She appeared on the famous center court on June 23, 1931 dressed in an outfit of her own creation featuring short trousers. Observers thought the innovation would not last long, even though the freedom of movement it permitted was an advantage, because it was unbecoming. (She did not, incidentally, win the tournament.)

FIRST EIGHT-TIME WIMBLEDON WINNER

Tennis Hall of Famer Helen Wills Moody of the United States was the first, and so far the only, woman to win eight Wimbledon women's singles titles. She did it in 1927, 1928, 1929, 1930, 1932, 1933, 1935 and 1938. Moody's closest female competitor is Suzanne Lenglen, who won the singles title six times (see **First Pro Tour**). Her closest male competitor is Willie Renshaw, who won the Wimbledon men's singles title seven times—from 1881 through 1886, and again in 1899.

FIRST GRAND SLAM VICTORIES BY MEN AND WOMEN

Only four players, two men and two women, have won the "grand slam" of tennis—singles victories in the same year at the U.S. Open, at Wimbledon and at the Australian and French championships.

American Don Budge was the first to accomplish the feat, taking the grand slam in 1938.

Australian Rod Laver was the first, and so far the only, man to win the grand slam twice. He did it in 1962 and again in 1969.

Maureen Connolly of the United States was the first woman to win the grand slam, in 1953. In 1970 Margaret Smith Court from Australia also accomplished the feat.

FIRST TELEVISED MATCH

The first tennis match to be televised was played Aug. 9, 1939 at the Country Club in Westchester County, N.Y. The broadcast featured the Eastern Grass Court Championships.

FIRST BLACK WOMAN TO WIN BOTH THE U.S. OPEN AND WIMBLEDON

Althea Gibson, a one-time Harlem tomboy, broke the color barrier at the U.S. Open Tennis Championships at Forest Hills, N.Y. in 1950, where she almost scored a storybook upset. Gibson battled her way through the preliminary rounds and found herself across the net from that year's Wimbledon champion, Louise Brough, in the championship round. They split the first two sets; Brough led 7-6 in the third, decisive set when the skies opened and rain forced postponement of the match. When play resumed the next day, Gibson lost.

In 1957, Gibson and Brough faced each other once again at Forest Hills in the women's singles final of the U.S. Open. Gibson stopped Brough 6-3, 6-2 and accepted a silver vase and tray and a gold tennis ball from Vice Pres. Richard M. Nixon for her efforts. She also combined with Kurt Nielsen to win the U.S. Open mixed doubles title that year.

Gibson also became the first black woman to win the Wimbledon women's singles title in 1957. It took her just 50 minutes to beat Darlene Hard of San Diego, Calif. in the championship match. She then joined with Hard to win the 1957 Wimbledon women's doubles crown.

Gibson repeated as the women's singles champ at both Wimbledon and the U.S. Open in 1958; that same year she also paired with Maria Bueno to win the women's doubles title at Wimbledon.

FIRST FEDERATION CUP COMPETITION

The International Lawn Tennis Federation inaugurated the Federation Cup for women's competition in 1963 to celebrate the organization's 50th anniversary. The Cup competition draws women's teams from more than 20 countries annually. The United States women's team won the First Federation Cup in 1963 by beating the Australian team, 2-1, at London, England.

FIRST WOMAN ATHLETE TO EARN OVER $100,000 IN ONE SEASON

Tennis star Billie Jean King was the first woman athlete in any sport to earn more than $100,000 in a single season. She earned $117,400 in 1971. Major tournaments King won that year included the U.S. Open women's singles match, the Wimbledon women's doubles match (with fellow American Rosemary Casals) and the mixed doubles matches at both Wimbledon and the U.S. Open (with Australian Owen Davidson).

FIRST BROTHER-SISTER COMBINATION TO WIN WIMBLEDON MIXED DOUBLES CHAMPIONSHIP

Americans Tracy and John Austin became the first brother and sister to win the Wimbledon mixed doubles championship on June 5, 1980. The Austins won in the finals against Mark Edmondson and Diane Fromholtz, 4-6, 7-6 and 6-3.

BADMINTON

ORIGINS

Badminton is an inexpensive game. A badminton set, including racquets, shuttlecocks and a net, can easily be acquired for a few dollars, and an unofficial badminton "court" can be set up on any treeless patch of grass or dirt, permitting instant competition among two or more players. The simplicity and low cost of the equipment required for badminton no doubt accounts for its considerable popularity.

But the relatively recent popularization of the game belies its distinguished background—in particular, that of the event that gave it its name.

Badminton is, somewhat surprisingly, not an offshoot of tennis—or, for that matter, of any other court game. The game originated in India centuries ago, where it was known as "poona." English army officers played the game there in the 19th century and introduced it to Great Britain in the early 1870s. The Duke of Beaufort, in turn, introduced it to royal society at Badminton, his country house in Gloucestershire, in 1873. The game soon became known as "the game at Badminton," which was eventually shortened to just "badminton." It continued to be played under the rules originally established in India until 1887, when a group of English badminton players formed the Bath Badminton Club and adjusted and regularized the rules. Those rules have largely continued in force to this day. A successor to the Bath Club, the Badminton Association of England, was formed in 1895 to succeed the Bath club; it further modified the rules which govern the modern game.

Badminton spread quickly from England to the United States. The first badminton club in the U.S. was the Badminton Club of the City of New York, formed in 1878. The first U.S. national championship tournament, however, was not held until the mid-1930s (see **First U.S. National Championship Tournament**).

FIRST U.S. NATIONAL CHAMPIONSHIP TOURNAMENT

The first United States National Badminton Championship Tournament was played in April 1937 at the Naval Armory Pier in Chicago. Trophies were donated for competition in five classes: Walter Rysam Jones of New York contributed a trophy for men's singles in memory of Bayard Clarke, E. Langdon Wilkes and Howland Pell, organizers of badminton in the U.S.; the trophy for the men's doubles championship was contributed by Col. Leander McCormick-Goodhart of the British Embassy in Washington; Alouise Boker of New York presented a trophy for women's singles; a friend of Boker's, Connie Ford, also of New York, donated a trophy for women's doubles; and the Geneva, Ill. Badminton Club gave the trophy for mixed doubles.

There were some 150 entrants in the various classes for the first tournament. Walter R. Kramer won the men's singles title; Mrs. Del Barkhuff took the women's singles crown; Chester Goss and Donald Eversoll won the men's doubles; Mrs. Del Barkhuff and Zoe G. Smith won the women's doubles title; and Mrs. Barkhuff joined with Hamilton Law to win the mixed doubles title.

FIRST THOMAS CUP COMPETITION

Although badminton was introduced into both the United States and England in the 1870s, it was not until 1939 that the International Badminton Federation decided to hold an international championship competition. The president of the IBF, Sir George A. Thomas, offered a trophy for the winning team which would become known as the Thomas Cup. Although the cup matches were proposed in 1939, World War II prevented them from actually being held until the 1948-49 season. The team from Malaya won the first Thomas Cup matches.

Preliminary Thomas Cup play is held every third year in four zones: American, European, Asian (eastern and western) and Australasian. The site for the inter-zone semi-final and final rounds is chosen by the IBF.

FIRST UBER CUP COMPETITION

A women's international team competition in badminton was first proposed in 1950 but the first matches did not actually take place until the 1956-57 season. Mrs. H.S. Uber of England donated a trophy for the women's competition that has become known as the Uber Cup.

The first cup competition was held in England in March 1957. The United States team, captained by Margaret Varner, won the inaugural cup competition, defeating Denmark, 6-1.

Uber Cup matches are held every three years.

SQUASH

ORIGINS

Squash racquets, or squash, as it is commonly known, was invented in about 1850 by a group of students at Harrow, the exclusive English boys' school, who played hard racquets and wanted a game that was slower and easier to learn. While the students waited their turns in the racquets court, they developed a version of racquets in the smaller court just outside, which had probably been used originally for the English game "fives." Because the court was smaller, they used a slower ball. It was made of India rubber and made a "squash" sound when it hit the wall or was squeezed in the hand; hence the name of the game.

The game quickly gained popularity in England, spreading to other schools and to the homes of the wealthy. By 1882 the game had crossed the Atlantic and was being played at St. Paul's, the preparatory school in Concord. N.H.

The first court in a club in the U.S. was built on 43rd Street in New York City, the original site of the Racquet and Tennis Club, in 1891.

FIRST MAN TO WIN THE NATIONAL CHAMPIONSHIP IN SQUASH RACQUETS

John A. Miskey of Philadelphia won the first Men's Singles National Championship in 1907. He repeated in 1908 and 1910.

FIRST TOURNAMENT SPONSORED BY THE NATIONAL SQUASH ASSOCIATION

In 1911 the National Squash Association held its first tournament in New York City. Dr. Alfred Stillman beat J.W. Prentiss, 15-5, 17-15.

FIRST FOREIGNER TO WIN THE U.S. NATIONAL CHAMPIONSHIP IN SQUASH

Gerald Roberts, an Englishman, became the first foreigner to win the United States Squash Racquets Championships men's single title in 1924.

FIRST U.S. WOMEN'S CHAMPION

In 1928 Eleanora Sears won the first U.S. women's squash racquets singles championship at the Round Hill Club in Greenwich, Conn.

FIRST MEN'S DOUBLES NATIONAL CHAMPIONS IN SQUASH RACQUETS

In 1933 Roy R. Coffin and Neil J. Sullivan II won the first United States Squash Racquets Championships men's doubles title. The two men from Philadelphia also won the title in each of the subsequent four years.

FIRST FOREIGNER TO WIN U.S. WOMEN'S CHAMPIONSHIP IN SQUASH RACQUETS

In 1935 Margot Lamb became the first foreigner to win the U.S. women's squash racquets title.

FIRST U.S. OPEN CHAMPION IN SQUASH RACQUETS

The first U.S. open championship competition in squash racquets was held at the University Club in New York City in 1954 and was won by Henri Salaun.

TABLE TENNIS

ORIGINS

Although the beginnings of table tennis are unrecorded, it seems likely that the game was originated by British Army officers in India in the last part of the 19th century. James Gibb, a founder of the Amateur Athletic Union, is credited with introducing a celluloid ball. He sold the U.S. distribution rights to Parker Brothers Co., which marketed table tennis as a family game. The game is sometime called ping-pong because of the sound the ball makes when it hits the table or the racquet.

Table tennis is the unofficial national sport in China and is also quite popular in other countries in the Far East. In 1971 a team of table tennis players from the United States played a series of exhibition games in the People's Republic of China; they were the first U.S. athletic team to be invited to China since the end of World War II. The team were popularly described as ambassadors of "ping-pong" diplomacy. The next year a Chinese team paid a return visit, playing in several U.S. cities.

World championship matches have been held every two years since 1927. The U.S. won its first two world titles in 1936, when Jimmy McClure and Bud Blattner won the men's doubles and Ruth Aaron the women's singles.

PADDLE TENNIS

ORIGINS

The Rev. Frank Beal invented paddle tennis in 1898 in Albion, Mich. as a game for children, who could easily play the game with its small court and short-handled racquet. When Rev. Beal was transferred to New York he introduced the game there. Beal conducted the first paddle tennis tournament in Washington Square Park in 1922 in cooperation with the City of New York Dept. of Parks and Recreation. Dalio Santini, a recreation assistant at Beal's church, won the first tournament.

In 1923 the American Paddle Tennis Association was formed. In 1934 it became the United States Paddle Tennis Association.

8/WATER SPORTS:

SWIMMING, ROWING, ANGLING, SURFING, YACHTING, CANOEING, DIVING (SKIN AND SCUBA), WATER POLO, MOTORBOATING, WATER-SKIING AND NIAGARA FALLS

SWIMMING

ORIGINS; FIRST RECORDED SWIMMING COMPETITION IN THE UNITED STATES; FIRST U.S. RECORDS IN THE 100-YARD SWIM

One would no doubt be safe in assuming that human beings learned how to swim for one reason: in order to survive. Our ancestors probably learned how to swim by watching animals—perhaps by watching dogs paddle. As with other survival skills that evolved out of necessity—archery, for example—the survival instinct soon came to be accompanied by an equally basic human instinct—the competitive instinct.

That, in turn, led to swimming competition.

The American Indians were, not surprisingly, the first competitive swimmers in the United States. Evidence exists that the American Indians held swimming competitions of one sort of another, and we know that two American Indians once competed for a medal at a London swimming club to which they had been invited for a competition. No formal records exist, however, from swimming competitions in the United States prior to 1883. That was the year in which the New York Athletic Club inaugurated swimming competition; it held annual meets through 1887, when the Amateur Athletic Union began sponsoring the meets.

A.F. Camacho of the Manhattan Athletic Club took first prize in the 100-yard swim in the New York Athletic Club's first competition, with a time of 88¼ seconds, 15 seconds slower than the existing record in England.

J. Scott Leary of the Olympic Club in San Francisco, Calif., a specialist in the Australian crawl, became the first American to swim 100 yards in 60 seconds on July 18, 1905. That was four seconds faster than the existing U.S. record at the time.

Charles M. Daniels, who modified the Australian crawl into the so-called American crawl, surpassed Leary's record in the 100-yard swim on Feb. 22, 1906 at the New York Athletic Club. His time of 57.6 seconds tied what was then the world record. Just a month later, on March 23, 1906, at St. Louis, Mo., Daniels reduced his time for the 100-yard swim to a flat 56 seconds, establishing a new world mark.

BENJAMIN FRANKLIN

Few of Benjamin Franklin's achievements require retelling. Every schoolchild knows that Franklin flew a kite in a thunderstorm, which led eventually to the harnessing of electricity. He is equally remembered as one of the nation's Founding Fathers, the first postmaster general and the founder of the *Saturday Evening Post*. But Franklin's athletic feats are less well known.

Franklin, an avid swimmer, believed that swimming contributed importantly to physical conditioning. Franklin's love of swimming led him to develop the first wet suit, used to keep skindivers warm at extreme depths. He also created a pair of webbed sandals that were the forerunners of today's swimming flippers. There is no evidence, however, that Franklin ever devised a breathing device that would allow divers to remain underwater for long periods.

Had more pressing concerns not intervened, Franklin might have been the father of water-skiing. While flying a kite one day near a lake, it occurred to Franklin that a giant kite might be used to pull people across bodies of water. Franklin tested his idea and found that, yes, indeed, giant kites could harness enough of the wind's energy to pull a "rider" across the water. Franklin then began to wonder what would happen if such a rider attached barrel staves to his or her feet. He wrote about the subject, designed a few primitive water skis and even took his designs to a carpenter. Apparently the business of starting a new nation proved too time-consuming, however, and the idea eventually fell by the wayside.

FIRST SWIMMERS TO CROSS THE ENGLISH CHANNEL

Since the mid-19th century many swimmers have attempted to cross the 21-mile English Channel, which separates England and France. The first to accomplish the feat was merchant captain Matthew Webb. He crossed the Channel, using the breaststroke, between Dover, England and Cap Gris-Nez, France in 21 hours and 45 minutes on Aug. 24-25, 1875. It is estimated that Webb actually swam 38 miles, even though the crossing, "as the crow flies," is only 21 miles.

The first man to swim from France to England was Enrique Tiraboschi, a wealthy Italian who lived in Argentina. He made the crossing in 16 hours and 33 minutes on Aug. 11, 1923. He won $5,000 for his efforts.

The first woman to swim across the English Channel was an American, Gertrude Ederle, who swam from Cap Gris-Nez to Dover on Aug. 6, 1926. She made the crossing in record time—14 hours and 39 minutes. The first woman to swim from England to France was Florence Chadwick, also from the United States. She did it in 16 hours and 19 minutes on Sept. 11, 1951. (See also **First Woman to Swim Across the English Channel in Both Directions.**)

The first double crossing of the English Channel was accomplished by Antonio Abertondo from Argentina on Sept. 20-21, 1961. Abertondo crossed from England to France to 18 hours and 50 minutes. He rested a mere four minutes before diving back into the Channel; he then made his way back to St. Margaret's Bay in England in 24 hours and 16 minutes, for a total elapsed time of 43 hours and 10 minutes.

The first woman to complete a double crossing of the English Channel was 19-year-old Cynthia Nicholas, a Canadian. She did it on Sept. 7-8, 1977 in the remarkable time of 19 hours and 55 minutes—surpassing the previous record, set by a man, by more than 10 hours.

FIRST WOMAN TO WEAR A ONE-PIECE BATHING SUIT

In 1907 Annette Kellerman appeared on Revere Beach in Boston in a one-piece bathing suit. She was promptly arrested. Kellerman is the first woman known to have appeared in public in such "shocking" attire. Kellerman was also the first woman to attempt to swim the English Channel. Her life story was made into a movie called *Million Dollar Mermaid*, starring Esther Williams.

FIRST WOMAN TO BREAK AN EXISTING MEN'S WORLD SWIMMING RECORD

In 1924, when Sybil Bauer won the Olympic backstroke event, she became the first woman to break an existing men's world swimming record. At one time or other Bauer held all existing backstroke records for women.

JOHNNY WEISSMULLER

Johnny Weissmuller broke many swimming records during his career. In the 1924 Olympics he became the first man to swim 100 meters in less than one minute, with a time of 59 seconds flat. He broke his own record, and won another gold medal, in the 1928 Olympics with a time of 58.6 seconds. Weissmuller also won a gold medal in the 400-meter race in the 1924 Olympics with a time of five minutes, 4.2 seconds, surpassing what was then the world record by 20 seconds. In both the 1924 and the 1928 Olympics, Weissmuller won gold medals in the 800-meter relays as a member of the U.S. team.

Some experts consider Weissmuller the greatest American swimmer of all time. While he never won as many gold medals in one year's Olympics as Mark Spitz did in 1972, he did win gold medals in the Olympics two different years. And, throughout his career, he set 67 world records in swimming, both in and out of the Olympics.

Weismuller went on to win fame in another field—for his portrayals of Tarzan on film.

FIRST WOMAN TO SWIM 100 YARDS IN ONE MINUTE

In 1932 Helene Madison of Seattle, Wash. became the first woman ever to swim 100 yards in one minute.

FIRST UNDERWATER PHOTO-FINISH

Underwater photography was first used to determine the finish of swimming races on April 15, 1939 at the Amateur Athletic Union national swimming meet in Detroit.

FIRST MAN TO SWIM ACROSS THE IRISH SEA

In 1947 Thomas Blower of Nottingham, England became the first man ever to swim across the Irish Sea. Blower swam from Donaghadee, Northern Ireland to a point five miles from Port Patrick, Scotland, a distance of 25 miles, in 15 hours and 25 minutes.

FIRST MAN TO SWIM ACROSS THE STRAIT OF GIBRALTAR

Daniel Carpio, from Peru, made the first recorded swim across the Strait of Gibraltar on July 22, 1948. He swam the eight miles from continental Spain to Morocco in nine hours and 20 minutes.

FIRST WOMAN TO SWIM ACROSS THE ENGLISH CHANNEL IN BOTH DIRECTIONS

Florence Chadwick was the first woman to swim both ways across the English Channel. Chadwick, an American, swam from France to England in 1950, setting a new record of 13 hours and 20 minutes, more than an hour faster than the previous record. The next year, on Sept. 11, she swam from England to France, completing her round trip. (See also **First Swimmers to Cross the English Channel.**)

FIRST MAN TO SWIM THE 200-METER FREESTYLE IN LESS THAN TWO MINUTES

Don Schollander became the first male swimmer to break the two-minute mark for the 200-meter freestyle on Aug. 24, 1963 at a meet in Osaka, Japan. His time was one minute, 58.4 seconds.

FIRST WORLD WOMEN'S INVITATIONAL SWIM MEET

The first World Women's Invitational Swim Meet was held at East Los Angeles College in February 1973. Only those swimmers who had been finalists in the 1972 Oympic Games were permitted to enter; these included Deena Deardruff and Shirley Babashoff from the United States and Shane Gould and Beverly Whitfield from Australia. Among the outstanding performers in the meet was Melissa Belote from the United States, who won in the 100-yard backstroke, the 200-yard backstroke and the 400-yard medley relay.

FIRST WORLD CHAMPION IN SOLO SYN-CHRONIZED SWIMMING

Terry Anderson from Santa Clara, Calif. was the first world champion in solo synchronized swimming. He won the title on Sept. 2, 1973 in a competition in Belgrade, Yugoslavia.

FIRST PERSON TO SWIM ACROSS LAKE ONTARIO

Diana Nyad became the first person ever to swim across Lake Ontario in 1975, covering the 32-mile distance in 20 hours. Nyad also set a record for swimming for the 28 miles around Manhattan—seven hours and 57 minutes.

FIRST MAN TO SWIM THE 200-METER BACKSTROKE IN LESS THAN TWO MINUTES

John Naber from the United States became the first man to break two minutes in the 200-meter backstroke in an Olympic final in 1976, with a time of one minute, 59.19 seconds. The outstanding male swimmer of the 1976 Olympic Games in Montreal, Naber won four gold medals and one silver. In addition to the 200-meter backstroke, he won the 100-meter backstroke, the 4 x 200-meter freestyle (relay) and the 4 x 100-meter medley (relay); he won his silver medal in the 200-meter freestyle.

FIRST WOMAN TO SWIM ACROSS THE ENGLISH CHANNEL FIVE TIMES

Greta Anderson was the first female swimmer to cross the English Channel five times. At one time she held the speed records for swimming both from France to England and from England to France, but Cindy Nicholas later surpassed Anderson's records. (See also **First Swimmers to Cross the English Channel.**)

Anderson has won a number of other swimming honors as well. Most notably, in 1948 she won a gold medal in the Olympics for the 100-meter sprint.

ROWING

ORIGINS

Boat and oar building was one of the earliest crafts practiced by human beings, as transportation along waterways was a necessity before the existence of good roads. Competitions among rowers probably began as soon as several boats crossed rivers or rowed their way up- or downstream at the same time.

Rowing was a sport in classical times. Virgil mentions in the *Aeneid*, which was completed in 19 B.C., that games Aeneas arranged for the funeral of his father, Anchises, included rowing competitions. In ancient times, however, rowing was generally not considered honorable work for freemen; rowers were usually slaves who were chained to their seats.

The English economy, in ancient and medieval times, depended upon rowboats for the transportation of both people and goods up and down the busy Thames. By the 1400s the rich frequently had their own luxuriously equipped barges. Parties held on boats were frequently the highlight of royal entertainment.

The first recorded rowing competition was held by Thomas Doggett, a Dublin-born actor, on Aug. 1, 1715. Doggett wanted the race to become an annual event; thus, in his will, he left a fund to pay for the continuation of the race after his death. As a result the Doggett's Coat and Badge race is the oldest rowing race in the world today.

The first college rowing competitions were held between Oxford and Cambridge in 1829 at Henley. The famous race has been held almost yearly since then.

Rowing is the oldest of American intercollegiate sports. The first match was held between Harvard and Yale in 1852 on Lake Winnepesaukee in New Hampshire.

FIRST RECORDED RUN OF THE COLORADO RIVER RAPIDS

In 1869 Maj. John Wesley Powell made the first recorded run of the Colorado River through the Grand Canyon. His party began the trip at Green River, Wyo. and reached what is now the Lake Mead area in 99 days.

FIRST MEN TO ROW ACROSS THE ATLANTIC

George Harbo and Frank Samuelson planned to become the first to travel the 3000 miles from New York to France in a rowboat—to be precise, in an 18-foot round-bottom boat without either a motor or sails. The boat was named *The Fox* in honor of Richard Fox, publisher of the *Police Gazette*, a peculiar montage of sordid police stories and sports news that was very popular at the time. The two Norwegian-born Americans spent two years planning their adventure. Many thought they were doomed to failure, if not certain death.

Harbo and Samuelson left New York on June 6, 1896, carrying with them 500 pounds of food, 60 gallons of water, an oil stove, five pair of oars, an anchor and, last but not least, emergency flares. Their plan was to ride the Gulf Stream all the way to Le Havre, France.

Several weeks had passed without incident when the adventurers ran into a storm. They were forced to stay awake for three days as they battled to remain afloat. On the third day a monstrous wave proved too much for the little boat; it flipped over. Harbo and Samuelson were able to remain near the boat because they were wearing life jackets that were tied to the boat. They eventually managed to get *The Fox* righted and climbed aboard, battered and bruised but still alive. They drifted into the Scilly Isles off the coast of Great Britain and rested there for a day before going on to Le Havre. They then rowed up the Seine to Paris.

The trip had taken 61 days.

FIRST AMERICAN TO WIN THE DIAMOND SCULLS AT THE HENLEY REGATTA

Ned Ten Eyck became the first American to win the Diamond Sculls at the Henley Regatta in 1897. Ten Eyck, who was coached by his father, the noted rower James A. Ten Eyck, was only 17 when he won the Diamond Sculls.

FIRST WOMAN COXSWAIN OF A MEN'S VARSITY ROWING TEAM

Sally Stearns of Rollins College in Winter Park, Fla., was the first woman coxswain of a men's collegiate varsity rowing team. She led a shell for the first time in a race against Marietta College on May 27, 1936.

FIRST COMMERCIAL WHITE WATER TRIPS DOWN THE COLORADO RIVER

Commercial white water trips down the Colorado River rapids have been made since 1938 when Norman Nevills started his business, using cataract boats.

FIRST WOMAN TO COMPETE IN THE OXFORD-CAMBRIDGE RACE

On April 4, 1981 Sue Brown from Oxford became the first woman to row against Cambridge in the 152-year history of the event (see also **Origins**). Brown coxed the Oxford crew to an eight-length victory over Cambridge.

ANGLING

ORIGINS

Angling is not merely fishing—it is making an art out of fishing. The angler is not interested just in catching fish. The handling of the frail rod, the casting of the line and the technique used in the operation of the reel all set angling apart from fishing. Angling today often involves casting competitions. In the early days of angling the competitors might cast into a barren field as often as into a river.

The ancient Egyptians may have been the first people actually to make fishing lines from braided animal hair and thornwood branches. The Egyptians may also have been the first to make crude hooks for catching fish.

It is not known who first fished with flies, or artificial bait, but the first to write about the practice was an Italian, Aelian, who lived from 170-230 AD An Englishman, Barker, wrote about fly fishing in 1651 in his book *The Art of Angling*. By 100 years later fly-casting contests were being held in England.

Informal angling clubs were formed in the United States even before the American Revolution. (See also **First American Angling Club**.) The first national angling tournament was held in 1893 by the Chicago Fly-casting Club during that year's World's Fair. The events included accuracy fly, delicacy fly, long-distance bait and long-distance fly. All of the contests were held on dry land because methods for measuring casts on water had not yet been perfected.

A permanent national association of anglers, called the National Association of Scientific Angling Clubs, was formed in 1906. Its nine local chapters were located in Chicago, Cincinnati, Fox River Valley, Wis., Grand Rapids, Kalamazoo, Kansas City, Racine, San Francisco and Illinois.

FIRST AMERICAN ANGLING CLUB

Thirty Quakers from Philadelphia founded the first angling club in the United States in 1732 while their city was in the grip of a smallpox epidemic. The group fished on the Schuylkill River on the farm of "Friend William Warner." They named their club the "Colony in Schuylkill" and modeled its organization on that of the colonial government. The anglers built a clubhouse, or courthouse, as they called it, 15 years later. There they opened each fishing season with a formal but inexpensive dinner prepared by the members.

The Colony in Schuylkill soon found its prestige challenged by a nearby club, the Society of Fort St. Davids, which was made up of Welshmen who also fished on the Schuylkill. Both clubs praised the perch and catfish found in the river; both also considered themselves the best group of anglers in the 13 colonies.

SURFING

ORIGINS

Surfing was by no means originated by the '60s surfing generation, with their sun-bleached hair and fiberglass boards. A museum in Peru exhibits a ceramic figurine, dating from pre-Inca times, of what may have been a prehistoric surfer on a short board. In 1777 Capt. Cook witnessed the Polynesians surfing in canoes; they may have been surfing for centuries before Cook's voyage. The Polynesians used wooden canoes and boards up to 18 feet long which weighed 150 pounds or more. After surfing was introduced to California in 1910 by Duke Kahanomoku—a noted Hawaiian swimmer who was to win Olympic gold medals in the 100-meter freestyle in 1912 and 1920—and George Freeth, most boards there were made of redwood. Surfers had to use boards that weighed about as much as they did in order to get sufficient buoyancy.

In the 1920s one Tom Blake introduced a lighter, hollow board, later called a paddleboard, which weighed only 100 pounds despite its 16-foot length. In 1935 Blake introduced the keel or "skeg" under the rear of the board, which gave it more directional stability. In 1950 balsa wood boards with a waterproof coating were introduced, and, in 1954, fiberglass boards. The most recent development in surfboard design was the replacement of fiberglass by foam plastic, which is so light that its weight is only seven percent of the weight of water.

YACHTING

FIRST SUCCESSFUL YACHT CLUB IN THE UNITED STATES

The first successful yacht club in the United States was the New York Yacht Club. The club was organized on July 30, 1844 in the cabin of the schooner *Gimcrack*, which was owned by John C. Stevens. The following year the club made its first home at the Elysian Fields in Hoboken, N.J.—where, incidentally, the Knickerbocker Baseball Club was playing exhibition contests (see also Chapter 1, "Baseball"—**Origins; First Game**).

For a quarter of a century the New York Yacht Club was the only such organization that was able to have regular squadron cruises, because it was the only club whose members owned large enough yachts in sufficient numbers.

The club, perhaps best known as the custodian of the America's Cup trophy, is still in existence. (See also **The America's Cup**.)

THE AMERICA'S CUP

The America's Cup, probably the most prestigious trophy in yachting, has been in the sole possession of the United States since 1851. As a result of its lengthy residence in the U.S., the trophy has been bolted to the floor at its home in the New York Yacht Club. Legend has it that the U.S. skipper who loses the cup will have his head bolted to the floor in its place.

In 1851 a syndicate of New York Yacht Club members built a 101-foot schooner named *America*. The *America* was launched May 3, 1851 and sailed to England—the intention was to show the British just who would dominate the competitive sailing world. Seventeen British vessels, ranging from the 47-ton *Aurora* to the 392-ton three-masted schooner *Brilliant*, accepted the *America*'s challenge. On Aug. 22, 1851 the 17 British vessels and the *America* gathered at the Isle of Wight for a race from Cowes eastward to the Nab lightship, then southwest to St. Catherine's Point and back into The Solent by way of the Needles.

Many of the British had initially been skeptical about the speed of the unusually designed schooner from the (former) colonies. The *America*'s sails were cut unconventionally, and were made out of cotton, rather than the usual flax. It was more sleekly designed than most schooners of the day—and, as it turned out, the *America*'s design was aerodynamically superior. It crossed the finish line in 10 hours and 37 minutes, 18 minutes ahead of the *Aurora*.

For their efforts the crew of the *America* received a trophy measuring more than two feet tall, then called the Hundred-Guinea Cup. In 1857 the commodore of the *America*, John Cox Stevens, and other members of the syndicate that owned the schooner presented the cup to the New York Yacht Club and specified that foreign yachts could challenge the Americans for possession of the cup. Since that time there have been 23 challenges for the America's Cup from England, Canada and Australia. None has succeeded.

Yachts taking part in the America's Cup races were traditionally of the largest classes, up to 145 feet long. But because of the ever-rising costs of building such large craft, the New York Yacht Club went to court in the 1950s and legally changed the America's Cup Deed of Gift. That action opened up Cup races to boats as small as 44 feet (waterline length). The court action also eliminated the requirement that America's Cup competitors had to be sailed to the site of the Cup races.

Today the America's Cup races take place off the coast of Newport, R.I. in 12-meter (about 40-foot) yachts which cost in the neighborhood of three-quarters of a million dollars.

FIRST TRANSATLANTIC YACHT RACE

The first transatlantic yacht race was held on a course from Sandy Hook Lightship, off New Jersey, to a finish at the Needles in England. The race began on Dec. 11, 1866. Pierre Lorillard Jr. set up the race because he had been dissatisfied with the competitions in regular yacht regattas during 1866. Lorillard raced his centerboard schooner, the *Vesta*, against the *Fleetwing*, owned by George and Franklin Osgood, and the *Henrietta*, a keel schooner owned by James Gordon Bennett Jr.

The race began in heavy weather. On Dec. 25 the *Henrietta* reached the finish more than eight hours ahead of the *Fleetwing*. The winner had sailed 3106 miles in 13 days, 21 hours and 55 minutes.

FIRST SOLO VOYAGE AROUND THE WORLD

Nova Scotia-born Joshua Slocum made the first solo voyage around the world in his 37-foot boat named *Spray*. Slocum left Boston, Mass. on April 24, 1895, sailing from east to west. He arrived in Newport, R. I. on June 27, 1898, more than three years later, after traveling 46,000 miles.

FIRST SOLO TRANSATLANTIC CROSSING BY A WOMAN

British-born Ann Davison was the first woman to make a solo transatlantic crossing, in her 23-foot sloop *Felicity Ann*. She left Plymouth, England on May 18, 1952 and spent 15 months traveling to Miami via France, Spain, Africa, the Canary Islands and the West Indies. Davison arrived in Miami Aug. 13, 1953.

FIRST MAN TO CROSS THE ATLANTIC ALONE IN A SMALL BOAT

On Oct. 20, 1956 Hannes Lindemann, a German, left the Canary Islands on a solo voyage across the Atlantic in a 17-foot boat (a day sailer). Lindemann rarely slept more than an hour at a time on his trip to Philipsburg, St. Martin. He was the first person ever to sail the Atlantic alone in so small a boat.

FIRST WOMAN TO SAIL SOLO TRANSPACIFIC

Only one woman has sailed solo across the Pacific Ocean. In 1969 Sharon Sites, an American, sailed her 25-foot sloop 5,000 miles from Yokohama, Japan to San Diego, Calif., in 74 days, completing the trip on July 24.

FIRST INTERNATIONAL WOMEN'S RACE

The first international women's yachting competition was held in May 1974 at Quiberon, France. Eighty women from 11 countries participated in the event, which was sponsored by a French national sailing group. Competing against 28 other women, Martine Allix of France won the single-handed dinghy class, while Gonnede de Vos of the Netherlands, competing against 25 other women, won in the 420, or two-handed dinghy, class.

FIRST WOMAN TO SAIL SOLO AROUND THE WORLD

Krystyna Choynowska-Liskiewicz of Poland was the first woman to sail around the world singled-handed. She left Las Palmas in the Canary Islands on March 28, 1976, sailing westward in her 32-foot fiberglass sloop. After making numerous stops, she crossed her outward bound course in the Atlantic Ocean on March 26, 1978.

CANOEING

ORIGINS OF COMPETITION

The canoe, a means of transportation whose origins can be traced back to thousands of years before the birth of Christ, began to be used widely for sport and competition in the last half of the 19th century.

A British barrister, John Macgregor, is credited with popularizing the canoe for sport and recreation through his creation of the Rob Roy-type canoe in 1865. Macgregor was also instrumental in the formation of the Royal Canoe Club on July 26, 1865 in London. The formation of the club led to the development of other types of canoes.

In 1871 William L. Alden and M. Roosevelt Schuyler formed the first canoe club in the United States, the New York Canoe Club, at a meeting of canoeing enthusiasts at Staten Island, N.Y. Other canoeing clubs were formed shortly thereafter in New York State, New Jersey and Pennsylvania.

The American Canoe Association was formed at a meeting Aug. 3, 1880 at Lake George, N.Y. Alden, then commodore of the New York Canoe Club, was elected the first commodore of the national organization. Nathaniel Bishop, who was famous for his 1874 trip from Quebec to the Gulf of Mexico in the paper canoe *Maria Theresa*, was the first secretary-treasurer of the national group. The ACA began sponsoring races during the 1880s; competitions for many of the trophies first offered as prizes in the early years of the ACA are still held on a regular basis in the U.S.

The first international canoeing organization, International Representation for the Canoeing Sport, was formed in the 1920s. Dr. Max Eckert of the German canoeing organization was the first president of the international organization. As a result of the efforts of the international group, canoeing became an official Olympic sport at the 1936 games in Berlin. (There had been demonstration canoeing events at earlier Olympiads.) The following canoeists won gold medals during the first Olympic canoeing competition:

> Gregor Hradetzky of Austria, in the 1000-meter kayak singles
> Ernst Krebs of Germany, in the 10,000-meter kayak singles
> Francis Amyot of Canada, in the 1000-meter Canadian singles
> The Austrian team of Adolf Kainz and Alfons Dorfner, in the 1000-meter kayak pairs
> The German team of Paul Wevers and Ludwig Lamden, in the 10,000-meter kayak pairs
> Gregor Hradetzky of Austria, in the 10,000-meter folding kayak singles
> The Swedish team of Sven Johansson and Eric Bladstroem, in the 10,000-meter folding kayak pairs
> The Czechoslovakian team of Vladimir Syrovatka and F. Jan Brzak, in the 1000-meter Canadian pairs
> The Czechoslovakian team of Vaclav Mottle and Zdenek Skrdlant, in the 10,000-meter Canadian pairs

Ernest Riedel of the Pendleton Canoe Club of Yonkers, N.Y. finished third in the 10,000-meter kayak singles; this was the best performance by a U.S. entrant in the first Olympic canoeing competition.

THE INTERNATIONAL CHALLENGE CUP

One of the oldest trophies offered for canoe racing is the International Challenge Cup, which was first offered in 1885 by the New York Canoe Club. C. Bowyer Vaus, a member of the New York Canoe Club, was the first to win the Challenge in 1886.

American, British and Canadian canoeing organizations still compete for the Challenge Cup on a challenge basis.

1. The 1869 Cincinnati Red Stockings, the first professional baseball team (see p. 6, **First Professional Team**).
(Photograph courtesy of the National Baseball Hall of Fame and Museum, Inc.)

2. Moses Fleetwood Walker, who became the first black player for a college baseball team in 1881 (see pp. 10–11, **First Black College Baseball Player**) and, in 1884, the first black to play professional baseball (see pp. 11–13, **First Black in the Major Leagues**).
(Photograph courtesy of the National Baseball Hall of Fame and Museum, Inc.)

3. Honus Wagner, of the Pittsburgh Pirates, was the National League's batting champion in 1903, with an average of .355. But his average against the Boston Red Sox in the first World Series, held that same year, was only .222. (See p. 14, **First World Series**.)
(Photograph courtesy of the National Baseball Hall of Fame and Museum, Inc.)

4. Neal Ball of the Cleveland Indians (second from left), shown here with the three players from the Boston Red Sox he put out in the first unassisted triple play in major league history in July 1909 (see p. 15, **First Unassisted Triple Play**). Ball's victims were Amby McConnell (far left), Heinie Wagner (second from right) and Jake Stahl (far right).
(Photograph courtesy of the National Baseball Hall of Fame and Museum, Inc.)

5. (Top left) Shoeless Joe Jackson, one of the eight members of the 1919 Chicago White Sox who were banned from major league baseball for life in the wake of the "Black Sox" scandal (see pp. 17–18, **First Modern Major League Scandal**). Jackson is shown here earlier in his career, wearing the uniform of the Philadelphia Athletics.
(Photograph courtesy of the National Baseball Hall of Fame and Museum, Inc.)

6. (Top right) Ty Cobb, who on July 18, 1927, while a member of the Philadelphia Athletics, became the first—and, so far, the only—major league player to make 4000 safe hits (see p. 20, **First Man to Make 4000 Safe Hits**). Cobb is shown here wearing the uniform of the Detroit Tigers, with whom he spent most of his career.
(Photograph courtesy of the National Baseball Hall of Fame and Museum, Inc.)

7. Mel Ott of the New York Giants, who on Aug. 4, 1934 became the first man to score six runs in a major league game (see p. 22, **First Major League Players to Score Six Runs in One Game**). Some 12 years later, while managing the Giants, Ott also became the first manager ever to be ejected from two games in one day (see p. 26, **First Manager to Be Ejected from Games Twice in One Day**).
(Photograph courtesy of the National Baseball Hall of Fame and Museum, Inc.)

8. (Top left) Ernie Nevers, player-coach for the St. Louis Cardinals, who became the first professional football player ever to score six touchdowns in one game, on Nov. 28, 1929, against the Chicago Bears (see pp. 43–44, **First Player to Score Six Touchdowns in a Professional Game**).
(Photograph courtesy of the Pro Football Hall of Fame.)

9. (Top right) Jay Berwanger, a back for the University of Chicago Maroons, who became the first winner of the Heisman Memorial Trophy in 1935 (see pp. 44–45, **Origins of the Heisman Trophy**) and the first player selected in an NFL draft in 1936 (see pp. 45–46, **First College Football Draft**).
(Photograph courtesy of the Downtown Athletic Club).

10. George S. Halas, renowned coach of the Chicago Bears, who was largely responsible for introducing the T-formation to professional football (see pp. 46–47, **Origins of the T-Formation**).
(Photograph courtesy of the Pro Football Hall of Fame).

11. (Top left) Willie Thrower of the Chicago Bears, who in 1953 became the first black quarterback in the National Football League (see p. 50, **First Black Pro Quarterback**).
(Photograph courtesy of the Pro Football Hall of Fame.)

12. (Top right) Harlon Hill, a receiver for the Chicago Bears, who in 1955 became the first recipient of the National Football League's most valuable player award, the Jim Thorpe Trophy (see p. 50, **First MVP**).
(Photograph courtesy of the Pro Football Hall of Fame.)

13. Pat Palinkas, who became the first woman to play in a professional football game on Aug. 15, 1970 (see pp. 51–52, **First Woman in Professional Football**).
(Photograph courtesy of the Orlando **Sentinel Star**.)

14. Dr. James A. Naismith, the creator of modern basketball (see pp. 53–54, **Origins**). (Photograph courtesy of the Basketball Hall of Fame.)

15. Ann Meyers, who became the first woman to sign a contract with a professional basketball team on Aug. 30, 1979 (see pp. 61–62, **First Woman to Sign a Pro Contract**). Meyers never actually played for the Indiana Pacers, the team that signed her.
(Photograph courtesy of Peter C. Borsari, Photography.)

16. Bill Smith of the New York Islanders, who became the first goalie in NHL history ever to score a goal on Nov. 28, 1979 (see **First Goalie to Score a Goal**).
(Photograph courtesy of the New York Islanders Hockey Club.)

17. Aristides, the winner of the first Kentucky Derby in 1875 (see p. 76, **Origins of the Kentucky Derby**).
(Illustration courtesy of **The Throughbred Record.**)

18. Sir Barton, the first horse to win the Triple Crown, in 1919 (see p. 78, **First Triple Crown Winner**).
(Illustration courtesy of **The Throughbred Record.**)

19. Diane Crump, who became the first woman to ride a horse in the Kentucky Derby on May 2, 1970 (see p. 8, **First Woman Jockey to Ride in the Kentucky Derby**).
(Photograph courtesy of **The Throughbred Record.**)

20. Ray Harroun, the winner of the first Indianapolis 500 on May 30, 1911, shown here in his Marmon Wasp (see p. 91, **First Indianapolis 500**).
(Photograph courtesy of the Indianapolis Motor Speedway.)

21. Janet Guthrie, who became the first woman to race in the Indianapolis 500 in 1977 (see pp. 94–95, **First Woman to Drive in the Indianapolis 500**).
Photograph courtesy of the Indianapolis Motor Speedway.)

22. (Top left) Kathy Whitworth, who won the Ladies Professional Golf Association's first Player of the Year Award in 1966 (see p. 106, **First LPGA Player of the Year Award**). (Photograph courtesy of the Ladies Professional Golf Association.)

23. (Top right) Richard D. Sears, the winner of the men's singles title at the first U.S. Open tennis tournament in 1881 (see p. 110, **First U.S. Open**). (Photograph courtesy of the International Tennis Hall of Fame and Tennis Museum.)

24. Ellen F. Hansell (far right), shown here with three other noted players of the day (Bertha Townsend, far left; Margie Ballard, second from left; and Louise Allerdice, second from right), won the women's singles title at the U.S. Open in 1887, the first year that the competition was open to women (see p. 110, **First U.S. Open**). Townsend won the title the following two years.
(Photograph courtesy of the International Tennis Hall of Fame and Tennis Museum.)

25. The America's Cup, shown here bolted to the floor at the New York Yacht Club (see pp. 131–132, **The America's Cup**).
(Photograph courtesy of Morris Rosenfeld & Sons Inc.)

26. Blondin, the first man ever to cross the Niagara Rapids on a cable, shown here Aug. 17, 1859 carrying a man across the rapids (see p. 139, **First Person to Cross the Niagara Rapids on a Cable**).
(Photograph courtesy of the Earl W. Brydges Public Library.)

27. Anna Taylor, who became the first person ever to ride Niagara Falls in a barrel in 1901 (see p. 140, **First Person to Ride a Barrel over Niagara Falls**), shown here after emerging from the barrel.
(Photograph courtesy of the Earl W. Brydges Public Library.)

28. Sonja Henie, probably the most famous ice skater in history (see pp. 144–145, **First Ice Skating Superstar;** also p. 145, **First Two-Time Grand Slam Winner**).
(Photograph courtesy of the United States Figure Skating Association.)

29. John L. Sullivan, who was the last bare-knuckle heavyweight boxing champion in the United States, and may have been the first (unofficial) champion in boxing with gloves as well (see pp. 165–167, **Origins of American Boxing; First U.S. Heavyweight Champion**).
(Photograph courtesy of Ring Magazine.)

30. James J. ("Gentleman Jim") Corbett, who knocked out John L. Sullivan on Sept. 7, 1892 to become the first official heavyweight boxing champion in the United States (see pp. 165–167, **Origins of American Boxing; First U.S. Heavyweight Champion).**
(Photograph courtesy of Ring Magazine.)

31. Jack Johnson, the first black heavyweight boxing champion in the United States (see pp. 170–171, **First Black Heavyweight Champion).**
(Photograph courtesy of Ring Magazine.)

32. Rocky Marciano, the first heavyweight boxing champion to retire undefeated (see p. 174, **First Undefeated Heavyweight Champion**).
(Photograph courtesy of Ring Magazine.)

33. The *Gossamer Condor,* the craft in which the first human-powered flight took place in August 1977 (see p. 188, **First Human-Powered Flight**).
(Photograph by Scot Morris.)

DIVING (SKIN AND SCUBA)

FIRST PRACTICAL SCUBA EQUIPMENT

In 1865 a mining engineer named Rouquayrol and a naval officer named Denayrose invented scuba equipment consisting of a steel drum, strapped to the diver's back, which held compressed air that was fed to its wearer through a mouthpiece. The drum contained sufficient air for about 20 minutes at a depth of 30 feet or 10 minutes at 90 feet.

INVENTION OF "FROG FEET" FOR SKIN DIVING

French naval commander Corlieu invented "frog feet" for skin diving in 1926. He took an idea from Leonardo da Vinci, who had suggested the use of webbed gloves for diving, and made webbed attachments for the feet.

WATER POLO

ORIGINS

Water polo is almost completely misnamed. It has nothing to do with horses, and the ball used in water polo is not made of wood, which was the original meaning of the Tibetan word "pulu." It is, however, played in the water.

The sport was developed in England at a time when swimming competitions had become so monotonous that they no longer attracted crowds. The London Swimming Club developed the first formal rules for water soccer, as it was then called, in 1870. After several years of attempts to popularize the sport, the first official match was held at the Crystal Palace in London in 1874. Because of disputes over rules the English Amateur Swimming Association did not recognize water polo as a sport until 1885.

In its early years water polo was a rough sport, as dunking was used frequently to obtain the ball. Teams had to have reserve players, because injuries were frequent.

The first international water polo match was held in 1890 between England and Scotland. Scotland won the match 4-1.

Water polo was first included in the Olympics in 1900 in Paris.

MOTORBOATING

ORIGINS

Gottlieb Daimler, father of the internal combustion engine, not only produced the first crude motorcycle (see Chapter 5, "Racing," **Origins**, in the section on "Motorcycling"); he also turned out the first, equally crude motorboat. Daimler had first attached his small internal combustion engine to his bicycle, in 1885, turning it into the first motorcycle. In 1887 he hooked his engine up to a rowboat. The engine successfully propelled the rowboat a few feet around the river Seine in Paris.

The motorboat made its first appearance in the U.S. toward the end of the 19th century. The early motorboats in the U.S. were quite similar to Daimler's original creation: rowboats propelled by small engines, which were powered by naphtha.

With the coming of the 20th century, however, more sophisticated and powerful boats were introduced—and so was the first international motorboating race. An Englishman, Sir Alfred Harmsworth, who later became Lord Northcliffe, donated a trophy, which soon became known as the Harmsworth Trophy, for a motorboating competition. The first race was held at Queenstown, Ireland. An English-registered boat, *Napier I*, owned by S.F. Edge, won the race with a speed of 19.53 miles per hour. In 1912, for the first time, a hydroplane won the Harmsworth Trophy. It was the English-registered *Maple Leaf IV*; it won the race, held at Huntington Bay, N.Y., with a speed of 43.18 mph. All earlier winners had been displacement craft. The Harmsworth Trophy race was held annually from 1903 through 1913; it has, however, been held only irregularly since then, and not at all since 1961.

The American Power Boat Association was formed in 1903 to govern motorboating in the U.S. The first national motorboat competition was the Gold Cup race in 1904, held at the Columbia Yacht Club on the Hudson River in New York. The race was won by the *Standard*, a 59-foot displacement boat owned by C.C. Riotte. The *Standard* turned in a speed of 23.6 mph over the 32-mile course. The Gold Cup race has been held annually since 1904, except during World War II.

The President's Cup race, three heats over 15 statute miles at Washington, D.C., was established in 1926. The race has been held regularly, although not annually, since then. The boat *Cigarette*, owned by L.G. Hamersley, won the first President's Cup race with a speed of 55.20 mph.

FIRST OFFSHORE MOTORBOAT RACE

A motorboat race across the English Channel, from Calais, France to Dover, England, was held in 1904. This was the first recorded ocean motorboat race. The winner, M. Sauer, piloted a 39-foot Mercedes IV. Sauer averaged 22 mph on the 22-mile course.

FIRST MAN TO DRIVE A
SPEEDBOAT 200 MILES PER HOUR

On July 23, 1955, on the Ullswater, a lake in the Cumbrian Mountains, Donald Campbell accomplished a feat that many experts had claimed was impossible—he piloted his speedboat *Bluebird* faster than 200 mph. Campbell's new world record, 202.32 mph, was almost 25 mph faster than the old record, 178.497 mph. Several men had previously died in the attempt to break 200 miles per hour.

In 1959 Campbell set a new world record, driving a speedboat 275 mph in a test on Coniston Water, a lake in England.

FIRST WOMAN TO WIN A MAJOR
OFFSHORE MOTORBOAT RACE

A petite grandmother who had not taken up motorboating until she was 50, Betty Cook, became the first woman to win a major offshore motorboat race on March 5, 1977 when she won the Bushmills Grand Prix off Newport Beach, Calif. She also won the world championships in offshore powerboat racing in 1977 and 1978 and the U.S. open class in 1978 and 1979. During her first three years of racing Cook won 11 races in all.

Not only did Cook win races, she also changed the nature of the sport: she was the first person to prove the suitability of catamarans for offshore powerboat racing. Tunnel hull boats, as they are often called, had always been considered too cumbersome or fragile in the expensive world of offshore powerboating, where boats often cost $100,000 to $125,000 and transporting them from race to race can cost tens of thousands of dollars for boat and crew.

When Betty Cook first set out to enter what had been the exclusively male world of offshore powerboat racing, she was often dismissed as a little lady with a fat checkbook. In what has been described as one of the most physically demanding sports in the world, because of the rough waves that can reach eight or even 12 feet, Cook has shown that she knows what she is doing. She gives part of the credit to her crew, John Connor and Bill Vogel

Jr., who have helped her bring her V-bottom *Scarab* (which she pilots in rough water) and her twin-hull *Cougar Cat* (for smooth water) to consistent victory.

WATER-SKIING

ORIGINS

Water-skiing as we know it was introduced in 1922 by Ralph W. Samuelson of Minnesota. (See also, however, **Benjamin Franklin**, in the section on "Swimming.") Samuelson turned two pine boards, each measuring eight feet long and nine inches wide, into water skis. He curved the ends of the boards by steaming the tips in boiling water. He then water-skied successfully for the first time behind a motorboat on a lake at Lake City, Minn.

The first water-skiing tournament in the United States was held in 1936 at Massapequa, N.Y. The event was won by Jack Andresen.

The American Water Ski Association was formed in 1939 by Dan Hains and Bruce Parker. The Association conducted the first U.S. national water-skiing tournament in 1939 at Jones Beach State Park, on Long Island, N.Y.

FIRST WATER SKI JUMP

Water-skiing pioneer Ralph W. Samuelson (see also **Origins**) is credited with making the first jump on water skis. He reportedly made the first jump off a greased ramp at Lake Pepin, Minn., in 1925.

FIRST WOMEN'S ALL-AROUND WATER-SKIING CHAMPION

Esther Yates won the women's all-around championship at the first national water-skiing championships in 1939 in Long Island, N.Y. (See also **Origins**.)

FIRST MAN TO WATER-SKI BAREFOOT

Dick Pope, Jr., is credited with being the first person to water-ski while barefoot. He did it March 6, 1947 at Lake Eloise, Fla.

NIAGARA FALLS

FIRST PERSON TO CROSS THE NIAGARA RAPIDS ON A CABLE

A 35-year-old French gymnast named Blondin started a craze for crossing the Niagara Rapids on a cable, crossing not once but several times in 1859.

Blondin had earlier walked ropes across the Seine in Paris and the Thames in London, and had given numerous exhibitions in the United States as well. It was his crossings of the Niagara Rapids, though, that made him famous and wealthy. On each new crossing he did yet another daring feat—going so far as to carry his manager across on his back. Once he crossed at night by the light of locomotive headlights—which failed halfway through his walk. He continued safely, and was greeted with cheers when he reached the other end.

FIRST AMERICAN TO CROSS THE NIAGARA RAPIDS ON A CABLE

The first American to walk across the Niagara Rapids on a cable was probably Harry Leslie, in 1865.

FIRST WOMAN TO CROSS THE NIAGARA RAPIDS ON A CABLE

The first woman to cross the Niagara Rapids on a cable was Maria Spelterina, in 1876. She crossed over once with her feet in baskets and once with her wrists and ankles manacled.

FIRST PERSON TO RIDE THE NIAGARA RAPIDS IN A BARREL

Carlisle Graham, a Philadelphia barrel maker, started the craze of riding river rapids in barrels when he rode the Niagara Rapids in a barrel on July 11, 1886. Graham had designed a big buoy-shaped barrel for the trip and pretested it with sandbags equal to his weight.

A month after Graham's first trip down the rapids he did it again. The second time his head was protruding from the top of the barrel; he suffered a permanent hearing loss as a result of the noise of the water. Graham made his last such voyage in 1901, when he was caught in a whirlpool for so long that he nearly suffocated inside the barrel before he was rescued.

FIRST PERSON TO RIDE A BARREL OVER NIAGARA FALLS

Anna Taylor, a middle-aged schoolteacher, rode a barrel over Niagara Falls in 1901. Her barrel was cushioned inside, equipped with a leather harness and arm straps and weighted to keep it upright. Air entered the barrel through a rubber tube connected to a small opening near the lid. Curiosity seekers came out by the thousands to watch her successful attempt. Although Taylor was able to walk away from the scene, she was battered and bruised by her ride; she warned others not to make the attempt.

9 / WINTER SPORTS:

SKIING, ICE SKATING, ICE BOATING, TOBOGGANING AND BOBSLEDDING

SKIING

ORIGINS

Skiing was an important survival skill for early inhabitants of northern climates. The origin of the first skis is unknown, but a pair of skis held by the Djugarden Museum in Stockholm, Sweden may be as much as 5000 years old. The earliest skis were made from the bones of large animals and were strapped to shoes like snowshoes. Skis were used for hunting and simply for getting from one place to another on a snow-covered landscape.

The first recorded use of skis during warfare was in the Battle of Oslo in 1200 AD. Scouts for King Sverre of Norway used skis for their reconnaissance missions against the Swedes. A few years later, during a Norwegian civil war, another king's son was carried over the mountains to safety in the dead of winter by two of his aides who were skiers. This event is still commemorated in the annual *lauglauf* race in Norway. By 1521 the Swedes equipped all their soldiers with skis or snowshoes for warfare in wintertime.

It was not until the 19th century that skis were widely used for sport. In 1860 the royal family of Norway donated a trophy to be awarded to the winner of a ski jumping tournament. The first recorded downhill race was held outside Stockholm, Sweden in 1879. The entrants had to ski around flags or poles toward a frozen lake. The skier whose speed carried him the farthest distance on the lake was the winner.

Cross-country skiing was dramatized in 1888 when explorer Fridtjof Nansen led a crossing of Greenland from east to west. The party dragged sleds on skis over some 300 miles, climbing to altitudes of almost 9000 feet during the 40-day crossing.

There is no record of the first skis used in North America. They may have been invented by Indians or imported from Europe. (It is known, incidentally, that snowshoes have been used in Canada for many generations.) Americans were, however, definitely using skis by the 1850s, during the gold rush in the Sierra Nevadas.

The first U.S. ski club was formed by Scandinavians at Berlin, N.H. in 1872. The club is still in existence, and is now known as the Nansen Ski Club, in honor of the Norwegian explorer.

Skiing was one of the main events during the first Winter Olympic Games in Chamonix, France in 1924, but it was not until after the first Winter Olympics in the United States, at Lake Placid in 1932, that skiing became a major sport in the United States. During the winter of 1936-37 a skiing exhibition at Soldier Field in Chicago drew 57,000 spectators. Ski resorts began opening all over the country and man-made snow machines were developed so that the only natural requirements for skiing were a slope and cold weather. Technology could take care of the rest.

Regional competitions are held in the U.S., leading to the National Championship. The Olympics, the World Championship, the World Cup and various national championships provide competition for the world-class skier.

THE FATHER OF SKI JUMPING

Sondre Norheim devised the first effective ski binding in the mid-19th century. He made the first officially measured jump in 1860. During a meet in Norway six years later, he wrapped cables around his heels, giving him control of his skis while in flight. His contribution earned him the title "father of ski jumping."

FIRST ORGANIZED SKI JUMPING TOURNAMENT

The first organized ski tournament was held by the Aurora Ski Club of Red Wing, Minn. on Feb. 8, 1887. Mikkel Hemmestvedt won the men's jumping championship.

FIRST WOMEN'S ALPINE SKIING CHAM-PIONSHIP

The first world alpine skiing championships for women were held in 1931 at Murren, Switzerland. Esme MacKinnon of Great Britain won both the alpine skiing and slalom events in the inaugural competition.

FIRST WORLD CUP

The World Cup for skiing is awarded annually to the year's best overall skier. In certain designated races, such as the slalom, giant slalom and downhill, players receive points based on how they finish. The skier with the highest total for any three events at the end of the series is awarded the World Cup.

Jean-Claude Killy of France won both the first World Cup, in 1967, and the second, in 1968.

ICE SKATING

ORIGINS

Primitive bone skates dating back as far as 4000 years have been found in the Scandinavian countries. Our forebears apparently made primitive ice skates by grinding bones down to make flat surfaces; they put on these skates and used spiked poles to help them move over the frozen surfaces of rivers and lakes.

Skating on wooden skates was quite common in Holland by the Middle Ages. Canals froze over, and were generally not covered with snow, so skating was the easiest and fastest way of getting from one place to another. All classes of people joined in the skating, but for the well-to-do skating was more than a way to get from place to place. Skating became something of an art; skaters tried particularly to glide gracefully and to skate on the inside and outside edges of the skate. When the Stuart dynasty returned to England from Holland they brought skating with them. Skating soon became quite a fad in England, and many people learned at least the basics of skating.

The first ice skating club was the Edinburgh Skating Club, formed in 1742. Applicants for membership were required to pass a test, measuring such skills as the ability to brake, before they could join the club.

The iron skate, which had been invented in 1572, had represented a distinct improvement over the waxed wooden runners which had been used before. It was not until 1850, however, when E.W. Bushnell invented skates with steel blades, that skating became very popular in the United States. The new skates' sharper edges made it much easier for skaters to maneuver on the ice.

An American ballet teacher, Jackson Haines, who had gone to Europe to escape the business conditions prevailing in the United States during the Civil War, revolutionized ice skating in the 1860s when he combined ballet movements with skating. (See also **The Father of Ice Skating**.) A man named Louis Rubinstein brought the "new" sport to Canada shortly thereafter, resulting in the formation of the Amateur Skating Association of Canada in 1878. It was not until 1887, however, that the first Haines-style skating club in the U.S., the Skating Club of the United States, was formed in Philadelphia.

THE FATHER OF ICE SKATING

A tombstone in Finland is inscribed "American Skating King." The stone marks the last resting place of Jackson Haines, an American who set the rather aimless figure skating of the 1860s to waltz music, added modified ballet movements and popularized his creation throughout Europe. Haines was a former ballet master who had moved to Europe to escape the Civil War. Old-style skating was already popular in Europe. But when Haines revolutionized the sport, adding glides, twists and spirals similar to those used in the ballet, the "Haines method" became the rage throughout Europe; Haines himself soon came to be known as "the American Ice Master." His students spread the new sport throughout Europe and took it to the United States and Canada as well. The major moves used in figure skating today are derived from the Haines method.

FIRST CHAMPIONSHIP COMPETITION IN THE UNITED STATES

In 1914 the first U.S. ice skating championship competition was held in New Haven, Conn. It was open not just to U.S. figure skaters, or fancy skaters, as they were called then, but to outstanding skaters from all countries.

Norman N. Scott of Montreal, Canada won the men's title. Theresa Weld of Massachusetts won the women's singles, and the pairs were won by two more Canadians, Scott and Jeanne Chevalier.

FIRST ICE SKATING SUPERSTAR

Norwegian ice skater Sonja Henie revolutionized the sport. Her program was choreographed like a ballet; spins and jumps blended together in beautifully executed figures.

Henie won 10 world championships in a row, from 1927 through 1936; six European titles between 1931 and 1940; and three Olympic gold medals, in 1928, 1932 and 1936. Already a household name from her amateur triumphs, Henie turned professional after the 1936 Olympics.

Henie was not, however, famous only for winning competitions. She was the first woman to dress in an abbreviated skirt instead of the ankle-length dresses and hats female ice skaters had traditionally worn. She starred in 11 films between 1938 and 1960, and toured the world with extremely successful ice shows. Henie greatly popularized ice skating and inspired generations of aspiring skaters.

FIRST TWO-TIME GRAND SLAM WINNERS

The grand slam of figure skating consists of victories in the world, Olympic and European competitions in the same year. Obviously it is a feat that can be accomplished only in a year during which an Olympiad is held.

Only one man and one woman have won the grand slam twice—coincidentally, in the same two years. Skating legend Sonja Henie of Norway (see also **First Ice Skating Superstar**) was the first woman to accomplish the feat twice. She took the grand slam for the first time in 1932 and repeated in 1936. Karl Schafer of Austria won the men's grand slam in the same two years, 1932 and 1936.

FIRST U.S. WOMAN TO WIN THE WORLD TITLE IN ICE SKATING

Tenley Albright became the first American woman to win the world title in ice skating on Feb. 15, 1953 in Davos, Switzerland. The same year she also won the North American and U.S. championships. Albright won the world championship a second time in 1955. She was also an Olympic winner, with a silver medal in the 1952 Olympics and a gold in the 1956 Olympics. After winning the gold medal she retired from skating to pursue medical studies.

FIRST WOMAN TO WIN THE SAME GOLD MEDAL IN SPEED SKATING TWICE IN ONE DAY

At the 1972 Olympic Games in Japan, Anne Henning scored the best time in the 500-meter speed skating race, but one of her opponents, Sylvia Burka of Canada, had failed to yield to Henning at the crossover. Burka was disqualified by the judges and Henning was offered another run by herself after the other skaters had finished. The incident had not affected the outcome of the race—Henning was clearly the winner—but she decided to take the penalty run so that she could attempt to set a world record. In her second run Henning covered the course in record-breaking 43.3 seconds, winning the same gold medal the second time in one day.

FIRST QUADRUPLE TWIST LIFT; FIRST SIMULTANEOUS TRIPLE JUMP

The extremely difficult quadruple twist lift was performed for the first time in international competition on Jan. 26, 1977. Soviet skaters Marina Tcherkasova and Sergei Shakrai did it in an international competition at Helsinki, Finland.

The two Russian skaters were also the first to complete the difficult simultaneous triple jump successfully in international competition, doing so at Strasbourg, France on Feb. 1, 1978.

ICE BOATING

ORIGINS

The first ice boaters were the Dutch. They brought their creation to the New World with them, and as early as 1790 Dutch settlers were using sleigh sailboats on the frozen Hudson River.

The first ice boating club in the U.S. was the Poughkeepsie Ice Yacht Club, which was formed in 1865. The members used craft that consisted of a simple framework on which the crew perched. Sails and rigging were like those used on conventional gaff-rigged sloops.

By the turn of the century ice boats were no longer necessarily small. John E. Roosevelt, an uncle of Pres. Franklin D. Roosevelt, built a ice yacht called the *Icicle* which was 70 feet long and was transported to the ice on a railroad flatcar. By the 1920s, however, the trend was back toward smaller ice boats, which were accessible to more people.

TOBOGGANING

FIRST INTERNATIONAL TOBOGGAN RACE

Probably the first international toboggan race was the Davos International Race, held in 1883 at Davos, Switzerland. The winner was Peter Minch, a postman from a nearby village.

BOBSLEDDING

FIRST BOBSLEDDING RUN IN THE UNITED STATES

The first bobsledding run, or bobrun, in the U.S. was built in 1931 at Lake Placid, on Mt. Van Hoevenberg, for the 1932 Olympics.

10/TRACK AND FIELD: _____

ORIGINS, WALKING AND RUNNING, HIGH JUMP, SHOT PUT, POLE VAULT AND MISCELLANEOUS FIRSTS

ORIGINS

The first man to run the hundred-yard dash was probably being pursued by a wild animal. His (or her) time was not recorded. Human beings did not begin running for sport, but for a much more basic reason: to survive. Those who ran fastest—or at least fast enough—lived to run another day. As our ancestors began to find life a little less dangerous, and no longer needed to worry solely about survival, it was only natural that they would want to compete against other human beings rather than against animals—to race, just to find out who was fastest. Similarly, other skills that had once been essential for survival persisted, but in the form of sport—those who had once wrestled with animals began instead to wrestle with other men. Those who had a talent for throwing a rock found that they could also throw a discus or a shot put. When it was no longer necessary—or socially acceptable—to throw spears, one could still throw a javelin. The end result? Track and field.

The ancient Greeks glorified the athlete. It was they who established the world's best-known sporting event, the Olympic Games. The first Olympics, held in 776 BC, included only one athletic event, the 200-yard dash. The winner, a cook named Koroibos, was honored with a torch, presented to him by a priest, with which he lit a sacrificial pyre dedicated to the god of gods, Zeus. He also received a laurel wreath from the sacred olive grove at Olympia. It is thought that Koroibos may also have been granted an exemption from paying taxes for the rest of his life; it is also possible that he may have received free food and lodging for life. The Greeks eventually added longer races to the Olympic program, and, later still, discus throwing, jumping and various forms of wrestling and boxing. After the Romans conquered Greece in 456 BC, Romans began to compete against the Greeks in the games until they were banned by the Roman emperor Theodosius in 392 AD. After the demise of the ancient Olympics, events were not revived in an organized fashion until the 12th century, when the English began to hold competitions. Interest in running, jumping and throwing had reached such proportions in England by the early 19th century that minimum standards of performance were established to determine whether a man was qualified to compete in contests of major significance.

The first major track and field competition in America was held by the newly-formed New York Athletic Club in 1868. In 1888 the Amateur Athletic Union of the United States was formed. It, too, began holding competitions, which were open to all amateur track and field enthusiasts.

WALKING AND RUNNING

THE FATHER OF PEDESTRIANISM; FIRST MAN TO WALK ACROSS THE UNITED STATES

Edward Payson Weston started a 19th-century sports craze, "pedestrianism," when he won a bet that he could walk the 478 miles from Boston to Washington in ten consecutive days. His goal was to arrive in Washington in time for the inauguration of Pres. Lincoln on March 4, 1861. He did, in fact, arrive on March 4; he was too late to see the inauguration itself, but did make it in time to dance at an inaugural ball.

Weston collected only a bag of peanuts on his bet. He did, however, take advantage of the publicity it engendered by becoming a professional walker. In 1867 he won $10,000 for walking from Portland, Maine to Chicago. He covered the 1200-mile distance in a month, taking Sundays off.

In 1909 Weston celebrated his 70th birthday by walking across the United States. His trek began in New York on March 15; he walked the 3795 miles to San Francisco in 104 days and 7 hours. Along the way he endured, among other obstacles, heavy blizzards.

The next year Weston walked back to New York from Los Angeles. He covered the 3600-mile distance in 76 days and 23 hours.

FIRST MAN TO RUN 100 YARDS IN 10 SECONDS

In 1877 Horace Lee, from Philadelphia, Pa., became the first man ever to run the 100-yard dash in 10 seconds. Lee's record stood until 1890.

FIRST MAN TO RUN THE 100-YARD DASH IN LESS THAN 10 SECONDS

John Owens became the first man to run the 100-yard dash in under 10 seconds in championship competition on Oct. 11, 1890. Owens ran the dash in nine and four-fifths seconds in the AAU Track and Field Championships, held in Washington, D.C.

ORIGINS OF THE MARATHON

The marathon dates back to antiquity. In 490 BC a fully-armed Greek courier ran from the battlefield on the Plains of Marathon to Athens to announce that a badly outnumbered Greek army had turned back Persian invaders. After running 24 miles, the courier announced, "Rejoice! We've won!" He then collapsed and died.

This was not, however, the first such accomplishment by a Greek runner. Before the Battle of Marathon the champion Athenian runner Pheidippides was sent to ask the Spartans for their help in stopping the Persians, who wanted to conquer and enslave all of Greece. Pheidippides ran for two days and two nights, traversing rivers, mountains and all kinds of other natural obstacles. After covering 158 miles, Pheidippides talked with the Spartans for a full day and then returned home with the news that the Spartans would help in the fight against the Persians as soon as one of their religious festivals was finished. Pheidippides had covered more than 300 miles in just four days, an astonishing feat. The Athenians honored Pheidippides by building a temple in his honor.

The marathon was not a part of the ancient Olympic Games, but it was included in the program when the modern games were revived in Athens, Greece in 1896. The first Olympic marathon was run over the original 24-mile course. The winner of the first Olympic marathon was, appropriately enough, a Greek, Spiridon Loues, whose time was two hours, 55 minutes and 20 seconds. T.J. Hicks became the first American to win the Olympic marathon at the 1904 games in St. Louis, Mo., with a time of three hours, 28 minutes and 53 seconds. That was the only occasion on which the winning time in the Olympic marathon has been in excess of three hours.

In the 1908 Olympics in London, the length of the marathon was increased as a favor to King Edward VII and Queen Alexandra. The race began on the grounds of Windsor Castle and ended at White City Stadium, 26 miles and 385 yards away. That has remained the official Olympic marathon distance since then. John J. Hayes from the United States was the first runner to win the longer Olympic marathon with a time of two hours, 55 minutes and 18 seconds.

FIRST BOSTON MARATHON

The Boston Marathon is run each year on April 19, Patriot's Day. The 26-mile, 385-yard course begins in Hopkinton, halfway between Boston and Worcester, and meanders its way to the finish line in Boston. Every year some 1500 runners compete in what is certainly the best-known marathon race in the United States. The marathon, sponsored by the Boston Athletic Association, was first held in 1897. The winner was John J. McDermott of New York.

FIRST RUN ACROSS THE UNITED STATES

The first race across the U.S. began on the afternoon of March 4, 1928 from the Ascot Speedway in Los Angeles. 199 men, competing for $48,500 in cash prizes, began the 3422-mile race to Madison Square Garden in New York.

The promoter of the race, Charles C. Pyle, hoped to make a fortune from the race—he intended to collect $100 entry fees, to sell programs, to secure promotional fees from the cities along the route and, when the race was over, to sell endorsements of commercial products by the winner. The race did not, however, inspire the interest that Pyle had hoped, and cities along the route began to withdraw their promotional fees. Seventy-six of the starters had quit the race within the first 16 miles.

The winner of the race was a farmboy from Claremore, Okla., Andrew Payne, who ran the distance in 573 hours, 4 minutes and 34 seconds—just under 24 days (not counting rest stops).

Pyle lost $15,000 on the race. Thinking that he had learned from his mistakes, he staged a repeat transcontinental derby, from New York to Los Angeles, in 1929. The second time Pyle lost $100,000.

FIRST MAN TO RUN A MILE IN FOUR MINUTES

When the 20th century began it was generally agreed that no one would ever run a mile in four minutes. Such an accomplishment, it was thought, was simply beyond human capabilities. After all, at that time no one had ever run a mile in less than four minutes, 15.6 seconds. In a sport where new records surpass old ones by mere tenths of seconds, one might say that the difference between a four-minute mile and a four-minute, 15.6-second mile was as good as a mile.

Still, during the 1920s five seconds were shaved off the old record. By 1945 the record time had been reduced to four minutes, 1.4 seconds. But many still thought that a four-minute mile was impossible.

Not Roger Bannister.

On May 6, 1954 Bannister and two friends, Chris Brasher and Chris Chataway, gathered at Iffley Stadium at Oxford for an assault on the four-minute mile. It was a windy, damp day—hardly ideal for a record-setting performance. Because of the weather, Bannister did not actually decide to attempt the historic run until just 15 minutes before the race was scheduled to begin.

Only a few spectators were on hand as Bannister lunged from the starting blocks. With Brasher, a former Cambridge steeplechase runner, supplying a fast early pace, Bannister was able to run the first quarter in 57.5 seconds and the second quarter in 60.7 seconds. At the halfway mark Chataway, a teammate of Bannister's at Oxford, took over for Brasher; running with Chataway, Bannister passed the three-quarter-mile mark with a time of three minutes and five-tenths seconds.

Three hundred yards from the finish line, Bannister surged onward, despite a stiff wind, and crossed the finish line with a time of three minutes, 59 and four-tenths seconds.

Since Bannister broke what he considered to be largely a psychological barrier, about 300 men have duplicated, or surpassed, his feat. As of this writing, the record for the mile stands at three minutes, 49.4 seconds. This mark was set in 1975 by John Walker of New Zealand.

And Bannister himself believes a three-minute, 30-second mile is within reach before the dawn of the 21st century.

FIRST MAN TO RUN A MILE IN UNDER FOUR MINUTES IN THE UNITED STATES

Don Bowden was the first man ever to run a mile in less than four minutes in the United States. Bowden clocked a time of three minutes, 58.7 seconds on June 1, 1957 in Stockton, Calif.

FIRST AMERICAN TO RUN A MILE IN LESS THAN FOUR MINUTES INDOORS

Jim Beatty was the first American to run a mile in less than four minutes indoors. He did it in three minutes, 58.9 seconds on Feb. 10, 1962 in Los Angeles, Calif.

FIRST WOMAN TO COMPETE IN THE BOSTON MARATHON

Roberta Gibb Bingay was the first woman ever to run in a Boston Marathon, in 1966. While Bingay did not win the race, she did finish well ahead of most of the 415 male starters in the race.

FIRST WOMAN TO RUN 100 YARDS IN 10 SECONDS

Chi Cheng of Taiwan was the first woman to run 100 yards in ten seconds flat. She did it on June 13, 1970 in Portland, Ore.

HIGH JUMP

FIRST HIGH JUMP OVER SIX FEET

The first recorded high jump of over six feet took place on March 17, 1876 at Marston, Oxford, England. An Englishman, Marshall Jones Brooks, jumped six feet and one-eighth inch.

FIRST WOMAN TO CLEAR FIVE FEET IN THE HIGH JUMP

The first woman to clear the five-foot barrier in the high jump was Phyllis Green of Great Britain. She accomplished the feat July 11, 1925 in London.

FIRST WOMAN TO CLEAR SIX FEET IN THE HIGH JUMP

The first woman to clear six feet in the high jump was a Rumanian, Iolanda Balas of Rumania. She did it in Bucharest on Oct. 18, 1958.

SHOT PUT

FIRST 60-FOOT SHOT PUT

At the beginning of the 20th century human beings were thought to be no more capable of heaving a 16-pound shot 60 feet than of running a mile in four minutes. In 1954 American William Parry O'Brien held the world mark of 59 feet, 2¼ inches, and the gold medal from the 1952 Olympics, when he decided to throw the shot put a little differently. He began to throw with his back to the toeboard from which the shot put was heaved. This gave him the force of a 180-degree turn rather than a 90-degree turn behind his throws. Using the new method on April 24, 1954, O'Brien put the shot 59 feet, 9¼ inches. This took place, however, during an exhibition; it was therefore not considered a new world mark.

On May 1, 1954 another American, Stan Lampert, upped the world mark with a throw of 59 feet, 5⅞ inches. His role as world leader usurped, O'Brien was motivated to try a little harder.

On May 8, 1954 in Los Angeles, O'Brien placed a board in the ground near the 60-foot mark. It read: "Lampert 59 5⅞." Then, employing his new 180-degree turn, O'Brien heaved the shot 60 feet, 5¼ inches. It was a new world mark. And it was the first time a 16-pound shot had been put beyond the 60-foot barrier.

Between 1953 and 1955 O'Brien broke the world shot put record a total of 14 times. He won a second Olympic gold medal in 1956 and a silver medal in 1960; he placed fourth in 1964. O'Brien's best effort was a put of 19.7 meters (64 feet, 7½ inches)—a feat he accomplished at the age of 34.

POLE VAULT

FIRST MAN TO POLE VAULT 16 FEET

On Feb. 2, 1962, before a capacity crowd in Madison Square Garden, 24-year-old Marine corporal John Uelses jumped 16 feet and ¼ inch—the first time anyone had ever surpassed the 16-foot barrier in the pole vault. But his jump didn't count as an official world record. Fans who rushed in to congratulate Uelses knocked askew the standards supporting the crossbars—and regulations required that the bar be measured both before and after a jump.

Uelses was, naturally enough, disappointed. He vowed, however, to make another 16-foot jump the next day—and he did. Even though he was suffering from a groin injury and pains in his legs, Uelses easily cleared a crossbar set at 16 feet, ¾ inches at a track meet in Boston.

FIRST MAN TO POLE VAULT 17 FEET

At a track meet in Miami, Fla. on Aug. 24, 1963, 23-year-old John Pennel became the first man ever to pole vault over 17 feet. The 170-pound vaulter had broken the world pole-vaulting record six times during 1963; in Miami he finally passed the 17-foot barrier, with a mark of 17 feet, ¾ inches.

MISCELLANEOUS FIRSTS

FIRST NATIONAL CHAMPIONSHIP MEET IN TRACK AND FIELD IN THE UNITED STATES

The New York Athletic Club, which had been formed in 1868, conducted the first national track and field competition in 1876 in New York. The club continued to conduct the national championship track and field meets through 1878; then, from 1879 through 1887, the annual event was sponsored by the National Association of Amateur Athletes of America. In 1888 the Amateur Athletic Union took charge of the meets; it has held the national championship track and field meets annually since then.

The winners in the first meet were:

100-yard dash: F.C. Saportas. (Time: 10½ seconds.)
440-yard run: Edward Merritt. (Time: 54½ seconds.)
880-yard run: H. Lambe. (Time: Two minutes, 10 seconds.)
One-mile run: H. Lambe. (Time: Four minutes, 51⅕ seconds.)
120-yard high hurdles: George Hitchcock. (Time: 19 seconds.)
High jump: H.E. Ficken. (Distance: Five feet, five inches.)
Long jump: I. Frazier. (Distance: 17 feet, four inches.)
Shot put: H.E. Buermeyer. (Distance: 32 feet, five inches.)
16-pound hammer throw: William B. Curtis. (Distance: 76 feet, four inches.)

FIRST NATIONAL COLLEGIATE MEET IN TRACK AND FIELD IN THE UNITED STATES

The first national collegiate track and field meet was held in 1921 in Chicago. The National Collegiate Athletic Association has conducted championship outdoor meets annually since then; in 1965 it established a separate indoor championship meet.

The winners in the first national meet were:

100-yard dash: Leonard Paulu, Grinnell College. (Time: 20 seconds.)
220-yard dash: Eric C. Wilson, University of Iowa. (Time: 22.6 seconds.)

440-yard run: Frank J. Shea, University of Pittsburgh. (Time: 49 seconds.)

880-yard run: Earl Eby, University of Pennsylvania. (Time: One minute, 57.4 seconds.)

One-mile run: Ray Watson, Kansas State University. (Time: Four minutes, 23.4 seconds.)

Two-mile run: John Romig, Pennsylvania State University. (Time: Nine minutes, 31 seconds.)

120-yard high hurdles: Earl J. Thomson, Dartmouth College. (Time: 14.4 seconds.)

220-yard low hurdles: August Desch, University of Notre Dame. (Time: 24.8 seconds.)

Long jump: Gaylord Stinchcomb, Ohio State University. (Distance: 23 feet, three and three-eighths inches.)

High jump: John Murphy, University of Notre Dame. (Distance: Six feet, three inches.)

Pole vault: Tie among Welch, Georgia Tech; Jenne, Washington State University; Wilder, University of Wisconsin; and Gardner, Yale College. (Height: 12 feet.)

Shot put: Gus Pope, University of Washington. (Distance: 45 feet, four and one-half inches.)

Discus throw: Gus Pope, University of Washington. (Distance: 142 feet, two and one-quarter inches.)

Javelin throw: Flint Hanner, Stanford University. (Distance: 191 feet, two and one-quarter inches.)

Hammer throw: Charles Redmon, University of Chicago. (Distance: 133 feet, nine and three-quarters inches.)

The University of Illinois won the team title at the first national collegiate meet.

FIRST MAJOR WOMEN'S OUTDOOR TRACK AND FIELD MEET

The first major outdoor track and field meet for women was sponsored by the Amateur Athletic Union in 1923. The AAU women's outdoor meet has been held annually since then.

The winners in the 1923 meet were:

100-meter dash: Frances Rupert. (Time: 12 seconds.)
80-meter hurdles: Hazel Kirk. (Time: 9.6 seconds.)

400-meter relay: The Meadowbrook Club team of Rupert, Bough, Rittler and Adams. (Time: 52.4 seconds.)

High jump: Catherine Wright. (Distance: Four feet, seven and one-half inches.)

Long jump: Helen Dinnehey. (Distance: 15 feet, four inches.)

Eight-pound shot put: Bertha Christophel. (Distance: 30 feet, 10½ inches.)

Discus throw: Babe Wolbert. (Distance: 71 feet, nine and one-half inches.)

Javelin: Roberta Ranck. (Distance: 59 feet, seven and three-quarters inches.)

FIRST TELEVISED COLLEGE MEET

The first college track meet to be televised took place on March 5, 1940 at Madison Square Garden in New York City. It was the 19th annual American Amateur Athletic Association meet that was broadcast. Twenty-three colleges participated in that meet; New York University won.

FIRST WOMAN TO WIN THE U.S. PENTATHLON CHAMPIONSHIP FIVE CONSECUTIVE TIMES

Stella Walsh won the U.S. pentathlon championship five consecutive times, from 1950 through 1954. She was in her forties at the time. Walsh was the first woman ever to accomplish that feat.

Stella Walsh began her international track and field career as Stella Walasiewicz when she won the gold medal in the women's 100-meter race in the 1932 Olympics as a Polish citizen. After her Olympic win she moved to the United States and changed her name to Stella Walsh. She continued to enter international competitions as a broad jumper, high jumper, shot putter, discus thrower and hurdler until she was past 50. Walsh won more than 1100 major track and field competitions during her career and set about 100 national and world records.

FIRST NATIONALLY-TELEVISED PROFESSIONAL TRACK MEET

The first nationally-televised professional outdoor track meet was held in El Paso, Texas in 1974. Among the participants were Steve Smith, John Carlos and Wyomia Tyus Simburg.

FIRST WOMAN TO THROW THE JAVELIN OVER 200 FEET

Karin Smith was the first woman to throw the javelin over 200 feet. Her new record was 203 feet, 10 inches, set in 1976.

11/TARGET SPORTS:

ARCHERY AND MARKSMANSHIP

ARCHERY

ORIGINS; FIRST COMPETITIONS

The bow and arrow, of course, originated as instruments of warfare; over thousands of years the bow and arrow evolved into what they are today—tools for sports, both for competition and for hunting. The bow and arrow were in use thousands of years before the birth of Christ; they may have originated in Egypt. The Egyptians first used the bow and arrow for hunting. But they soon realized that the bow and arrow could be put to another use—war. The Egyptians rightly figured that an arrow, which could be shot up to 300 feet, would make a superior weapon against the slingshot, with a range of about 140 feet, and the javelin, whose range was about 175 feet. The Egyptians thus began to train their warriors in the use of the bow and arrow. Not long thereafter the Egyptians went to war with Persia and, using the bow and arrow, wiped out the Persians, who were armed with slingshots and javelins. Other nations gradually took up the bow and arrow; they remained the most important instruments of warfare until the 16th century, when they were largely replaced by firearms. The bow and arrow did, however, continue to see use in warfare until well into the 19th century.

The earliest recorded bow and arrow competitions took place in the 16th and 17th centuries in Japan. Occasional tournaments were held in Tokyo and Kyoto, in which arrows were shot at targets from a distance of 384 feet. It is reported that sometime in the 17th century one Japanese bowman shot 8133 arrows during the course of a 24-hour endurance contest. That's a rate of over five shots per minute.

In 1673 a group of archers in Yorkshire, England held the first Scorton Arrow Contest; the winner received a small silver bow. The contest, now known as the Ancient Scorton Arrow Contest, is the oldest continuing archery tournament in existence today.

Archery for sport came into being in the United States during the 1600s, but it was not until the 1800s that it gained any real popularity. The United Bowmen of Philadelphia, formed in 1828, probably conducted the first bow and arrow competition in the United States. The organization, however, disbanded in 1859. (See also **First Archery Club in the United States.**)

The popularity of archery in the U.S. surged again in the 1870s, leading to a meeting, held on Jan. 23, 1879 in Crawfordsville, Ind., at which eight local archery clubs formed the National Archery Association. Later that year, on Aug. 12-14 in Chicago, the first U.S. grand archery tournament was held; 69 men and 20 women competed. Will Thompson won the men's division, scoring 172 hits for a total of 624 points. Mrs. S. Brown was the women's division winner.

Interest in archery throughout the world led to the formation of the *Federation Internationale de Tir a l'Arc* and to the first world archery tournament, held in 1931 in Poland. (See also **First World Tournament.**)

FIRST ARCHERY CLUB IN THE UNITED STATES

America's first archery club was the United Bowmen of Philadelphia, formed in 1828. The group of 25 gentlemen adopted a natty uniform of light blue jackets and white trousers. They believed in healthful recreation, not in frivolity: Their bylaws specified that nothing but water could be drunk at their meetings.

The group held yearly competitions and awarded silver trophies until it was disbanded in 1859.

FIRST WORLD TOURNAMENT

The growth in the popularity of archery in the United States and throughout the world in the 1920s led to the formation of the international archery organizations, *Federation Internationale de Tir a l'Arc* (FITA). The organization held its first international tournament in 1931 at Poland. France won the men's team title with 1277 points, while M. Sawicki of Poland won the men's singles championship. The world tournament was expanded to include women archers in 1933 (see also **First International Women's Competition**). Janina Spychajowa-Kurkowska of Poland won the women's singles championship and Poland won the women's team title with 2627 points.

The FITA world championship tournament was held annually until 1959; it has been held biannually since then.

FIRST INTERNATIONAL WOMEN'S COMPETITION

The first international women's archery competition was held by the *Federation Internationale de Tir a l'Arc* (FITA), the international archery organization, in 1931. Poland won the women's team title with 2627 points; Janina Spychajowa-Kurkowska of Poland won the women's singles title. Spychajowa-Kurkowska won the tournament again in 1934, then repeated in 1936, 1939 and 1947. No other woman archer has ever come close to matching her international tournament record.

MARKSMANSHIP
ORIGINS OF RIFLE SHOOTING

Sportsmen have been competing with firearms since their invention. Although marksmanship was once more valuable as a survival skill than as a sport, as the importance of hunting as a source of food declined, the element of sport became more and more pronounced.

In the United States shooting first gained great popularity as a sport after the Civil War. In 1871 the National Rifle Association was formed by a group of officers in the National Guard who felt that there should be some executive control in the sport. The organization standardized targets, distances and other aspects of competition. It was also the sponsor of the first championship tournament held in the United States (see also **First International Rifle Match in the United States**).

Rifle shooters of the 1870s were national heroes, lionized as Jack Dempsey and Babe Ruth would be in later years. Although the sport does not have that kind of prestige today, national championship competitions are still held in rifle shooting; it is also an Olympic sport.

ORIGINS OF TRAPSHOOTING

Trapshooting is derived from an 18th-century English sport called "high hats," in which marksmen placed live birds under their hats. After a signal they lifted their hats to release the birds. They were permitted to shoot at the birds only after they had replaced their hats, allowing the birds to gain some distance. As the supply of captive birds dwindled, the gunners tried various substitutes. The first was a glass ball placed in a cup with a spring. When the spring was released the ball would fly out. Demand for more difficult targets led to the development of the revolving trap, which sent glass balls in different directions, and clay pigeons.

Trapshooting was introduced to the United States in the 1870s. By the early 1880s the sport was so popular that the Interstate Association of Trap-shooters was formed. In 1900 the organization sponsored the first Grand American Trapshoot, which was won by R.O. Heikes. The same year the IAT changed its name, to the American Trapshooting Association.

FIRST INTERNATIONAL RIFLE MATCH IN THE UNITED STATES

The first international rifle match in the U.S was held on Sept. 26, 1871 between an eight-man Irish team from the Ulster Rifle Club, which had beaten a team representing England this year before, and a team from the newly-formed National Rifle Association. Gen. George W. Wingate led the American team. The Americans used breech-loading rifles; the Irish, muzzle-loaded. Some 5,000 people turned out at Creedmoor, Long Island to see the day-long contest. It turned out to be so close that it was decided by the final shot, made by Col. John Bodine. The colonel made his shot and the Americans won by a score of 935-931. The prize for winning the match was $500.

ORIGINS OF SKEET SHOOTING

Skeet shooting is an American invention which derived from trapshooting. The sport was developed around 1910 by a group of trapshooters who often practiced shooting on the grounds of the Glen Rock Kennels in Andover, Mass., including C.E. Davies, William H. Foster and Henry W. Davies. The group had developed a friendly rivalry and wanted to compete against each other on absolutely even terms, so they devised a method by which each contestant could be given precisely the same series of shots.

In 1936 William H. Foster and the publishers of *National Sportsman* and *Hunting and Fishing* made a few changes in the rules and introduced the sport to the public. The name skeet shooting was contributed by Mrs. Gertrude Hurlbutt of Dayton, Mont., who won a $100 prize in a contest sponsored by *National Sportsman* to name the new sport. "Skeet" derived from an old Scandinavian word meaning "shoot."

FIRST PERFECT SCORE IN THE WORLD PISTOL SHOOTING COMPETITION

Al Hemming of Detroit won the 1940 world pistol shooting championship on July 6 with the first perfect (300) score ever in world championship competition. In the .22 caliber shot Hemming won the title from 17-year-old Gloria Jacobs, who had won the competition the previous year.

FIRST MARKSMAN TO HOLD THE NATIONAL TITLES IN BOTH SKEET SHOOTING AND TRAPSHOOTING IN THE SAME YEAR

In 1947 D. Lee Braun became the first professional marksman ever to hold the U.S. titles in both skeet shooting and trapshooting in the same year.

FIRST WOMAN TO WIN THE GRAND AMERICAN TRAPSHOOT

In 1950 Joan Pflueger became the first woman ever to win the Grand American Trapshoot (see also **Origins of Trapshooting**) in competition against an otherwise all-male field in Vandalia, Ohio. Competing against the champions from the other 49 states and from Cuba, the 18-year-old woman from Miami broke 100 clay pigeons in a row, then won a 75-bird shoot-off against four men.

12/COMBAT SPORTS:

WRESTLING, KARATE, BOXING AND JUDO

WRESTLING

ORIGINS

Wrestling, like swimming and running, was inspired by the need to survive. It is more than a little likely that the first wrestling match took place between a man and an animal; the prize was life itself.

Wrestling between men dates back to antiquity, thousands of years before the birth of Christ. The ancient Greeks founded wrestling schools, and wrestling was a part of the ancient Olympic Games. When the Olympic Games were revived in Athens in 1896, Greco-Roman wrestling was part of the program. Only five athletes competed that year; Karl Schumann from Germany was the freestyle featherweight winner. Wrestling was dropped from the 1900 Olympic program but restored for the 1904 games in St. Louis, Mo., where the U.S. took all the freestyle events. Wrestling, both Greco-Roman and freestyle, has been a part of the Olympic program ever since.

During the early 19th century wrestling in the United States was primarily confined to the Greco-Roman style, with rules closely regulating the kinds of holds that could and could not be used. But grapplers, less interested in form, used the catch-as-catch-can style which permitted the wrestler to use any type of hold except the stranglehold. Tom Jenkins became the first American wrestler to use the freer style during the late 19th century. Jenkins, a professional from Cleveland, Ohio, was generally recognized as the champion of freestyle wrestling for many years; he often wrestled for purses of up to $500. Jenkins lost his title in 1905 to Frank Gotch, who some considered the greatest catch-as-catch-can wrestler of all time. Gotch retired in 1913, after winning 154 out of 160 matches during his professional career.

Since the 1930s professional wrestling in the U.S. has generally declined to the level of showboat exhibitionism. It now possesses little credibility except among its ardent followers, who protest vehemently when others suggest that pro wrestling now involves little more than fakery.

The Amateur Athletic Union presides over annual Greco-Roman and freestyle wrestling tournaments each year in the U.S. as well as intercollegiate competition.

KARATE
ORIGINS

Karate means "empty hand"—appropriately enough for a sport that grew out of the Eastern tradition of weaponless combat. Unlike judo, karate was devised for self-defense, not as a sport.

Karate developed in Okinawa during the early part of the 17th century. The Japanese Satsuma clan had invaded Okinawa, set up their own administration and forbidden the possession of arms by native Okinawans. The people of Okinawa began to train secretly in self-defense in preparation for a revolt. Through arduous training they learned to use their fists, elbows, knees and feet to maim, smash or kill opponents. They borrowed and refined from earlier self-defense techniques, some of which can be traced back to humankind's early history. The techniques of karate spread eventually to Japan and elsewhere, but it was not formally introduced to Japan until the 1920s, when the karate master Gichin Funakoshi began to offer instruction there.

With refinements afforded by the application of Japanese jujitsu traditions, karate eventually grew from a secret form of self-defense into an international sport, complete with competitions and tournaments.

BOXING
ORIGINS OF AMERICAN BOXING; FIRST U.S. HEAVYWEIGHT CHAMPION

It seems that wherever there have been men there has been fighting, although not always in the name of sport. Boxing was introduced to the United States, for example, as a result of a grudge fight during the early days of the nation.

The rules devised by the Marquis of Queensberry, which gave birth to boxing with gloves, weren't yet known when the first American laid claim to the title "champion." His name was Jacob Hyer. His claim to the title was based on a bare-knuckle grudge fight he had won against one Tom Beasley in 1816. After the fight Hyer claimed to be the "champion"—the champion of *what*, it is not exactly clear. One can assume, however, that Hyer considered himself the U.S. champion. Apparently no one felt the need—or perhaps the inclination—to challenge him, since there is no record that he ever put his alleged title on the line.

Twenty-four years later, in 1840, Hyer's son Tom claimed to be successor to his father's title. Apparently his claim was based more on inheritance than on pugilistic competition, although he did fight a few times in 1840 and once in 1841; he then beat Yankee Sullivan from Great Britain on Feb. 7, 1849 in 16 rounds. The younger Hyer's claim to the title of world bare-knuckle champion was not supported by any organization; still, based on his defeat of Yankee Sullivan, he might be considered the first U.S. citizen to become world boxing champion. After beating Sullivan, Tom Hyer went into retirement without putting his title on the line.

The first generally recognized U.S. bare-knuckle boxing champion was Paddy Ryan. The first recorded fight in Ryan's career, which took place in 1880 near Collier's Station, W. Va., was fought under the London Prize Ring bare-knuckle rules. Ryan defeated an Englishman, Joe Goss, who claimed to be the world champion under the London Prize Ring rules. Ryan knocked out Goss in the 87th round of the bout. Ryan and Goss had bet $1000 on the fight.

Ryan did not, however, hold the title very long. The first time he defended his title, in a bout held in Mississippi City, Miss. on Feb. 7, 1882, he was knocked out in the ninth round by the legendary John L. Sullivan. Sullivan won a purse and a bet with Ryan for a total prize of $5000.

Sullivan was the last of the bare-knuckle champions. It is also possible that he may have been the first American to hold the world title under the Marquis of Queensberry rules for boxing with gloves. There is some evidence that Sullivan fought Dominick McCaffery from Pittsburgh under the Marquis of Queensberry rules in 1885 in Cincinnati. That fight went six rounds; referee Billy Tait, so the story goes, left the bout without announcing a decision. Two days later, in Toledo, Ohio, Tait was reminded that no decision had been announced; Tait announced then and there that Sullivan had won.

If this story is true, then Sullivan would have been not only the last of the bare-knuckle champs but also the first under the Marquis of Queensberry rules for boxing with gloves. It is known, however, that Gentleman Jim Corbett knocked out Sullivan in the 21st round of a fight held under the Marquis of Queensberry rules on Sept. 7, 1892 in New Orleans. The two men fought for a purse of $25,000 and a $10,000 side bet. It was the first and only time in Sullivan's career, which spanned 18 years and 17 fights, that he was knocked out, although he did have three draws and one no-decision bout. It also made Corbett the first official heavyweight boxing champion in the United States.

FIRST U.S. BANTAMWEIGHT CHAMPIONS

The smallest boxers are called "bantamweights"; the word "bantam" refers to miniature chickens. The weight limit was originally 105 pounds, but has now been raised to 118. The first American bantamweight was Charlie Lynch. He had lost a 95-round fight to English bantamweight Simon Finighty in 1856 in England. Three years later, though, Lynch beat Finighty in 43 rounds and laid claim to the bantamweight title. Lynch retired undefeated in 1861.

In 1890 George Dixon, a black from the United States, defeated Lynch's successor, Tom Kelly, to become the first black bantamweight champion. Dixon later outgrew the class and went on to become the first black featherweight champ as well. (See also **First Featherweight Champions**.)

FIRST U.S. MIDDLEWEIGHT CHAMPIONS

The first unofficial middleweight fight in the United States took place in 1867. That year Tom Chaney defeated Dooney Harris in 33 rounds in a bare-knuckle match in San Francisco, Calif., for a bet of $5,000. Chaney laid claim to the championship of his class, which was about 155-156 pounds, and which as yet had no name.

Five years later, in 1872, George Rooke challenged Chaney to a fight. Chaney didn't respond to the challenge; Rooke therefore claimed the middleweight title. Rooke, however, lost the title to Mike Donovan in 1874; Donovan successfully defended the title—which was still unofficial—until he retired in 1882.

In 1884 boxer George Fulljames coined the term "middleweight" and issued a challenge to all comers. Jack "The Nonpareil" Dempsey accepted; on

Aug. 30, 1884, in Toronto, Ontario, Dempsey defeated Fulljames in 22 rounds to become the first officially recognized middleweight champ.

On Aug. 19, 1926 Tiger Flowers outpointed Harry Greb in New York City to become the first black middleweight champion.

FIRST LIGHTWEIGHT CHAMPIONS

The lightweight division, now set at 135 pounds, originated with a bout held in Perrysville, Mo. in 1868. Abe Hicken beat Pete McGuire at 130 pounds; the two were the first to call themselves lightweights. As a result of that fight, Hicken claimed to be lightweight champion, and no one cared enough to argue with him. Hicken retired in a few years, the undefeated—if unofficial—champion.

During a visit to the United States in 1872, an Englishman, Joe Collyer, beat Billy Edwards, an American, and Arthur Chambers, another Englishman; he then claimed the lightweight title. Collyer also retired as champ.

On March 27, 1879 Chambers, fighting at 133 pounds, beat John Clark in Chippewa Falls, Canada on a 33rd-round foul. Chambers received a belt emblematic of world lightweight champion; he was thus the first recognized (i.e., other than by himself) lightweight champion.

FIRST WOMEN'S BOXING MATCH IN THE UNITED STATES

Rose Harland was defeated by Nell Saunders in the first U.S. women's boxing match. The event was held in Hill's Theater on March 16, 1876. Saunders received a silver butter dish as a prize.

FIRST FEATHERWEIGHT CHAMPIONS

The Belfast Spider, Ike Weir, was the first fighter actually rated a featherweight champion. The class was originally for boxers weighing between 118 pounds and 122 pounds; the upper limit has since been increased to 126 pounds. Weir held the featherweight crown during the 1880s, but when American Harry Gilmore challenged him to a bout in 1887, Weir declined. Two years later, in 1889, Weir fought an 80-round draw with Frank Murphy near Kouts, Ind. Billy Murphy of New Zealand defeated Weir Jan. 13, 1890 in San Francisco, Calif., to become the new featherweight champ.

After Murphy outgrew the class, George Dixon, an American black, defeated Nunce Wallace of England in an 18-round fight, held in London in

1890, for a $2000 bet and the championship. Dixon was the first black featherweight champ.

FIRST WELTERWEIGHT CHAMPIONS

The word "welter" comes from an English weight term used in horse racing. In the last decade of the 18th century some English fighters weighing around 145 pounds began fighting as "welters"; Paddington Tom Jones became the first "welter" champion in 1792 and retained the title for several years thereafter. Fighting in the "welter" class generally faded, though, after the turn of the century. English fighters in the welter class continued to box, but there was no officially recognized champion of the class.

American welter Paddy Duffy beat all challengers in the late 1880s and became the first boxer in the United States to lay claim to the title of welterweight champion. Since no one seemed to be interested enough to challenge him, Duffy retired. The title fell to Billy Smith on Dec. 14, 1892 when he knocked out Danny Needham in 14 rounds at San Francisco.

On Dec. 18, 1901 Joe Walcott defeated Rube Ferns in five rounds in Fort Erie, Ontario to become the first black welterweight champion.

FIRST LIGHT HEAVYWEIGHT CHAMPIONS

Shortly after the turn of the century Chicago newspaperman and boxing promoter Lou Houseman proposed creating a division for boxers who were too heavy for the middleweight division, which had a weight limit of 158 pounds, and too light for the heavyweight class. Houseman had a vested interest in the new division: He managed a fighter named Jack Root who had outgrown the middleweight division. Houseman proposed creating a light heavyweight class for boxers weighing between 158 and 175 pounds. Root laid claim to the light heavyweight title when he defeated Kid McCoy in 10 rounds on April 22, 1903 in Detroit. He only held the title until July 4, however, when George Gardner knocked him out in Fort Erie, Ontario.

A fighter known as the Battling Siki, who was Senegalese, was the first black to hold the light heavyweight crown. He knocked out reigning champ Georges Carpentier, a Frenchman, on Sept. 24, 1922 in Paris to win the title.

FIRST HEAVYWEIGHT CHAMPION TO RETIRE WHILE HOLDING THE TITLE

Jim Jeffries was the first world heavyweight boxing champion to retire while still holding the crown. Jeffries retired in 1905; he was later defeated in a comeback attempt.

FIRST BLACK HEAVYWEIGHT CHAMPION

He came out of Galveston, Texas in the late 1800s to become not only the first black heavyweight champion but also one of boxing's most colorful and controversial figures. He was Jack Johnson, who held the heavyweight crown longer than any other boxer except Joe Louis. Not bad for a rube who had found himself fighting for survival, not sport, on the Galveston streets and docks where he worked. After beating all the bullies Galveston had to offer, Johnson headed north to Dallas, where fate started him on the road toward the heavyweight championship.

Johnson worked for a man in Dallas who was himself an amateur boxer. The man, learning of Johnson's days as a street fighter, began to work out with him, helping to turn him from a bully into a boxer. After a degree of success as an amateur boxer in Dallas, Johnson returned to Galveston, where he turned back all challengers, bully and boxer alike. Johnson was eventually offered $25 for a four-round bout with a man named Bob Thompson. At last the street fighter was a professional boxer.

On the road again after finding that Galveston offered few prospects for an aspiring professional boxer, Johnson began to fight bout after bout with local champions in such diverse locales as New York City and a Colorado mining town. As undramatic and financially unrewarding as those many fights may have been, they did present Johnson with an opportunity to meet George Gardner, who claimed the championship of the light heavyweight class. Johnson apparently won his 22-round bout with Gardner on March 31, 1902 in San Francisco, which would have made him the first black to hold the light heavyweight crown. The light heavyweight class was not, however, yet an officially recognized one at that time; Gardner was not formally the light heavyweight title holder until he beat Jack Root in July 1904. A fighter known as the Battling Siki is thus acknowledged as the first black to hold the light heavyweight title (see also **First Light Heavyweight Champions**). Johnson's performance against Gardner nevertheless gave his boxing career impetus. Between 1902 and 1907 Johnson defeated dozens of challengers. But he faced an obstacle he couldn't have overcome even if he had wanted to—the color of his skin. A white man had what Johnson most wanted: The heavyweight championship of the world. And the champion, a French-Canadian boxer named Tommy Burns, just wasn't going to offer a black boxer a chance to take it away from him. Finally he had no choice: Johnson had beaten every challenger that stood between him and Burns. Johnson made offer after offer to lure Burns into a ring. Burns simply couldn't deny Johnson any longer. The terms of the fight overwhelmingly favored Burns: He was to get $30,000 for the bout while Johnson would receive $5,000. Johnson also made an incredible concession—he accepted Burns' manager as referee.

Finally, on Dec. 26, 1908, the two men met in Sydney, Australia. And Johnson was not denied. He pummeled Burns, who could not find his way through the Johnson defense, in round after round. The fight was supposed to go 20 rounds, but Burns was so badly beaten that police climbed into the ring in the 14th round and stopped it. Johnson was the heavyweight champion of the world. More than that, he was the first black heavyweight champion of the world.

Johnson's victory was, however, marred by the fact that Burns' claim to the title had been somewhat dubious. In 1905 the reigning heavyweight champion, Jim Jeffries, had retired. Subsequently a promoter had arranged a bout between heavyweights Marvin Hart and Jack Root. The winner of the bout, the promoter had said, would be the new heavyweight champion. He had even arranged for Jeffries to referee the bout, which Hart won, only to lose to Burns in 1906, leading to the 1908 Burns-Johnson title fight in Sydney.

Jeffries, however, claimed that he had not sanctioned the fight between Hart and Burns. Jeffries, possibly spurred by racially motivated sentiments, asserted his own claim to the heavyweight title. Thus Jeffries, the "White Hope," and Johnson met in Reno, Nev. on July 4, 1910. Jeffries was the betting favorite for the fight, perhaps mainly because he was white. Johnson was not, however, intimidated by the odds. Under a hot sun, Johnson dominated round after round of the fight until finally, in the 15th, he knocked Jeffries out to become, officially, the first black heavyweight champion.

Johnson was 32 years old when he stopped Jeffries. He held the title until April 5, 1915, when he fought Jess Willard in Havana, Cuba and was knocked out in the 26th round. That fight spawned years of controversy—many alleged that it had been fixed. His loss to Willard, of course, also made Johnson the first black heavyweight champion to lose the heavyweight crown.

When the Boxing Hall of Fame was founded in 1954, Johnson was among the first group of fighters chosen for the shrine. The honor came eight years after he had died in an automobile accident in North Carolina in 1946 at the age of 68.

FIRST FLYWEIGHT CHAMPIONS

The flyweight class, for 112-pound boxers, originated around 1910. Frankie Mason, the winner of many bouts, came to be generally recognized as the U.S. flyweight champion, while Jimmy Wilde, an Englishman, was considered the world champion after he knocked out Johnny Rosner in a 1916 bout in Liverpool. Apparently Mason and Wilde never met; for a number of years afterwards there were separate U.S. and world flyweight title holders.

FIRST FIGHT BETWEEN TWO BLACKS FOR THE HEAVYWEIGHT CHAMPIONSHIP

Once Jack Johnson had become the first black to hold the heavyweight title (see also **First Black Heavyweight Champion**), the stage was set for the first fight between two blacks for the heavyweight crown. That bout took place Dec. 19, 1913 in Paris, where Jack Johnson met challenger Jim Johnson. Jack Johnson won the bout with a decision in 10 rounds to retain his title.

FIRST RADIO BROADCAST OF A BOXING MATCH

The first U.S. prize fight broadcast on radio took place at the Pittsburgh Motor Garden on April 11, 1921 between featherweights Johnny Ray and Johnny Dundee. Pittsburgh *Post* sports editor Florent Gibson called the action as Ray won the fight in ten rounds.

FIRST RADIO BROADCAST OF A HEAVYWEIGHT TITLE FIGHT

An estimated 300,000 people heard the first radio broadcast of a heavyweight title fight. The fight, between champion Jack Dempsey and challenger Georges Carpentier, took place July 2, 1921 at Boyle's Thirty Acres in Hoboken, N.J. Dempsey knocked out Carpentier in the fourth round to retain his title; J. Andrew White, sitting next to David Sarnoff, called the blow-by-blow action.

ORIGINS OF THE GOLDEN GLOVES

The Golden Gloves matches, in which many professional boxing champions got their start, were originated in 1927 by the New York *Daily News*. The matches were originally confined to the New York metropolitan area, but soon spread to Chicago and, eventually, to the rest of the nation and the rest of the world. Proceeds from the matches are used for charitable purposes.

The Golden Gloves championships are awarded in two areas, east and west. Winners of local tournaments within each region meet in regional championships, held in New York City and Chicago. Finally national championships are held, in which the eastern and western champions in the various weight classes contend for the national title. The Golden Gloves are awarded in nine weight classes: 106 pounds, 112 pounds, 118 pounds, 126 pounds, 135 pounds, 147 pounds, 160 pounds, 175 pounds and heavyweight.

Most of the youngsters who compete in the Golden Gloves do not, unsurprisingly, go on to become professional fighters. But many have: Joe Louis, Rocky Marciano, Ray Robinson, Ezzard Charles, Barney Ross and Tony Zale, among many others.

Arch Ward, the late sports editor of the Chicago *Tribune*, who launched the professional baseball and football all-star games, also helped make the Golden Gloves international by arranging All-American and All-European title bouts in the 1930s. Except during World War II international bouts have been held annually.

FIRST MAN TO WIN THE FEATHERWEIGHT, WELTERWEIGHT AND LIGHTWEIGHT CHAMPIONSHIPS IN ONE YEAR

On Oct. 29, 1937 Henry Armstrong won the featherweight boxing championship of the world in New York City, beating Petey Sarron. A few months later, on May 31, 1938, he won the welterweight championship from Barney Ross in Long Island City, N.Y. And finally, on Aug. 17, 1938, Armstrong beat Lou Ambers in New York City for the world's lightweight boxing title. The little former slum kid was the first man ever to win all three championships within a year, the first "triple world boxing champion." Armstrong believed that his three victories were a sign that he had been chosen to speak the word of God, so he left the boxing ring to become an evangelist.

FIRST FIGHT TO BE TELEVISED IN THE UNITED STATES

The first prize fight to be televised in the United States took place between Lou Nova and Max Baer, two heavyweights, on June 1, 1939 at Yankee Stadium in New York City. The fight was broadcast over WNBT-TV; Sam Taub was the announcer. Nova scored a technical knockout in the 11th round.

FIRST FEMALE BOXING REFEREE

Belle Martell of Van Nuys, Calif., was the first woman boxing referee. She was licensed by the State of California on April 30, 1940. She refereed her first card, eight bouts, on May 2, 1940 at San Bernardino, Calif. She retired the next month when she was assigned to referee bouts in Los Angeles.

FIRST HEAVYWEIGHT TITLE FIGHT TO BE BROADCAST ON TELEVISION; FIRST $100 TICKETS

The first heavyweight title fight to be televised was the Joe Louis-Billy Conn bout held June 19, 1946 at Yankee Stadium in New York City. WNBT-TV in New York City televised the fight to just a handful of television sets as Louis knocked out Conn in the eighth round of a dull fight. This was also the first boxing match at which the top price for tickets was $100.

FIRST DEFEAT OF A MIDDLEWEIGHT CHAMPION BY A WELTERWEIGHT CHAMPION

Sugar Ray Robinson won the middleweight boxing title Feb. 14, 1951, defeating Jake LaMotta in Chicago. This was the first time a welterweight champion had defeated a middleweight title holder. It was also the fifth time in six fights that Robinson had beaten LaMotta.

FIRST HEAVYWEIGHT TITLE BOUT TO BE BROADCAST COAST TO COAST ON TELEVISION

The first heavyweight title fight to be broadcast coast to coast on television in the United States was a match between champ Jersey Joe Walcott and Ezzard Charles, held June 5, 1952 at Municipal Stadium in Philadelphia. Walcott out-pointed Charles to retain the crown.

FIRST UNDEFEATED HEAVYWEIGHT CHAMPION

Rocky Marciano was the first—and so far the only—heavyweight boxing champion to retire undefeated. Marciano fought 49 professional fights and never lost one. He won the heavyweight championship Sept. 23, 1952, knocking out Joe Walcott in 13 rounds in Philadelphia. Marciano defended his title successfully in six other bouts, the last time on Sept. 21, 1955, when he knocked out Archie Moore in nine rounds at Yankee Stadium.

Marciano was killed in an airplane crash on Aug. 31, 1969.

FIRST WOMAN IN THE UNITED STATES TO BE GRANTED A LICENSE AS A JUDGE FOR BOXING MATCHES

Carol Polis was issued a license by the New York State Athletic Commission as a judge for boxing matches in July 1974. She the first woman ever to be granted such a license.

JUDO

ORIGINS

Throughout Japan's long history its young men have been trained in unarmed combat of various types, such as jujitsu. Judo, however, was not developed until 1882. In that year Prof. Jigoro Kano established a school for teaching judo, "the gentle way," in Tokyo. He turned a way of fighting into a sport.

But judo was to be more than a sport. The judo concept of yielding in order ultimately to conquer was a maxim that would come to govern the students' entire lives. The fundamental principal behind judo was to obtain maximum efficiency in the use of the mind and the body with minimum effort.

Kano began his school with ten mats thrown in the front room of the Eishoji Temple. He never dreamed that his sport would someday be practiced by millions of people throughout the world.

13/SOCCER

ORIGINS

If there is any sport that can be considered a worldwide game, it's soccer, known outside the United States as football. Soccer is played in well over a hundred countries. In many of these nations, particularly in Europe and South America, it is the national sport and games frequently attract more than 100,000 spectators, many thousands more than even the most heavily attended baseball or football games draw in the United States.

Soccer may well have its roots in games played in Rome and Greece in the first two or three hundred years after the birth of Christ. By the 14th century the game of football had gained such popularity in England that Edward III felt compelled to forbid playing the game because it was taking too much time away from archery practice. (In the 15th century Edward IV banned cricket for that same reason.) Although subsequent monarchs also forbade the playing of football, the game had achieved such popularity that it continued to flourish through the 15th century. Royalty continued to frown on the game, both officially and unofficially, for many years, but were never successful in stopping its play.

When the first settlers, particularly the English, Irish and Scots, reached the American colonies, they brought football with them. By the 1880s soccer's popularity had reached such proportions in the United States that the American Football Association was formed in 1884 to regulate the game.

The first international soccer match featuring a U.S. team was played in 1886, when a team composed of players from local New Jersey teams went to Canada for a series of three games against a Canadian all-star team. The next year the Canadian team came to the United States for another three-game series. After these six games the record stood at two wins and two losses for each team (two games ended in ties).

The St. Louis Kensingtons, a soccer team, were formed in 1890 in St. Louis; this team may have been the first composed entirely of native U.S. citizens. Soccer continued to expand westward along with the country, completing its coast-to-coast trek with the formation of the California Association Football Club in 1902.

The first British team to play in the United States, known as the Pilgrims, arrived in 1904; they posted a 21 wins-two losses record before returning home.

By the first years of the 20th century the American Football Association presided over the professional leagues and teams in New England, New Jersey and Pennsylvania. The American Amateur Football Association, a competing group, had its power base in the New York State Amateur Football Association League. In 1912 the two organizations went to a meeting in Stockholm, Sweden of the Federation Internationale de Football Association, the international soccer football association, both seeking to be recognized as soccer's governing body in the United States. But the international organized refused to be drawn into the fray and sent the two organizations home to work out their differences, form one organization and apply again for international recognition. Committees representing both organizations held a series of meetings between September and December of 1912, when the American Football Association withdrew from the talks.

The American Amateur Football Association meanwhile garnered considerable support from other soccer football organizations and clubs, and at a meeting in New York City on April 5, 1913 the United States Football Association, which was in reality an augmented version of the American Amateur Football Association, was formed. In June Dr. G. Randolph Manning of the American Amateur Football Association was elected as the first president of the U.S. Football Association.

Even though the American Football Association still had an application pending to be recognized as soccer's governing organization in the United States, the International Federation awarded the honor to the United States

Football Association at a meeting in Copenhagen, Denmark in 1913. Recognizing its defeat, the American Football Association voted to join the United States Football Association, bringing peace to the U.S. soccer world.

In 1945 the national organization changed its name to the United States Soccer Football Association. Within the past few years its name has been changed again—it is now known as the United States Soccer Federation.

FIRST NATIONAL CHALLENGE CUP

The most coveted prize in soccer football in the United States is the National Challenge Cup. British sportsman Sir Thomas R. Dewar donated the trophy, then worth $500, to the American Amateur Football Association in 1912. The trophy was originally offered for amateur play only, but is now available to professional teams as well.

The Yonkers, N.Y. Football Club won the Challenge Cup in 1913, beating the Hollywood Inn Football Club, also of Yonkers, by a score of 3-0 in New York City.

After the formation of the United States Football Association (now the United States Soccer Federation) in 1913 the trophy was turned over to the new association, which has administered the competition ever since.

The Challenge Cup is the prize in an annual competition in which the winners of eastern and western regional playoffs meet in a championship game. The winning team keeps the Cup for one year under a bond to guarantee its return without damage.

FIRST NATIONAL AMATEUR CHALLENGE CUP

Interest in the National Challenge Cup had reached such large proportions by the 1922-23 season that the United States Football Association decided to offer a National Amateur Challenge Cup, which would, of course, be awarded to amateur teams only, as the National Challenge Cup itself originally had been. The Cup was placed into competition in 1923, but because of bad weather the tournament never progressed to the championship round. The Fleisher Yarn Football Club of Philadelphia and the Roxbury, Mass. team had made it to the eastern division finals, while the Jeannette, Pa. Football Club and the Swedish-American Athletic Association of Detroit were the western finalists.

The Fleisher Yarn club won the Cup the following year when it was awarded for the first time.

FIRST WORLD CUP

As befits the most truly international of sports, soccer boasts the most classically international competition: The World Cup. It isn't just a sporting event. For the competitors, national honor is at stake. For the fans, it is sometimes literally a matter of life and death. The fans at one World Cup final chanted "victory or death." During another World Cup final, a fan committed suicide when his television failed during the broadcast of the game.

The World Cup was born in 1930 under the auspices of the international soccer organization, Federation Internationale de Football Association (FIFA). When the cup competition was first proposed, interest was not overwhelming. Only four European teams agreed to participate in the first competition: Belgium, France, Rumania and Yugoslavia. Four other European countries, Spain, Italy, Sweden and the Netherlands, had wanted to host the first World Cup matches, but boycotted the competition when Montevideo, Uruguay was chosen as the site. FIFA decided on Montevideo because Uruguay was celebrating its 100th anniversary of independence that year and because Uruguay had won the gold medals in soccer at both the 1924 and 1928 Olympics. Great Britain had dropped out of FIFA several years earlier and was thus not eligible for the tournament. Other European countries decided against sending teams because of the distance and cost involved. The United States sent a team, and eight Latin American nations completed the lineup: Argentina, Bolivia, Brazil, Chile, Mexico, Peru, Paraguay and, of course, the host country, Uruguay.

Argentina was favored to win as the tournament began. The United States, fielding a team composed mainly of naturalized Americans originally from Great Britain, did unexpectedly well, defeating both Belgium and Paraguay in the preliminary rounds. After those two victories the U.S. team suddenly found itself favored to win the first World Cup. But the early favorite, Argentina, also won its preliminary rounds with victories over France, Mexico and Chile. That set the stage for a match between the United States and Argentina in the semifinal round.

After a ferocious first half the U.S. team trailed 1-0. But the team's situation was not as good as the score seemed to indicate. Ralph Tracy had suffered a broken leg in the first half—and, at that time, no substitutes were allowed. That meant that the U.S. team had to play the second half with only ten men. Two other Americans suffered injuries during the second half of the brutal game as Argentina rose to beat the U.S., 6-1.

In the finals Argentina played Uruguay in a rematch of the final game of the 1928 Olympics, which Uruguay had won. A home-town crowd of 100,000 was on hand as Uruguay won 4-2 to become the first recipient of the Jules Rimet Trophy, named for the president of FIFA at the time—more commonly known as the World Cup.

ORIGINS OF THE NORTH AMERICAN SOCCER LEAGUE

While soccer is perhaps the most popular game in the world, it has never become as prevalent in the United States as it is elsewhere. It is therefore not surprising that skeptics were abundant in the mid-1960s when some well-heeled businessmen decided to form the first major professional soccer league in the United States. What was, perhaps, surprising was that a total of three rival groups decided to form professional soccer leagues at the same time.

In 1966 two such groups, one headed by Jack Kent Cooke and the other by Richard Millen, sought approval from the United States Soccer Football Association (now the United States Soccer Federation). Even though the national association had only one full-time employee in 1966 and an average annual income of just $40,000, it decided it wanted $25,000 from each professional team, plus four percent of all gate receipts and 10 percent of any income from television. The founders of the would-be professional soccer leagues found the association's demands amusing, to say the least. They couldn't see any reason why they should pay any more than the $25 annual fee the American Soccer League, a more or less semi-professional operation, had been paying. Representatives of the fledgling leagues met with association officials at the association's New York office in the spring of 1966. Each of the new leagues wanted to gain the association's approval for itself; the other proposed league would then presumably fall by the wayside. After representatives of the two new leagues had outlined their plans, association officials came up with what they thought was an acceptable compromise: The proposed leagues should merge into one operation. The proposal, however, was rejected by the representatives of both leagues, partially because more than one franchise was planned for at least five cities.

The failure of the merger plan left the association in a difficult position since the international soccer organization, FIFA, wanted only one professional league operating in the United States. FIFA officials believed that more than one league would doom professional soccer in the United States to failure. The association thus formed a committee to recommend which of the new leagues should be recognized. The committee was to make its report at the association's convention in June 1966, where the various state associations would be given a chance to vote on the issue. But before the convention opened a group headed by Bill Cox proceeded to form the North American Professional Soccer League (NAPSL) without the association's approval.

Angered by the Cox group's unilateral action, the association made clear its position that no professional soccer league could be formed without the association's sanction.

At the conventional in June the committee gave its approval to the group headed by Jack Kent Cooke, which later became known as the North American Soccer League. The Cox group, undaunted, announced that it was merging with Richard Millen's National Soccer League to form the National Professional Soccer League (NPSL), which would begin play in the spring of 1967. Cooke's league followed by announcing that it too would begin play in 1967, importing teams from overseas until the 12 teams in the league had completed their rosters.

The national association, faced with an outlaw league, announced that any player joining an NPSL team would be suspended by FIFA. The threat apparently had little effect; many foreign players signed up to play for NPSL teams. The overall quality of NPSL players, however, left something to be desired—many of the top foreign stars had no intention of risking suspension.

The NPSL soon announced that it had made an agreement with one of the major television networks to broadcast one game every week over a 10-year period. The NASL, meanwhile, had no television contract. Someone, perhaps a public relations man looking for something to give the official league more pizzazz, came up with the idea of renaming it the United Soccer Association, giving it the patriotic acronym "USA."

The founders of the USA/NASL must have patted themselves on the back as exhibition games early in 1967 produced paying crowds ranging in size from 20,000 to 35,000. Nevertheless, as the regular season began, average attendance fell off to less than 10,000 a game.

The NPSL did even less well. Because its teams were composed mostly of foreign has-beens, attendance at NPSL games averaged only about 4000. The NPSL also got a bit of unfavorable publicity when it was disclosed that referees were cooperating with the television network by calling dubious penalties in order to stop action while the network inserted commercials, thereby disrupting action and creating the first "official" time-outs in soccer's history.

The inaugural season ended with the Oakland Clippers defeating the Baltimore Bays in a two-game series to win the NPSL crown (Baltimore won the first game, 1-0, and Oakland won the second, 4-1; the aggregate score was thus 4-2 in Oakland's favor). The Los Angeles Lakers meanwhile slipped by the Washington Whips, 6-5, to win the USA title.

As the first season for both leagues ended, some team owners found themselves in the red by as much as a half-million dollars. Propelled, perhaps, more by pains in the pocketbook than by a spirit of brotherhood, owners in both leagues reached the same conclusion: If professional soccer were to survive in the United States, then only one league could operate. Prompted by the team's losses and by the NPSL's $18 million antitrust suit against the USA, the United States Soccer Football Association and FIFA met with representatives of the two rival leagues in late 1967; all parties agreed to form a 17-team league which would be called the North American Soccer League.

The merger resulted not only in improved finances but also in better soccer in 1968, when the Atlanta Chiefs won the first NASL title by defeating San Diego 3-0 in the last game of the season. Chicago's John Kowalik was the first NASL scoring king, with 30 goals and nine assists for 69 points in the 1968 season. Kowalik edged out San Diego's Cirilo Fernandez by just two points.

14/FLYING:

BALLOONS, SKYDIVING, AIRPLANES AND OTHER FORMS OF FLIGHT

BALLOONS

FIRST CROSSING OF THE ENGLISH CHANNEL BY BALLOON

On Jan. 7, 1785 Jean Pierre Blanchard and J. Jeffries crossed the English Channel, from Dover, England to a forest 12 miles from Calais, in a balloon. Blanchard, who was to make the first balloon flight in the United States on Jan. 9, 1793 in Philadelphia, and Jeffries, an American doctor, found it necessary to throw out every bit of ballast, including their clothing, to keep their balloon in the air.

FIRST BALLOON RACE IN THE UNITED STATES

The first American hot air balloon race was a disaster. More than 100 hot air balloonists gathered with their craft at Dayton, Ohio in 1876 for a race to suburban Chicago. About three-quarters of the entrants failed to last the first mile. Many collided with trees, with results that were fatal for the balloons, although none of the aeronauts were seriously injured. Other balloons drifted, uncontrolled, to various points in Indiana and northern Ohio.

None of the balloons managed to land anywhere near Chicago.

FIRST WOMAN TO PILOT HER OWN BALLOON

Mary H. Myers became the first woman to pilot her own aircraft, a balloon, at Little Falls, N.Y. in 1880. Later billed professionally as "Carlotta, the Lady Aeronaut," Myers was often hired to perform at festivals. She established a new world altitude record—four miles—in 1886 after filling her balloon with natural gas rather than hydrogen. The record was even more impressive in light of the fact that Carlotta did not use oxygen equipment.

FIRST USE OF A PRESSURIZED CABIN IN A MANNED FLIGHT

Two Germans, Auguste Picard and his assistant, Charles Kipfer, took off from Augsburg, Germany on May 27, 1931 in a hot air balloon. During their 16-hour flight they set a new altitude record, rising to a height of 51,775 feet. It was also the first time a pressurized cabin had been used for a manned flight.

SKY DIVING

ORIGINS

Human beings have long dreamed of flying through the air. Greek mythology, of course, features Icarus' attempt to construct wings, with disastrous results. He who could fly could also fall to his death. Leonardo da Vinci designed a contrivance to lower a person safely from high places, but he never got around to trying to make a parachute himself. The Montgolfier brothers experimented with some devices for descent, but eventually invented the hot air balloon instead. Professor Lenormand of Montpellier tested a type of parachute in 1783; it was intended to save people trapped on upper floors of burning buildings. So, strangely enough, parachutes predate flying machines.

Early parachutes were usually made of muslin or similar fabrics. Jean Pierre Blanchard (see also **First Crossing of the English Channel by Balloon**) probably used the first silk parachute in 1793. In the 1800s further advances were made in the design of parachutes. At the same time many experiments meant to improve parachute design proved unworkable, often at the expense of the experimenter's life.

Early parachutists were concerned only with getting to the ground safely. After it became clear, however, that it was possible to dive into thin air and survive, people began to wait for a few seconds before pulling the rip cord. Thus sky diving was born. Exhibition parachute jumping made up a thrilling portion of early air shows. (Charles Lindbergh was a wing walker and parachute jumper before he started his flying career.) It was not until after World War II, however, that parachuting for sport was done in any significant way in the United States, although it had caught on earlier in Europe. Still, some sky diving "firsts" had already been recorded. In 1924 Captain A.W. Stevens jumped out of a plane at 26,000 feet and waited until he was only a few thousand feet off the ground before opening his parachute. Equally daring chutists tried to set new, even more impressive records for height or free fall.

The first international competition in sky diving was held in Yugoslavia in 1951, but it was not until the second world championship competition, held in Saint-Yan, France in 1954, that the United States was represented. Fred Mason placed 21st in the individual standings. In 1960 Jim Arender won top honors in a style event. He was the first American to win first place in an international sky diving competition.

FIRST WOMEN'S PARACHUTE JUMPING COMPETITION

The first world parachute jumping competition for women was held at Lesce-Bled, Yugoslavia in 1951. Monique Laroche of France won the overall title.

AIRPLANES

FIRST INTERNATIONAL AIRPLANE RACES

The first international air races were the events of the *Grand Semaine d'Aviation de la Champagne*, held in 1909 northeast of Reims, France. The finest aviators of Europe participated; so did one lone American, Glenn Curtiss.

There were six events during the eight-day meet, but the most important was the Grand Prix de Champagne. Prize money donated by the local vintners, amounting to some $20,000, was to be awarded for the longest continuous flight. Henry Farnam won the competition in his Voisin biplane; his distance of 111.85 miles in three hours, four minutes and 56.4 seconds broke all records for distance and endurance. When he landed Farnam was so stiff from the cold that he could not move, so he was carried back to the hangar, where the celebratory champagne had already begun to flow.

FIRST INTERNATIONAL AIR RACE IN THE UNITED STATES

The first international air race in the United States, held at Belmont Park on Long Island in 1910, consisted of a nine-day schedule of races. The most important was the second Gordon Bennett Trophy. The Bennett trophies were already the most sought after awards in auto racing and balloon racing; the Bennett air trophy, which had been donated by James Gordon Bennett Jr., publisher of the New York *Herald*, also promised to be very prestigious.

Claude Grahame-White from Great Britain was the first to start in the competition, flying his 100-horsepower Bleriot over the 100-kilometer distance (62 miles) in one hour, one minute and 4.73 seconds for an average speed of 66.2 mph. None of the other entries were able to beat White's time; thus he won the second Bennett trophy and the first major air race in the United States.

FIRST WOMAN TO FLY SOLO IN AN AIRPLANE

Blanche Scott became the first woman to solo in an airplane in 1910 in Dayton, Ohio. This was not, however, her first daring feat. She was hired earlier by the Willys Overland Company to drive an Overland car coast to coast as a publicity stunt. Thus Scott was also the first woman to drive coast to coast.

FIRST FEMALE PILOT KILLED IN AN AIRPLANE CRASH IN THE UNITED STATES

Julia Clark was the first female pilot killed in an airplane crash in the United States. The accident occurred in 1912 at the Illinois State Fair in Springfield.

FIRST WOMAN TO FLY ACROSS THE ENGLISH CHANNEL

Harriet Quimby caught America's fancy with her flying exploits. Dressed in a plum-colored satin flying suit, she looped and whirled in exhibitions. She was also a well-known journalist and a drama critic for *Leslie's Weekly*, a popular magazine of the day. In 1912 Quimby became the first woman to fly across the English Channel. Unfortunately, that same year she was killed during a routine flying exhibition at the 1912 Harvard-Boston Meet.

FIRST PILOT TO WIN THE BENDIX TROPHY THREE TIMES

Paul Mantz scored his third consecutive win in the Bendix Trophy races on Sept. 4, 1948, making him the first pilot to win the 2080-mile air race three times. The race began in Long Beach, Calif. and ended in Cleveland, Ohio.

FIRST SOLAR-POWERED AIRCRAFT

The first solar-powered aircraft, the *Gossamer Penguin*, constructed largely of plastic foam and Mylar, a very light but strong plastic foam, was designed by Paul MacCready. Powered by banks of photovoltaic cells, which convert sunlight directly into the electricity that runs the plane's motors, the *Penguin* is a three-quarter-scale version of MacCready's earlier *Gossamer Condor*, which was the first plane to make a sustained flight on human power, and his *Gossamer Albatross*, the first aircraft to cross the English Channel on human muscle power. (See also **First Human-Powered Flight; First Human-Powered Flight Across the English Channel.**)

The first solar-powered flight took place on May 18, 1980 with MacCready's 13-year-old son as a pilot.

OTHER FORMS OF FLIGHT

FIRST SUCCESSFUL GLIDER FLIGHT

Sir George Cayley of England built the first successful glider in 1852. His coachman and a neighbor child flew Sir George's glider in a brief downhill trip the same year.

FIRST FATALITY RESULTING FROM THE CRASH OF A CRAFT HEAVIER THAN AIR

In 1891 Otto Lilienthal flew 100 meters in a "hang"-type glider, the longest such distance to that date. Shortly thereafter he became the first victim of a heavier-than-air crash in an accident with his glider.

FIRST SCHNEIDER TROPHY FOR WATERPLANES

The first major trophy offered for waterplane races was the Schneider Trophy, first awarded in April 1913. The trophy was the prize for one of a series of flying contests for waterplanes held over a two-week period by the

Aero Club de France in Monaco. The course for the Schneider Trophy race was 28 laps of a 10-kilometer course.

Only France and the United States were represented by entrants in the first Schneider Trophy race. The planes flew singly, competing against the clock. After the preliminary trials only four entrants were left; all of those but one had mechanical difficulties during the final that prevented them from finishing. Only Maurice Prevost managed to complete the course, in two hours, 50 minutes and 47 seconds. About an hour after he had landed, however, someone remembered that the rules required competitors to cross the finish line while still airborne. Prevost, who had crossed it on water, rushed back to his plane, circled and crossed the line again, this time in the air. Thanks to the delay, Prevost's recorded speed for the race was only 45.75 mph—less than his airplane's stalling speed.

The Schneider Trophy is no longer awarded.

FIRST MAN TO FLY 650 MILES WITHOUT AN ENGINE

In 1965 Al Parker flew close to 650 miles in a sailplane. He was first man to fly so far in a non-powered aircraft. The 45-year-old pilot used an all-metal Sisu, a high-performance sailplane which is capable of gliding 40 miles horizontally for every mile it descends vertically.

FIRST NATIONAL HANG-GLIDING CHAMPIONSHIPS

The first U.S. national hang-gliding championships were held in the Angeles National Forest, Sylmar, Calif. on Oct. 25, 1973. The winner was a pre-med student from Santa Ana, Calif. named Chris Wills.

FIRST HUMAN-POWERED FLIGHT

The first human-powered flight took place in August 1977 in the *Gossamer Condor*, which had been built by Paul MacCready and was flown by Bryan Allen. Allen pedaled rapidly to keep the craft afloat. The *Gossamer Condor* was made largely of plastic foam and Mylar. (See also **First Solar-Powered Aircraft; First Human-Powered Flight Across the English Channel.**)

FIRST HUMAN-POWERED FLIGHT ACROSS THE ENGLISH CHANNEL

The *Gossamer Albatross*, a craft made by Paul MacCready mostly of plastic foam and Mylar, made the first human-powered flight across the English

Channel in June 1979. The pilot, Bryan Allen, kept the craft in flight by pedaling furiously on a bicycle-type crank to spin the propeller. (See also **First Solar-Powered Aircraft; First Human-Powered Flight.**)

15/INDOOR SPORTS:

BOWLING, GYMNASTICS, BILLIARDS, WEIGHT LIFTING, VOLLEYBALL, DUCK PIN BOWLING, DANCE MARATHONS AND ROLLER DERBIES

BOWLING

ORIGINS

Almost every American town or city of more than a few hundred people has a bowling alley. Many of these are elaborate establishments replete with restaurants, cocktail lounges, billiard facilities and, in some cases, even day-care facilities for bowling moms. The game attracts millions of participants each year, ranging from the youngster with barely enough strength to roll the ball down the alley to the professional competing for thousands of dollars in prize money.

Bowling dates back to ancient Egypt, more than 5200 years before the birth of Christ. The Egyptians "bowled" at nine stone "pins" with a stone ball. The ball was tossed through a stone arch made of three pieces of marble. The ancient Polynesians also played a game with stone pins and balls; the ball was rolled from a distance of 60 feet—the same distance that applies today.

Bowling at wooden pins probably grew out of a religious ceremony practiced in Germany in the third or fourth century AD. The ancient Germans carried a club known as a "kegel" (which gave birth to the word "kegler"). The kegel was placed at the end of a runway similar to today's alleys. The kegel represented the "heide," or heathen in oneself. A stone was tossed at the kegel; those who were successful in hitting the kegel were thereby cleansed of their sins. By the 14th century the Germans had begun bowling with a wooden ball on a wooden surface. The number of pins ranged from three up to 17. Interestingly enough, Martin Luther is credited with establishing the custom of using nine pins.

Bowling spread throughout Europe and England in the 15th, 16th and 17th centuries. The British began bowling indoors rather than outdoors in 1450, propelling the game into its modern form.

It is not known precisely when bowling was introduced into the United States because the word "bowl" was used to describe both 10-pin bowling and lawn bowling, even though the two games bear no physical resemblance to each other. But it is believed that 10-pin bowling was played in New York City by the first part of the 19th century.

Indoor bowling lanes originated in the U.S. in New York State in the mid-19th century, then spread west to Ohio, Illinois and Wisconsin. The game's popularity grew slowly at first, however, perhaps because of the absence of uniform rules and regulations and equipment. The first effort to end local and regional variations came in 1875 when representatives of nine bowling clubs from the New York area met in lower Manhattan and formed the National Bowling Association. That, however, did not end such variations, which persisted for another 20 years. On Sept. 9, 1895, however, the American Bowling Congress (ABC), which governs the game in the United States today, was founded in New York City. The ABC soon established uniform rules and equipment specifications. The first ABC National Championship tournament was held six years later, in 1901, in Chicago. A man named Frank Brill won both the singles championship and the all-events championship, and the Standards from Chicago won the team championship.

FIRST MAN TO WIN FOUR AMERICAN BOWLING CONGRESS TITLES

John Koster was the first man to win four American Bowling Congress titles. Koster was a member of the tournament championship teams in 1902 and 1912. He also won the all-events title in 1902 and the doubles crown in 1913. Koster's record stood for nearly 50 years.

ORIGINS OF THE WOMEN'S INTERNATIONAL BOWLING CONGRESS

Women began bowling in the United States in the 1880s, often at some peril to their reputations.

The first women's bowling league was not, however, organized until 1907. That first league was established in St. Louis by sportswriter and bowling alley proprietor Dennis J. Sweeney. That same year, 1907, saw the first interest in forming a national women's bowling organization. Many women accompanied their husbands to the men's American Bowling Congress tournament in St. Louis, where they made plans to hold their own tournament the following year on ABC tournament lanes in Cincinnati after the men's tournament. Another women's tournament was held in 1909 in Pittsburgh, once again after the men's ABC tournament.

Little else memorable occurred on the women's bowling scene until 1915, when Ellen Kelly, a bowling enthusiast herself, formed the St. Louis Women's Bowling Association. Pleased with her success in St. Louis, Kelly wrote to bowling alley proprietors across the nation, asking for the names of women who might want to help form a national bowling organization for women. Kelly then wrote to those women, urging them to form local bowling associations.

By the fall of 1916 many women had begun to support Kelly's idea of founding a national women's bowling organization. Many of those women accompanied their husbands to the ABC tournament, again held in St. Louis, where Sweeney joined with Kelly in sponsoring the first "national" women's tournament. Eight teams were entered; they competed for team, doubles, singles and all-events championships. The prize fund amounted to $222. Mrs. A.J. Koester was the all-events winner with a score of 1423. Mrs. Koester also won the singles event with a score of 486. Mrs. Roy Acker and Mrs. Jack Reilly won the doubles event with a score of 1011. The Progress of St. Louis team won the five-woman team title with a score of 2082.

Following the tournament, the 40 women from 11 cities who had participated met at Sweeney's Washington Recreation Parlor to form what became, after several name changes, the Women's International Bowling Congress. From those 40 women, the membership of the WIBC has grown to over four million today.

FIRST MAN TO WIN TWO ABC ALL-EVENTS TITLES

James Smith was the first man to win two American Bowling Congress all-events titles. He did it the first time in 1911 and repeated in 1920. Smith was also the first man to roll four 1900s in ABC tournaments.

FIRST BOWLER TO ROLL BACK-TO-BACK 300 GAMES

Frank Carauna of Buffalo, N.Y. became the first bowler on record to roll back-to-back 300 games on March 5, 1924. After rolling the two perfect games, Carauna threw five more strikes on his way to a 247 third game for a three-game series total of 847, just 53 pins from perfect.

FIRST WOMAN TO BOWL A 300 GAME

The first woman to bowl a perfect game was Rose Jacobs. She did it in Schenectady, N.Y. in 1929.

FIRST AUTOMATIC PIN SETTER

An automatic pin setter was first used in Brooklyn, N.Y. in August 1952.

FIRST BLACK TO ROLL A PERFECT GAME IN ABC COMPETITION

Kirk Ramsey was the first black to bowl a 300 game in an American Bowling Congress match. Ramsey did it at the Garfield Bowl lanes in Chicago in 1952.

FIRST BOWLER TO ROLL 300 IN A TELEVISED MATCH

In a 1954 series Steven Nagy became the first bowler to roll 300 in a televised match. Nagy was later named to the American Bowling Congress Hall of Fame.

FIRST WOMAN TO BE SELECTED INTERNATIONAL BOWLER OF THE YEAR FOUR TIMES

Marion Ladewig of Grand Rapids, Mich. was named Bowler of the Year in 1957, 1958, 1959 and 1963, making her the first and, so far, the only woman to be selected International Bowler of the Year four times.

GYMNASTICS

ORIGINS

Gymnastics originated in ancient Greece, where athletic events, practiced in a gymnasium, were one of the most important aspects of life. "Gymnastics" derives from a Greek word which means "to exercise naked." Gymnasiums were often elaborate structures equipped with a running track, a field for throwing the discus and the javelin, baths and areas where the teachers of the city held classes. Many Greek boys and young men spent most of their time training at the gymnasium. Each city's best athletes were selected to represent their cities at the Olympic Games.

The Romans adopted gymnastics and integrated them into military training. Gymnastic training died out, however, about the time the Olympics were banned, in 392 AD. Not until the 1700s were gymnastics revived in Germany by Frederick Jahn, who introduced the side bar with pommels, the horizontal bars, the parallel bars, the balance beam and jumping standards.

Gymnastics were brought to the United States in the 1800s by immigrants, and the sport soon gained limited popularity. In 1881 Americans first participated in an international competition: The Milwaukee Turners traveled to a meet held in Frankfurt, Germany. Still, there was not enough interest in gymnastics or in the newly-revived Olympic Games to send gymnasts to the games in 1896. The Amateur Athletic Union did, however, assume control of gymnastics in the United States in 1897. The first all-around AAU gymnastics champion was Earl Linderman in 1897.

The first Olympic gold medal winners in gymnastics from the United States were Anton Heida, who won in the all-around individual, long horse (vault), side horse and horizontal bar events (the last in a tie); George Eyser, who won in the parallel bar, rope climb and long horse (vault) events; Herman T. Glass, who won the flying rings event; and E.A. Hennig, who tied for a gold in the horizontal bar event and won in the Indian club event. All four gymnasts won their medals in the 1904 Olympics.

The first Amateur Athletic Union championship tournament for women was held in 1931. Roberta C. Ranck of Philadelphia was the all-around winner, with specialties in the side horse and the parallel bars.

FIRST AMERICAN TO WIN A SILVER MEDAL IN WORLD CHAMPIONSHIP COMPETITION

U.S. gymnast Cathy Rigby captured the hearts of American television viewers during the 1968 Olympics, although she placed only 16th overall.

She went on, however, to win a silver medal in the World Games in Ljubljana, Yugoslavia in 1970. Rigby was the first American woman ever to do so well in gymnastics, traditionally dominated by Europeans. Unfortunately, Rigby injured her ankle ligaments early in 1972, which may have affected her performance in the Olympics that year. She did, however, improve greatly on her 1968 performance, finishing 10th overall and seventh in the balance beam.

FIRST WOMEN'S WORLD CUP GYMNASTICS COMPETITION

The first women's World Cup gymnastics competition was held in London in 1975. Ludmilla Tourischeva of the Soviet Union won all of the five gold medals that were offered.

FIRST TEAM MEDAL FOR THE UNITED STATES IN WORLD CHAMPIONSHIP COMPETITION

The U.S. men's gymnastics team won its first team medal ever in world championship competition—a bronze—in 1979 in Fort Worth, Texas. Kurt Thomas and Bart Conner were the stars of the U.S. team. Thomas won a gold medal on the high bar in an inspired performance, scoring 9.90 points out of a possible 10. He also won another gold and two silver medals. Conner's performance on the parallel bars, including a one-armed handstand like none that any other finalist attempted, earned him a score of 9.90 and a gold medal. He also won a bronze on the vault. Despite the youth and inexperience of the rest of the team, the American men felt that with their bronze medal they had really arrived in international competition.

BILLIARDS

ORIGINS

The origins of billiards are even more obscure than those of most modern games. It is likely that an early form of billiards was first played when an outdoor game similar to croquet was brought inside in bad weather, probably in the 14th or 15th century.

The game as it is played in the United States derives from the English style of billiards, played on a table measuring either six feet by 12 feet or $5\frac{1}{2}$ feet by 11 feet, equipped with either four or six pockets. Originally only four balls were used—one ball for each player and two object balls. The first billiards tournament in the U.S. was played in that style in New York June 1-9, 1863. Dudley Kavanaugh won out over seven other players.

In the years after that first tournament the two types of tables in use today evolved—the billiard table without pockets and the pocket billiards table.

Championship matches in the early part of the 20th century were formal affairs, held in ballrooms of large hotels; spectators wore formal clothes. After Willie Hoppe won a billiards championship abroad he was asked to give a performance at the White House.

The popularity of billiards in the United States reached its height in the 1920s. Winners of big billiards tournaments were household names. Perhaps Willie Hoppe was the most famous; he won his first tournament at the age of 18 in 1906 and his last in 1952 at 64.

FIRST 14.2 and 18.1 BALKLINE CHAMPION

George Slosson, a native of New York State, was the first world champion in 14.2 balkline billiards. He took the first world crown in 1884. Slosson also became the first world champion in 18.1 balkline billiards in 1897.

FIRST BLACK POCKET BILLIARDS CHAMPION

It was not until 1965 that pocket billiards had its first black champion. Cicero Murphy, competing in his first world tournament in Burbank, Calif., posted a 17-3 record to win the 36-day, $19,500 tournament.

WEIGHT LIFTING

ORIGINS

Weight lifting became popular in central Europe, particularly in Germany and France, during the early 19th century. From there it spread to the Scandinavian countries, the Middle East and Japan. During the 19th century men lifting huge weights were popular attractions on the vaudeville circuit. One of those men, Arthur Saxon of Germany, once lifted a total of 448 pounds over his head—the most weight ever held overhead by a single man without help. Saxon, who had been born Arthur Hennig but changed his name to Saxon when he and two brothers formed a vaudeville trio, shouldered a 336-pound barbell and pushed it over his head, then lifted a 112-pound weight overhead at the same time. It was an amazing accomplishment, especially in view of Saxon's relatively small size—he was five feet, five inches tall and weighed 210 pounds. Saxon thus actually lifted more than twice his own weight.

Weight lifting became a permanent part of the Olympic Games in the seventh modern Olympiad, held in 1920 in Antwerp, Belgium. Competition was based on the press, snatch and jerk. That practice continued through the 1972 games; since 1976, however, Olympic weight lifting competition has been based only on the snatch and jerk.

The gold medal winners in weight lifting in 1920 were:

Featherweight: L. de Haes, Belgium, 485 pounds
Lightweight: Alfred Neyland, Estonia, 567.68 pounds
Middleweight: B. Gance, France, 540.012 pounds
Light heavyweight: E. Cadine, France, 639.334 pounds
Heavyweight: Filippo Bottino, Italy, 595.24 pounds.

Otto C. Osthoff was the first American to win a gold medal in Olympic weight-lifting competition. Osthoff won his gold in the one-hand lift at the 1904 games in St. Louis with a lift of 191.25 pounds. Weight lifting was, however, temporarily dropped from the Olympic program after the 1904 games.

Featherweight Anthony Terlazzo was the first American to win an Olympic gold medal in the traditional two-handed press, snatch and jerk competition. Terlazzo won his gold medal at the 1936 games in Berlin lifting 688.937 pounds.

American John Davis became the first amateur weight lifter to clean and jerk 400 pounds in 1951. Davis also became the first American weight lifter to win an Olympic gold medal in the heavyweight class in 1948 in London with a total of 996.581 pounds. At the 1952 games in Helsinki, Finland, Davis became the first American to win gold medals in back-to-back Olympic competitions when he repeated as heavyweight champion with a total of 1012 pounds. That marked the first time the 1000-pound total had been surpassed in Olympic competition.

Paul Anderson of Toccoa, Ga. became the first man to lift a total of 1100 pounds in the press, snatch and jerk in 1955. He was also the first to press 400 pounds. Anderson succeeded Davis as the Olympic gold medal-winning heavyweight at the 1956 games in Melbourne, Australia with a total of 1102 pounds. This marked the first time the 1100-pound total had been surpassed in Olympic competition.

The Amateur Athletic Union conducts annual weight-lifting competitions in the United States. It also sanctions collegiate weight-lifting competition.

FIRST WOMAN TO LIFT 1000 POUNDS OR MORE IN THREE POWER LIFTS

In 1977 Jan Todd bench pressed 176¼ pounds, dead lifted 441 pounds and lifted 424¼ pounds from a squat to become the first woman ever to lift more than 1000 pounds in three power lifts.

VOLLEYBALL

ORIGINS

Volleyball, like basketball, has its roots in the United States and, more specifically, in the Young Men's Christian Association (YMCA). The game was invented in 1895 by William Morgan, a student at Springfield College and a director of the YMCA in Holyoke, Mass. Morgan originally called the game "mintonette," but it soon became known as "volleyball." As the first volleyball players left the Holyoke area they took the game with them; as a result it spread both throughout the United States and overseas.

The first national championship tournament in volleyball was held in 1922 at the Central branch of the YMCA in Brooklyn. The team from the Pittsburgh YMCA was the winner.

The United States Volleyball Association was formed in 1928. Dr. George Fisher was elected president and Dr. John Brown Jr. was elected secretary-treasurer.

DUCK PIN BOWLING

ORIGINS

Two members of baseball's Hall of Fame, John McGraw and Wilbert Robinson, are credited with creating duck pin bowling. The two owned a Baltimore bowling alley; in 1900 their manager, Frank Van Sant, proposed that a set of regular 10 pins be converted into smaller pins to conform with the six-inch bowling ball used in the games of five-back and cocked hat. A Baltimore woodturner, John Ditmar, produced the first set of the smaller pins. The first time McGraw and Robinson, both duck hunters, saw the little pins go flying, they commented that it looked like a flock of flying ducks. The next day, in the Baltimore *Morning Sun*, sportswriter Bill Clarke, describing the event, called the game "duck pins"; the name stuck.

Informal duck pin play continued on the eastern seaboard until 1927, when the National Duck Pin Bowling Congress was formed in order to standardize rules and play.

The first national duck pin bowling tournament was held in Baltimore in 1928, with 68 teams competing. Howard Campbell was the all-events winner of the inaugural tournament with a score of 1113. Irene Mischou was the women's all-events champ with a score of 973.

DANCE MARATHONS

FIRST BIG-TIME DANCE MARATHON

The first major dance marathon began June 10, 1928, in Madison Square Garden in New York. Health Commissioner Louis Harris ordered the marathon stopped June 30 after a contestant who had dropped out collapsed on the street from a bleeding ulcer. The promoter, Milton D. Crandall, split $8500 in prize money among the 18 contestants still on the floor.

ROLLER DERBIES

FIRST ROLLER DERBY

The first roller derby was presented by promoter Leo Seltzer on Aug. 13, 1935 at the Chicago Coliseum. At first the derbies were really little more than walkathons on wheels. Seltzer later banked the turns on the oval track. Soon roller derbies were sufficiently successful for Seltzer to take them on the road. The sport did not really catch on, though, until writer Damon Runyon suggested that what roller derbies needed was more body contact—this, he thought, would make for a real sport. The rules were thus changed, and the sport became a combination of roller skating, football, ice hockey, bicycle races and any number of other fast contact sports.

From the first, women's squads as well as men's squads participated in roller derbies. So roller derbies may have been the first professional sport in which women competed equally with men, under the same set of rules.

FIRST TELEVISED ROLLER DERBY

Roller derby promoter Leo Seltzer paid to have the derbies televised on a Chicago station in 1947. Television viewers loved it, and Seltzer had no trouble finding sponsors for roller derby games in the future.

16/OLYMPICS

ORIGINS

Because of their rich history and international scope, many consider the Olympic Games the ultimate event in amateur sports. Some have criticized the games, claiming that they are excessively commercialized and politicized and that many of the athletes are subsidized to such a degree that they are not really amateurs at all. Yet the games remain the most prestigious forum in which amateur athletes can compete.

The Olympics originated in ancient Greece, probably long before the first recorded Olympics in 776 BC. They were not merely athletic competitions, but religious festivals honoring the dead with spectacles that they might have enjoyed in life. The ancient Olympics were always held in Olympia, near the western coast of Greece. In the beginning the games included events such as oratory, art, music and poetry recitals. The first recorded Olympics in 776 BC included only one athletic event, a foot race of one stade (about 200 yards), which was won by a young cook, Koroibos of Elis. Over the years other events were added, such as the pentathlon and the pankration (a combination of boxing and wrestling).

Many of the ancient Olympic sports were extremely violent. In one chariot race only one man, Arcesilaus of Cyrene, out of a field of forty finished the race. Boxers were often mutilated for life; a boxer named Arrachion twisted his opponent's foot with such force that the man raised his hand in surrender. In the process, however, Arrachion was choked to death by his opponent. The dead man was judged the winner.

Not only were women not included as competitors in the ancient Olympics—they were not even allowed as spectators. Any woman found in attendance was thrown off a nearby cliff. Women did have their own games, the Heraea, which were held every five years, but their importance did not match that of the Olympics.

Even though Olympic events were often violent, the spectators were expected to be peaceful. Weapons were not allowed within the sacred bounds of Olympia. Wars between rival city-states were even halted for the duration of the games. Only once was the truce broken, in 364 BC, when the Eleians attacked the Pisates, who presided over the Olympics at that time.

Only freeborn Greeks were allowed to enter the early Olympic Games. Athletes had to devote themselves to training for 11 months before the games. The last month of practice took place under the supervision of the Olympic judges, who chose the athletes allowed to enter the actual games.

Winners of the earliest Olympic Games received only crowns of wild olive branches, but later on statues were erected to honor those who had been champions three times. Each city in Greece showered its winners with gifts and honors. Sometimes cities even broke a special opening in the city's walls for the athlete to enter, signifying that, with such an athlete among its populace, the city needed have no fear of enemies. Winners were often declared exempt from taxes for life.

In the later years of the ancient Olympics, non-Greeks were allowed to enter. In 66 AD the Roman emperor Nero entered several events. Naturally the tyrant won each of the events he entered, turning the games into a farce. The games continued uninterrupted until 394 AD, when the Emperor Theodosius of Rome, a Christian, formally abolished the pagan Olympic Games. The ancient games had been held every four years for approximately 1200 years, for a total of 291 Olympiads.

The Olympic Games were revived in modern times mainly through the efforts of one man, Baron Pierre de Coubertin, who had a dream that athletes of all nations might compete on an equal basis in international games and thus help to create goodwill among people of all countries.

Coubertin first proposed the revival of the ancient Olympic Games at a meeting of the Athletic Sports Union at the Sorbonne in Paris in 1892, but he received little encouragement from the other members. He brought up the idea once again at an international congress which he had assembled to study the question of amateurism in sports. Coubertin succeeded in spreading his enthusiasm about the Olympic idea to the others at the Congress; together they formed an international committee to study the revival of the games.

The first modern Olympic Games were held in Athens in April 1896. The Greek government, which was then on the verge of bankruptcy , was unable to finance the games. Crown Prince Constantine came to the rescue by setting up a 12-member committee to establish ground rules for the games and to raise funds. Collections were made throughout Greece and among Greeks living in other countries; their response allowed the games to proceed. A wealthy Greek businessman, Georgios Averoff, donated 920,000 gold drachmae for the reconstruction of the Panathenaic Stadium.

There were 311 athletes from 13 countries participating in the first Olympics of the modern era, which began on Easter Sunday, March 24, 1896 (April 6 by the calendar in use today). The games included 43 events in nine different sports. Two events were being held for the first time in modern history, the marathon and the discus. The Greek people considered it necessary to the national honor for a Greek citizen to win the marathon, an event created to celebrate a key event in Greek history. A young Greek shepherd, Spiridon Loues, won the event; his reward was not just a medal but the affection of the Greek people. One barber offered to shave him free for life; a restaurant owner promised to give him free meals for life. Loues did not enter the competition again.

Recalling ancient Olympic practice, the first modern Olympics included performances of ancient dramas (*Medea* and *Antigone*) and concerts.

The standard of the competitors in the first modern Olympics was quite low compared to what it is today, but the standards of cooperation and competition that we associate with the Olympics were firmly established in Athens in 1896.

The first Olympic Games held in the United States took place in 1904 in St. Louis during the World's Fair. The first Winter Olympic Games in the United States were held at Lake Placid, N.Y. in 1932.

Women were first allowed to participate in the Olympic Games in Stockholm in 1912, but only in swimming and diving events. Women were first allowed to participate in separate track and field events in 1928 in Amsterdam.

WOMEN IN THE OLYMPICS

While athletic competitions for women were not a part of the ancient Olympic Games, women were allowed to own chariots that were entered in the Olympic chariot competition. Cynisca of Sparta became the first woman whose chariot won an Olympic victory in 396 BC.

Women also did not participate in the first modern Olympic Games, held in 1896 in Athens, Greece. Tennis and golf competitions for women were, however, included on the program for the 1900 Olympiad in Paris. Margaret Abbott from the United States won the first gold medal in the women's nine-hole golf competition, while Charlotte Cooper from Great Britain won the gold for women's singles tennis.

AMERICAN WINNERS IN THE FIRST OLYMPICS

No Olympic committee was formed to send U.S. athletes to the first modern Olympics because most Americans considered the Olympic revival primarily a European event. Four Princeton students—Robert Garrett, Francis A. Lane, Herbert B. Jamison and Albert C. Tyler—decided, however, to go to the games; Garrett paid all their expenses. Harvard student James B. Connolly went along, paying his own way. The Boston Athletic Association raised money for a few others who wanted to attend: Thomas Curtis, Thomas E. Burke, Ellery H. Clark, William W. Hoyt and Arthur Blake.

The young men sailed for Europe on a small tramp steamer which arrived in Italy on April 1. Only then did they realize that the Greeks used a different calendar; the games they had thought would start on April 18 were instead starting on April 6. The Americans sailed to Greece on another small ship, then took an all-night train to Athens, arriving just in time for the first event. They were out of shape, having had no chance to exercise during their journey from the United States. Nevertheless, the first man to win a gold medal in the modern Olympic Games was James B. Connolly, the student from Harvard (see also **First Gold Medal Winner**). Several other Americans won gold medals as well: Robert Garrett won the shot put and the discus throw (see also **First Gold Medal Winner in the Discus Throw**). William W. Hoyt won in the pole vault with a vault of 10 feet, 9¾ inches. Ellery H. Clark won both the high jump and the broad jump, with distances of five feet, 11¼ inches and 20 feet, 9¾ inches, respectively, while Thomas E. Burke won the 100-meter dash, with a time of 12 seconds, and the 400-meter run, with a time of 54.2 seconds. Thomas Curtis also won a gold medal, in the 110-meter hurdles, with a time of 17.6 seconds. Arthur Blake came in second in the 800-meter race; he also entered the marathon, but was forced to withdraw after 15 miles. In all the Americans won nine out of the 12 track and field events while competing against some of the best athletes in Europe.

FIRST GOLD MEDAL WINNER

When the modern Olympic Games began in 1896 in Athens, Greece, an American had the distinction of winning the first gold medal. He was James B. Connolly, who won the gold medal in the triple jump (hop, step and jump) with a distance of 45 feet, and thus became the first Olympic champion in 15 centuries.

Connolly was a student at Harvard University when the games were planned. He requested a leave of absence to participate in the games, which Harvard denied, so, instead, he left Harvard for good. Connolly went on to become an author of sea stories.

FIRST GOLD MEDAL WINNER IN THE DISCUS THROW

Robert Garrett, a member of the Princeton University track team, gained the opportunity to participate in the first modern Olympics in 1896 in probably the simplest way: he paid his own fare to Athens. Garrett had never been a discus thrower; in fact, he had never even seen a discus a few weeks before the Athens games began. But he asked a friend to make him a discus so that he could give it a try. It worked. Garrett went to Athens and won the gold medal not only in the discus, with a throw of 95 feet, 7½ inches, but also in the shot put, with a throw of 36 feet, two inches.

FIRST MAN TO WIN FOUR GOLD MEDALS IN ONE OLYMPIAD

American Alvin Kraenzlein was the first man to win four gold medals in individual events in one Olympiad. He was also the first—and, so far, the only—man to win four gold medals in individual track and field events in one year's Olympics. In the 1900 games in Paris, Kraenzlein won gold medals in the long jump (running broad jump) with a distance of 23 feet, 6⅞ inches; in the 60-meter dash, with a time of seven seconds; in the 110-meter hurdles, with a time of 15.4 seconds; and in the 200-meter hurdles, with a time of 25.4 seconds.

FIRST OLYMPIAD HELD IN THE UNITED STATES

The third modern Olympiad, held in 1904, was the first in the United States. The games were held in St. Louis in conjunction with the 1904 World's Fair.

Because of the high cost of sending athletes to St. Louis, located in the middle of the United States, only nine of the 20 countries which had been invited to particiate sent representatives. Great Britain sent only one athlete; Germany, just seven; and France, none at all. But there were Americans everywhere one looked, it seemed. Eighty percent of the athletes there were from the United States. One observer called the track and field events a dual meet between the New York Athletic Club and the Chicago Athletic Association. Because of the overabundance of American athletes and the lack of foreign competitors, the games seemed like a display of bad manners on the part of the host country: U.S. athletes won 23 of the 25 track and field events and finished one-two-three in 18 of those events. Americans won all three medals—gold, silver and bronze—in boxing, archery, wrestling, bicycling and gymnastics. All told, U.S. athletes won 64 medals in 1904—22 gold, 22 silver and 20 bronze.

Somewhat chagrined by the poor foreign turnout and embarrassed by the U.S. domination of the 1904 games, the International Olympic Committee did not choose another site in the United States for the games until 28 years had passed. The 1932 Olympics were held in Los Angeles.

FIRST CUBAN TO COMPETE IN AN OLYMPIC MARATHON

Cuba's first representative in the Olympic marathon was Felix Carajal, a Havana postman who had never before competed in a race. Carajal heard about the St. Louis Olympics in 1904 and decided that he would compete. Cuba did not plan to provide financial assistance for athletes who wanted to participate in the Olympics, so Carajal raised the money himself by running repeatedly around a square in Havana and begging for money.

After collecting enough money, Carajal set off for the Olympics. Unfortunately he lost all of his money in a card game in New Orleans, but, undaunted, he ran the 700 miles to St. Louis, living on handouts along the way. Carajal arrived just hours before the marathon was to begin, clad in heavy walking shoes, a long-sleeved shirt and long trousers. He cut his pants short and took off in the marathon. Despite laughter from the crowd, Carajal not only finished; he placed fourth.

FIRST OLYMPIC PRANK

In the 1904 Olympic Games in St. Louis, Fred Lorz from the United States dropped out of the marathon because he could not keep up the pace. He caught a ride on the running board of a passing car and traveled in this fashion along five miles of the course before he resumed running in the direction of the stadium. When he entered the stadium the officials and crowd assumed that he had won the race. Lorz did not, however, accept the gold medal; he admitted what he had done. He didn't win the gold medal, but he had gained the distinction of being the first athlete to pull such a prank in the Olympics.

FIRST OFF-YEAR GAMES

The first and only "off-year" Olympics were held in Athens, Greece in 1906.

At that time many felt that the Olympics should be held only in Athens, their birthplace. Another group suggested that the games be held at two-year intervals: The regular Olympics would continue to be held every four years, and would rotate from city to city around the world; meanwhile, "off-year" games would be held two years after each regular Olympiad, in Athens only. Thanks partly to the feeble turnout at the 1904 games (see also **First Olympiad Held in the United States**), and partly to the efforts of the Athens-only group, the decision was made to hold off-year Olympics in Athens in 1906.

(The U.S. athletes, incidentally, wearing uniforms for the first time, did well in many events, taking home their share of medals.)

Thousands turned out to see the Athens games, as they had in 1896 when the modern Olympics began. But the cost of sending athletes to the games every two years was just too much for most countries, and support for off-year games largely disappeared after 1906.

FIRST AMERICAN TO WIN AN OLYMPIC MARATHON

On July 26, 1908, 17-year-old Johnny Hayes became the first American to win the Olympic marathon. Hayes had never before run a marathon race. Everyone expected Dorando Pietri of Italy, who was thought to be the world's best long-distance runner, to win the race.

Pietri held the lead throughout most of the race, but collapsed about 100 yards from the finish line. British Olympic officials helped him across the finish line, a few steps ahead of Johnny Hayes. At first Pietri was proclaimed the official winner, but there was an outcry from the public because it was against Olympic rules for a runner to receive assistance. Hayes was then declared the winner.

FIRST U.S. ATHLETE TO WIN 10 GOLD MEDALS

Ray C. Ewry was the first athlete from the United States to win 10 gold medals in the Olympic Games. Ewry participated in four Olympiads and won medals in each. His specialties were the standing broad jump, the standing high jump and the standing hop, step and jump, none of which are now Olympic events. His award-winning distances were as follows:

> Standing high jump (1900): Five feet, five inches
> Standing high jump (1904): Four feet, 11 inches
> Standing high jump (1906): Five feet, 1 5/8 inches
> Standing high jump (1908): Five feet, two inches
> Standing broad jump (1900): 10 feet, 6 2/5 inches
> Standing broad jump (1904): 11 feet, 4 7/8 inches
> Standing broad jump (1906): 10 feet, 10 inches
> Standing broad jump (1908): 10 feet, 11 1/4 inches
> Standing hop, step and jump (1900): 34 feet, 8 1/2 inches
> Standing hop, step and jump (1904): 34 feet, 7 1/4 inches.

Ewry had had polio as a child; later he took up calisthenics and jumping to strengthen his legs. He became so strong that he was able to dominate the standing jump events for almost the entire time they were included in the Olympics. (The standing hop, step and jump was an Olympic event only the two years Ewry won it; both the standing high jump and the standing broad jump were Olympic events only one year—1912—in which Ewry did not win them.)

FIRST MAN TO WIN BOTH THE PENTATHLON AND THE DECATHLON IN ONE OLYMPIAD; FIRST AMERICAN TO HAVE MEDALS REVOKED

Jim Thorpe, an American Indian, was famous for his performance in football, but he was also outstanding in track and field. In the 1912 Olympiad in Stockholm he became the first—and is so far the only—man to win both the decathlon and the pentathlon in the same Olympiad. To win both he had to compete in a total of 15 different events.

In the pentathlon Thorpe finished first in the 200-meter dash, the 1500-meter run, the broad jump and the discus throw. He placed third in the javelin throw. In the decathlon he won the gold medal by finishing first in the shot put, the high hurdles race, the high jump and the 1500-meter run. He placed third in the 100-meter dash, the discus, the pole vault and the broad jump. Thorpe came in fourth in the 400-meter race and the javelin throw. He scored twice as many points as his nearest competitor in both the pentathlon and the decathlon.

After Thorpe had been awarded the medals, however, charges were made that he had violated the Olympic code of amateurism by playing semi-professional baseball during summers while he was a student at Carlisle Indian School in Pennsylvania. He was consequently forced to return his medals. Several efforts were made at different times by his supporters to have the medals returned to Thorpe, but none succeeded.

In 1950 American sports writers and broadcasters in an Associated Press poll voted Thorpe the outstanding U.S. athlete of the first half of the 20th century.

Thorpe was to become one of professional football's pioneers. He served as the first professional football commissioner, although the post was largely ceremonial. (See also **First Professional Commissioner** in Chapter 2, "Football.")

(In 1912, the same year in which Thorpe won the pentathlon and the decathlon, famed Gen. George S. "Blood and Guts" Patton also entered the pentathlon competition. Thorpe and Patton were the first Americans to compete in the Olympics in this event. Patton, then a young lieutenant, finished fifth.)

FIRST U.S. WOMAN TO WIN AN OLYMPIC GOLD MEDAL; FIRST WOMAN TO WIN THREE GOLD MEDALS IN ONE OLYMPIAD

In the 1920 Olympics, held in Antwerp, Belgium, women were allowed to enter only three swimming events. Ethelda Bleibtrey from the United States won gold medals in all three, and probably would have won another if there had been a backstroke event, because at the time she held the world record for women in the 100-yard backstroke. First she won the 100-meter freestyle, with a time of one minute, 13.6 seconds, setting a world record and becoming the first woman from the United States ever to win an Olympic gold medal. In the 300-meter event, her time of four minutes, 34 seconds also set a world record. Bleibtrey won her third gold medal in the 400-meter freestyle relay, together with Margaret Woodbridge, Mrs. Frances C. Shroth and Irene Guest, with a time of five minutes, 11.6 seconds.

Bleibtrey set seven world records during her career, including her two individual gold medal-winning performances.

FIRST MAN TO WIN TWO OLYMPIC SCULLING TITLES ON THE SAME DAY

John B. Kelly from the United States won two medals in the 1920 Olympics in Antwerp, both in the same day. He won the double sculls in partnership with Paul Costello and beat Jack Beresford to win the single sculls. Kelly was the first man to win two gold medals in sculling in one day. He was to win the double sculls again in 1924. He was also to become the father of actress Grace Kelly, now Princess Grace of Monaco.

FIRST WINTER OLYMPIC GAMES

For the first quarter-century of the modern Olympics, only summer games were held. Limited ice-skating programs had been included in the 1908 Olympics in London and in the 1920 Olympics in Antwerp, but a movement to hold regular Winter Olympic Games as well as summer games, which had first arisen in the early 1900s, met with stiff resistance from many, including the International Olympic Committee, because the ancient Olympics had included only the summer events. It just wouldn't have been in keeping with Olympic tradition, they claimed, to include winter sports in the Olympiad, even though skiing, skating and other winter sports were gaining considerable popularity in Europe at the time.

The movement to include winter events in the Olympics persisted, however, and in 1924 the French Olympic Committee agreed to hold seperate winter games in Chamonix. The competition in five sports—hockey, speed skating, figure skating, skiing and bobsledding—together with demonstrations in curling and a form of biathlon, was strictly experimental, insisted the International Olympic Committee. The winter sports competitions were a success, however, and the Winter Olympics were given official sanction by the IOC.

The original intention of the IOC had been to hold both the summer and winter games in the same country during the same year. But there weren't proper facilities for winter games in the Netherlands, the site of the 1928 Summer Olympics; as a result the winter games were moved to St. Moritz, Switzerland. With that exception, the Summer and Winter Olympic Games were held within one country each year until the games were suspended for the duration of World War II. In the postwar years the games became separate entities; each year's games have since been held in two different countries.

In 1924 Charles Jewtraw became the first U.S. athlete to win a gold medal in the Winter Olympics, with a winning time of 44 seconds in the 500-meter speed skating event.

FIRST DIVER TO WIN SPRINGBOARD AND HIGHBOARD DIVING TITLES THE SAME YEAR

Albert C. White from the United States was the first diver to win both the springboard and highboard titles at the same Olympiad. White, a member of Stanford University's outstanding swimming team, won his medals in the 1924 games in Paris.

FIRST WOMAN TO WIN GOLD MEDALS FOR THE SAME EVENT AT TWO SUCCESSIVE GAMES

Martha Norelius represented the United States as a swimmer in the 1924 and 1928 Olympics. She was the first woman ever to win an Olympic gold medal for the same event at successive games, winning the 400-meter freestyle in 1924 and 1928. Her time in 1928, five minutes, 42.8 seconds, was a world record.

Norelius won 16 U.S. titles and set 19 world amateur records before turning professional. Her father had represented Sweden in the interim games in 1906 (see also **First Off-Year Games**); she married a Canadian, Joseph Wright, who won a silver medal at the 1928 Olympics for double sculls.

FIRST RUNNER TO WIN SEVEN GOLD MEDALS

Paavo Nurmi, a cross-country runner from Finland, competed in the Antwerp Olympics in 1920 when he was 23. He won the 10,000-meter event and led Finland's 10,000-meter cross-country team to victory.

In the next Olympic Games, in Paris, Nurmi won both the 1500-meter and the 5000-meter events within 90 minutes, setting new Olympic records for both. He also won the 10,000-meter cross-country race and led the Finnish relay team to a new record in the 3000-meter race.

Nurmi was 31 years old when he competed in his final Olympics, in Amsterdam in 1928, but his age did not prevent him from winning the 10,000-meter championship and his seventh gold medal. Nurmi was the first runner ever to win so many medals.

FIRST AMERICAN TO WIN GOLD MEDALS AT BOTH SUMMER AND WINTER OLYMPIC GAMES

Edward Egan was the first American to win gold medals at both summer and winter Olympic Games. He took the gold medal in light heavyweight boxing in the 1920 summer games in Antwerp, Belgium. Then in the 1932 Winter Olympics at Lake Placid, N.Y., he was a member of the four-man bobsled team from the United States, which finished first.

FIRST EQUESTRIAN TO WIN AN INDIVIDUAL GOLD MEDAL IN TWO CONSECUTIVE OLYMPIADS; FIRST HORSE TO COMPETE IN THREE CONSECUTIVE THREE-DAY INDIVIDUAL EVENTS

Charles Mortanges from the Netherlands set a record which has lasted for nearly 50 years when he won the three-day individual equestrian event in two successive Olympic Games, in 1928 and 1932. He competed in the individual events in four Olympiads, finishing fourth in 1924, first in 1928 and first in 1932; he did not place in 1936. He also won gold team medals in 1924 and 1928 and a silver team medal in 1932. Mortanges rode Marcroix for his two individual gold medals and for his unplaced finish in the 1936 Olympics, making the Anglo-Norman palomino the only horse ever to have competed in three successive three-day Olympic events.

FIRST SWIMMER TO WIN THE 200-METER OLYMPIC BREASTSTROKE EVENT TWICE

Japanese swimmer Yoshiyuki Tsuruta was the first and only person ever to win the Olympic 200-meter breaststroke twice. His time in the 1928 Olympics was two minutes, 48.8 seconds, which surpassed the existing Olympic record by a wide margin. He won the event again in 1932, setting another Olympic record with a time of two minutes, 45.4 seconds.

FIRST AMERICAN TO WIN A GOLD MEDAL IN FIGURE SKATING

Dick Button's new approach to figure skating, which combined extraordinary athleticism with elegant choreography, won him the first goal medal ever awarded to a U.S. figure skater in the 1948 Olympics in St. Moritz. In 1952 in Oslo he won his second gold in a free program highlighted by the first real triple loop jump to be used successfully in competition.

FIRST U.S. SKIER TO WIN A GOLD MEDAL

In the 1948 Winter Olympics in St. Moritz, Switzerland, Gretchen Frazier became the first skier from the United States ever to win a gold medal, in the women's slalom. She also won a silver in the alpine combined event. (This was the last time medals were awarded for that event.)

FIRST WOMAN TO WIN FOUR GOLD MEDALS IN TRACK AND FIELD

The greatest number of gold medals ever won by a woman in Olympic track and field competition is four. Two women have accomplished the feat. The first was Francina E. Blankers-Koen of the Netherlands. She won the 100- and 200-meter runs and the 80-meter hurdles at the 1948 summer games in London; she was also a member of the gold medal-winning 400-meter relay team. She was 30 years old and had two children at the time.

The other woman who won four Olympic gold medals in track and field competition was Betty Cuthbert from Australia. She won the 100- and 200-meter runs, and was a member of the winning 400-meter relay team, at the 1956 games in Melbourne; she also won the 400-meter run at the 1964 games in Tokyo.

FIRST U.S. SKIER TO WIN TWO GOLD MEDALS

In the 1952 Winter Olympics in Oslo, Norway, 19-year-old Andrea Mead Lawrence from Vermont won both the giant slalom and the slalom, making her the first American ever to win two gold medals in skiing. She fell once in the first heat of the slalom, but still managed to win the event.

FIRST AMERICAN TO PLAY ON TWO OLYMPIC BASKETBALL TEAMS

Former Oklahoma A & M All-American Bob Kurland was the first American to play on two Olympic basketball teams. After graduating from college in 1946, Kurland rejected several offers from professional teams and went to work for the Phillips Petroleum Company in Bartlesville, Okla. He played for the famous Phillips 66ers Amateur Athletic Union basketball team and thus retained his amateur status. He subsequently became a member of the U.S. basketball team that won a gold medal at the 1948 Summer Olympic Games in London. Kurland was also a member of the U.S. team that won the gold medal at the 1952 games in Helsinki.

Kurland, a member of basketball's Hall of Fame, is considered the first of the great seven-foot players.

FIRST MAN TO DEFEND THE GOLD MEDAL SUCCESSFULLY IN THE DECATHLON

Although Robert B. Mathias from the United States suffered from childhood anemia, he became the youngest athlete ever to win the gold medal in the decathlon at the age of 17. He achieved his first victory in the tiring 10-event competition in 1948 in London, and won again in 1952 in Helsinki.

FIRST AMERICAN WOMAN TO WIN A GOLD MEDAL IN FIGURE SKATING

In the 1956 Winter Olympics in Cortina d'Ampezzo, Italy, Tenley Albright's artistic, rhythmic performance to a Jacques Offenbach medley won her the gold medal in figure skating in a close contest with Carol Heiss, also from the United States. Albright was the first female figure skater from the United States ever to win an Olympic gold medal.

FIRST SKIER TO WIN ALL THREE ALPINE SKIING EVENTS IN ONE OLYMPIAD

The first skier to win all three alpine skiing events in one year's Olympic competition was not Jean-Claude Killy of France in 1968 but Anton Sailer of Austria in 1956. In fact, Sailer won all three events by a greater margin than Killy would 12 years later: 3.5 seconds in the downhill event, 4.0 seconds in the slalom and 6.2 seconds in the giant slalom.

During the four years or so that he was one of the world's top skiers, Sailer turned in beautiful performances at the Lauberhorn Cup competition in Wengen in 1955 and at the World Championship competition in 1958, both of which he won.

The handsome skier later made motion pictures, with only moderate success. In 1972 Sailer became the director of the Austrian alpine ski teams.

FIRST RIDER TO WIN TWO INDIVIDUAL GOLD MEDALS FOR DRESSAGE

Maj. Henri St. Cyr from Sweden became the first and only rider to win two individual Olympic gold medals in dressage by winning both in 1952, in Helsinki, and in 1956, in Melbourne. St. Cyr also contributed to Swedish team victories those same two years, giving him four Olympic gold medals in all.

St. Cyr also took part in individual Olympic events in 1948 and 1960. In addition, he had competed as a member of the Swedish three-day event team in 1936.

A consistently outstanding horseman, Maj. St. Cyr was Swedish National Champion in 1935, 1937 and 1939. He also won the world championship in dressage in 1953.

FIRST DIVER TO WIN BOTH SPRINGBOARD AND PLATFORM DIVING CHAMPIONSHIPS AT TWO CONSECUTIVE OLYMPIADS; FIRST WOMAN TO WIN FOUR GOLD MEDALS IN OLYMPIC SWIMMING COMPETITION

Patricia McCormick from Long Beach, Calif. won the Olympic championships in both springboard diving and platform diving at the 1952 Olympics in Helsinki. In 1956, at the age of 26, she won both championships again—this time just five months after giving birth to a son. At the 1956 games McCormick was in fourth place in the platform diving competition before taking her last two dives. Even the judges applauded her difficult two-and-a-half-somersault dive. She topped that, however, with a flawless one-and-a-half-somersault with a full twist, ending her Olympic career with two of the most perfect dives ever made by a woman.

McCormick's outstanding performance made her the first diver, male or female, ever to win both the springboard and platform diving championships at two consecutive Olympiads. It also made her the first female swimmer to win four Olympic gold medals. Dawn Fraser from Australia and Kornelia Ender from East Germany were later to match McCormick's record by winning four gold medals. McCormick herself became one of the first divers inducted into the U.S. Swimming Hall of Fame.

FIRST GOLD MEDAL WINNER FROM BLACK AFRICA; FIRST MAN TO WIN THE OLYMPIC MARATHON TWICE

In 1960 Abebe Bikila, a member of the Imperial Guard of Emperor Haile Selassie, was unknown outside his native Ethiopia, although he had already run a marathon in an impressive two hours, 21 minutes and 23 seconds. In the Summer Olympics in Rome that year he ran barefoot, easily outdistancing Rhadi Ben Abdesselam, his nearest competitor, becoming the first black African ever to win an Olympic gold medal. Bikila set a world record with his time of two hours, 15 minutes and 16.2 seconds. This was only his third marathon.

Bikila—wearing shoes this time—successfully defended his title in the 1964 Olympics in Tokyo, even though his appendix had been removed only a few weeks earlier. In 1968 Bikila tried for a third gold in the marathon, but had to drop out of the race after ten miles because of an injured leg.

In 1969 Bikila was injured in a traffic accident which left him unable to walk again. Before his death at the age of 41, however, Bikila competed again, this time in sports such as archery.

FIRST AMERICAN WOMAN TO WIN THREE GOLD MEDALS IN TRACK AND FIELD

Six-foot-tall Wilma Rudolph won the 100-meter and 200-meter events and anchored the 400-meter relay team to a win in 1960, becoming the first American woman to win three gold medals in track and field events. The black college student from Tennessee had already won a bronze medal in 1956 in the 400-meter relay. During her career Rudolph set new U.S. and world records in the 100- and 200-meter dashes, both indoors and outdoors.

FIRST TRIPLE JUMPER TO SURPASS THE 17-METER BARRIER

Jozef Schmidt from Poland set a record which remained unsurpassed for eight years when he broke two long-standing psychological barriers in the triple jump—55 feet and 17 meters—in the 1960 Olympics, with a jump of 17.03 meters (55 feet, 10½ inches). Schmidt was also to win the gold medal in the triple jump in 1964; he had already been named European triple jump champion, in 1958, and would be again, in 1962.

FIRST MAN TO WIN THE 110-METER HURDLES TWICE

Lee Q. Calhoun was the first—and so far the only—man to win the Olympic 110-meter hurdle event twice. In 1956 Calhoun defeated his teammate Jack Davis in a race that was so close that the outcome had to be determined by an official photo finish. His winning time was 13.5 seconds. After being suspended for a year by the Amateur Athletic Union for appearing with his wife on a television game show and receiving prizes, Calhoun won a second Olympic gold medal in Rome in 1960, where he set a world high hurdles record in another photo finish. Calhoun's time in 1960 was 13.2 seconds.

FIRST ATHLETE TO WIN FOUR GOLD MEDALS DURING ONE YEAR'S WINTER OLYMPICS

In 1964 in Innsbruck, Austria, Lydia Skoblikova, a 24-year-old Soviet skater, won the 500-, 1000-, 1500- and 3000-meter events, making her the first athlete ever to win four gold medals in a single year's Winter Olympic

Games. Her winning times were as follows: In the 500-meter event, 45 seconds; in the 1000-meter event, one minute, 33.2 seconds; in the 1500-meter event, two minutes, 22.6 seconds; and in the 3000-meter event, five minutes, 14.9 seconds.

FIRST AMERICANS TO WIN MEDALS IN MEN'S ALPINE SKIING

It was not until the 1964 Olympics in Innsbruck that skiers from the United States won medals in men's alpine skiing. Billy Kidd and Jim Heuga finished second and third, respectively, in the slalom for a silver and a bronze. A gold medal continued to elude the Americans.

FIRST MAN TO WIN NINE MEDALS IN CROSS-COUNTRY SKIING

Many regard Sixten Jernberg from Sweden as the best cross-country skier ever. He won a total of three Olympic gold medals in cross-country skiing: the 50-kilometer event in 1956, with a time of two hours, 50 minutes and 27 seconds; the 30-kilometer event in 1960, with a time of one hour, 51 minutes and 3.9 seconds; and the 50-kilometer event in 1964, with a time of two hours, 43 minutes and 52.6 seconds. Jernberg won his last gold just before his 35th birthday. He also won three silver medals and one bronze medal in individual Olympic competition, plus a gold medal and a bronze medal in relay cross-country races.

FIRST RIDER TO WIN TWO INDIVIDUAL GOLD MEDALS FOR SHOW JUMPING

Pierre Jonqueres d'Oriola from France was the first—and so far the only—rider to win two individual gold medals for show jumping in the Olympics. He won in 1952, riding Ali Baba, and in 1964, riding Lutteur B. He also won silver medals in team show jumping in 1964 and 1968.

D'Oriola went on to win the men's world championship in show jumping in 1966, after having placed second in 1953 and third in 1954.

FIRST SWIMMER TO WIN GOLD MEDALS IN THE SAME EVENT IN THREE SUCCESSIVE OLYMPICS

Dawn Fraser from Australia had a slender, boyish figure which was ideal for swimming. She also suffered from bronchial asthma, but that did not deter her from setting 39 world records in swimming. Her performance in the 100-

meter freestyle in the 1956 Olympics broke a 20-year-old world record and won her a gold medal. Her record of one minute, two seconds was bested by her own 59.5-second performance eight years later, a new record which itself stood for eight years. Fraser also won the 100-meter freestyle in 1960, with a time of one minute, 1.2 seconds, and was a member of Australia's winning 400-meter freestyle relay team in 1956. She won silver medals in the 400-meter individual freestyle in 1956, in the 400-meter freestyle relay in 1960 and in the 400-meter medley relay in 1960. Fraser's three gold medals in the 100-meter freestyle made her the first swimmer to win the same event in three consecutive Olympiads.

FIRST SWIMMER TO WIN FOUR GOLD MEDALS IN ONE OLYMPIAD

U.S. swimmer Don Schollander became the first swimmer ever to win four gold medals in one Olympiad in 1964. He was the first American to win so many medals in the Summer Olympics since Jesse Owens in 1936.

Schollander, an 18-year-old blond from Lake Oswego, Ore., who had been accepted as a member of the class of 1968 at Yale, won the 100-meter and 400-meter freestyle races with times of 53.4 seconds and four minutes, 12.2 seconds, respectively. He then swam anchor on the U.S. teams which won the 400-meter and 800-meter freestyle relays.

Schollander helped set a world record in the 400-meter relay; his team's time was three minutes, 33.2 seconds. He also helped set a world record in the 800-meter relay, with a time of seven minutes, 52.1 seconds. And his winning time in the 400-meter event set an individual world record.

FIRST MIDDLE-DISTANCE RUNNER TO WIN THREE INDIVIDUAL OLYMPIC GOLD MEDALS

Although New Zealander Peter Snell did not begin training seriously as a runner until he was 18, he became the first, and so far the only, middle-distance runner to win three individual Olympic gold medals. He won the 800-meter race in 1960, with a time of one minute, 46.3 seconds, and again in 1964, with a time of one minute, 45.1 seconds. Snell also won the 1500-meter event in 1964, with a time of three minutes, 38.1 seconds.

FIRST WOMAN TO WIN NINE GOLD MEDALS

No woman has won more Olympic gold medals than Larisa Latynina of the Soviet Union, who won nine gold medals in gymnastics in three Olympiads. She dominated the sport completely during the 12 years she took part in international competition, taking a total of 24 gold medals in the Olympics and in world and European championship competitions, as well as 15 silver medals and five bronze medals. During her career in international gymnastics she also gave birth to two children, which made her continuing achievements all the more unusual. Latynina was at her best in floor exercises, in which she moved easily from one intricate position to another. Latynina won Olympic gold medals in the individual combined exercises event in 1956 and 1960; in the horse vault in 1956, 1960 and 1964; in floor exercises in 1956, 1960 and 1964; and in the team combined exercises event in 1956, 1960 and 1964.

FIRST WOMAN TO CARRY THE OLYMPIC TORCH; FIRST OLYMPIC GAMES HELD IN LATIN AMERICA

Norma Enriqueta Basilio Satelo became the first woman ever to carry the Olympic torch in 1968. She carried the torch into the Olympic stadium in Mexico City in October 1968 and lit the Olympic flame to open the 1968 summer games. The Mexico City Olympics were the first to be held in Latin America.

FIRST AMERICAN TO WIN A GOLD MEDAL IN SHOW JUMPING

It took William C. Steinkraus four tries to win the first gold medal for the United States in show jumping. Steinkraus first competed in the Olympics in 1952, but it was not until 1968, his fourth Olympics, that he won the gold medal in individual show jumping, riding Snowbound. He also won silver medals in team show jumping in 1960 and 1972 and a bronze medal in team show jumping in 1952.

Steinkraus was the captain of the American show jumping team from 1955 until his retirement in 1972. Under his leadership the team won the President's Cup in 1966 and 1968.

FIRST SWIMMER TO WIN THREE GOLD MEDALS IN INDIVIDUAL EVENTS IN ONE OLYMPIAD

Deborah Meyer from the United States won three gold medals in individual events in the 1968 Olympic Games: the 200-meter freestyle, with a time of two minutes, 10.5 seconds; the 400-meter freestyle, with a time of four minutes, 31.8 seconds; and the 800-meter freestyle, with a time of nine minutes, 24 seconds. Thus she became the first swimmer, male or female, to win three gold medals in individual events in a single Olympiad.

The 1500-meter race, which was not included in the Olympic Games, was one of Meyer's specialties. She set world records in the 1500 four times; her best performance was 17 minutes, 19.9 seconds. In all Meyer set 16 world freestyle records during her career.

FIRST RUNNER TO WIN TWO CONSECUTIVE GOLD MEDALS IN THE 100-METER RACE

Wyomia Tyus won gold medals in the 100-meter race in both 1964 and 1968; she was the first athlete ever to win the race twice in a row. In 1964 Tyus was an unknown who had not even been expected to make the U.S. team; in fact, she placed only third in the Olympic trials. She kept getting better, however, and gained enough momentum to win the gold medal. Tyus won again in 1968 with a time of 11.0 seconds, even better than her 11.2-second time in the 1964 games.

After the 1968 Olympics Tyus retired for five years, but began competing again when the professional International Track Association was formed in 1973.

FIRST MAN TO EXCEED 29 FEET IN THE LONG JUMP

Robert Beamon from Jamaica, N.Y. achieved what may have been the most outstanding single performance of the 1968 Summer Olympics with his long jump of 29 feet, 2½ inches (8.90 meters), which added 21½ inches (55 centimeters) to the previous record, in Mexico City on Oct. 18. Beamon won a gold medal for the jump, which was the best of his amateur career.

FIRST MAN TO WIN GOLD MEDALS IN FOUR CONSECUTIVE OLYMPIADS

Al Oerter from the United States won gold medals in the discus throw in 1956 in Melbourne, in 1960 in Rome, in 1964 in Tokyo and in 1968 in Mexico City. He had not been favored to win any of those times. Before the 1956 Olympics Oerter was an unknown student at the University of Kansas whose personal record was 30 feet short of that of his teammate Fortune Gordien, who held the world record. Yet he won, with a throw of 184 feet, 11 inches. In 1960 another American, Rink Babka, was expected to win, but Oerter beat him by three feet with a toss of 194 feet, two inches. In 1964 Oerter was suffering from a slipped cervical disc and torn cartilage on his rib cage, but he nevertheless threw the discus 200 feet, 1½ inches. He won again in Mexico City in 1968 with a throw of 212 feet, 6½ inches. This made Oerter the first athlete ever to win gold medals in four consecutive Olympiads.

FIRST WINTER OLYMPICS HELD IN ASIA

The Winter Olympics were held in Sapporo, Japan, in 1972; this was the first time the winter games were ever held in Asia. Sapporo was to have been the site of the 1940 games, but they were not held because of World War II. Sapporo, with a population of about one million, was the largest city ever to host the Winter Olympics. The city spent some $40 million for Olympic facilities and $400 million for highways, subways and other improvements. The games were lavish and impressive; the trend since then has been in the direction of simplicity and economy.

FIRST WOMAN TO WIN GOLD MEDALS IN BOTH THE GIANT SLALOM AND THE DOWNHILL

Marie-Therese Nadig from Switzerland won gold medals in both the downhill and the giant slalom ski events in 1972. She was the first female skier ever to do so. Her time in the downhill event was one minute, 36.68 seconds; in the giant slalom, it was one minute, 29.9 seconds.

FIRST SWIMMER TO WIN THE 1500-METER FREESTYLE EVENT AT TWO SUCCESSIVE OLYMPIADS

Michael Burton took up swimming on the advice of his doctors after he was hit by a truck while cycling. Burton had severed tendons under his right knee, and the ball joint of his hip had been forced through his rib cage. Burton did a little more than the limited swimming his doctors had advised to strengthen his leg muscles. In 1968 he set Olympic records in the 1500-meter freestyle and the 400-meter freestyle, winning gold medals in both events. Burton set a total of five world records in the 1500-meter swim during his career. The last record-setting performance came at the 1972 Summer Olympics in Munich, making Burton the first swimmer to win the 1500-meter event at successive games.

FIRST FEMALE SWIMMER TO WIN GOLD MEDALS IN THREE INDIVIDUAL EVENTS WHILE SETTING NEW WORLD RECORDS IN ALL THREE AT ONE OLYMPIAD

In reaction to the Australian Shane Gould's awe-inspiring performance at the 1972 Olympic Games, the U.S. team wore T-shirts that read, "All that glitters is not Gould." It was thought that she might sweep all the women's swimming events. Although that did not happen, Gould did win three gold medals in 1972, setting a world record in each of the three events.

Gould had set her first world record at the age of 14 when she beat Dawn Fraser's 100-meter freestyle record (see also **First Swimmer to Win Gold Medals in the Same Event in Three Successive Olympics**). By 1971 Gould had become the first woman ever to hold the world record in every freestyle category from 100 meters to 1500 meters.

Shane Gould's record-setting times at the 1972 Olympics were as follows: in the 200-meter freestyle event, two minutes, 3.56 seconds; in the 400-meter freestyle event, four minutes, 19.04 seconds; and in the 200-meter individual medley, two minutes, 23.07 seconds.

FIRST MAN TO WIN SEVEN GOLD MEDALS IN A SINGLE OLYMPIAD

Mark Spitz, a swimmer from Carmichael, Calif., won seven gold medals at the 1972 Olympic Games in Munich. He won both the 100-meter and 200-meter butterfly races and both the 100-meter and 200-meter freestyle sprints; he was also on three gold medal-winning relay teams. Spitz was the first athlete ever to win so many golds in one Olympiad. He cashed in on the fame he won with his performance in the Olympics by means of a $1 million product endorsement and television appearance package. Spitz's winning times in Munich were as follows: in the 100-meter butterfly, 54.3 seconds; in the 200-meter butterfly, two minutes, 0.7 seconds; in the 100-meter freestyle, 51.2 seconds; and in the 200-meter freestyle, one minute, 52.8 seconds. Spitz also won gold medals for his participation on the 400-meter and 800-meter freestyle relay teams and the 400-meter medley relay team.

FIRST MAN TO WIN GOLD MEDALS IN WRESTLING AT THREE SUCCESSIVE OLYMPIADS

Aleksandr Medved from the USSR was the first man to win gold medals in wrestling in three successive Olympics. He won in the light heavyweight class in 1964, in the heavyweight class in 1968 and in the super heavyweight class in 1972. Between 1962 and 1972, when he retired, Medved lost only one Olympic or world title, the 1965 world championship, to Ahmer Ayik of Turkey.

FIRST MAN TO RECEIVE A MEDAL 50 YEARS LATE

Anders Haugen from the United States received a bronze medal for the 1924 Nordic combined ski event (cross-country skiing and ski jumping) 50 years late, after a Norwegian sports statistician discovered an error in the computations of the final standings for the event. The medal had originally been awarded to a Norwegian skier, but it was recovered and awarded to Haugen in Oslo in 1974.

FIRST U.S. MEDALIST IN CROSS-COUNTRY SKIING

The first—and so far the only—U.S. medalist in cross-country skiing was Bill Koch, who won a silver medal in the 1976 Olympics for his second-place finish in the 30-kilometer event.

FIRST GYMNAST TO RECEIVE A PERFECT SCORE IN OLYMPIC COMPETITION

A tiny 15-year-old Rumanian girl named Nadia Comaneci stole the Olympic spotlight at the 1976 Summer Olympic Games in Montreal when she was awarded 10.0 points—a perfect score—for her performance on the asymmetrical bars in the team competition. Comaneci was the first gymnast ever to receive a perfect score in the Olympics. She received a score of 10.0 six more times during the games, winning three individual gold medals, in the combined exercises, the asymmetrical bars and the balance beam. She also won a silver medal in the team combined exercises and a bronze medal in the floor exercises.

FIRST BLACKS FROM THE UNITED STATES TO PARTICIPATE IN THE WINTER OLYMPICS

Jeff Gadley and Olympic gold medal winner Willie Davenport became the first blacks from the United States to participate in the Winter Olympics when they were chosen for one of the two four-man bobsled teams representing the United States at the 13th Winter Olympic Games, held in 1980 at Lake Placid, N.Y. The two teams met with little success. Davenport and

Gadley's team finished 12th in the competition; the other U.S. team finished 13th. The poor performance cost Davenport a chance at becoming only the second American ever to win a gold medal at both the summer and winter games (see also **First American to Win Gold Medals at Both Summer and Winter Olympic Games**). Davenport had won a gold medal in the 110-meter high hurdle event at the 1968 summer games in Mexico City. He had also won a bronze medal in the high hurdles at the 1976 summer games in Montreal.

FIRST SISTERS TO QUALIFY FOR THE SAME OLYMPIC EVENT

Eighteen-year-old Sherri Howard and her 15-year-old sister Denean were the first sisters ever to qualify for the same event as members of the U.S. Olympic team. Sherri Howard finished first in the 400-meter freestyle swimming event in the 1980 Olympic trials, while her sister finished third.

The U.S. Summer Olympic team was selected in 1980, but did not actually compete in the Moscow Olympics. The United States boycotted the Moscow games in response to the Soviet invasion of Afghanistan a few months earlier.

Both Howards said that they were disappointed at not being able to compete in the 1980 Olympics. Both also promised that they would be back to try out for the 1984 Olympic team.

17/OTHER SPORTS:

HORSESHOE PITCHING, HURLING, CRICKET, CURLING, MOUNTAIN CLIMBING, CROQUET, LACROSSE, JAI ALAI, BIATHLON AND POLO

HORSESHOE PITCHING

ORIGINS

It seems natural that horseshoe pitching should have originated in a civilization that relied heavily upon horses, which is exactly what happened. Roman soldiers first played the game in their army camps shortly after they began protecting their horses' hooves with iron footwear, around 150 AD Common soldiers and camp followers played horseshoes as a substitute for throwing the discus or playing quoits, pastimes which were popular among officers and members of the nobility. The Roman legions took the game with them when they invaded England, where it remained popular with soldiers even after the Romans' departure.

English settlers and soldiers brought the game to America in colonial days; it became very popular in rural areas of the United States, where horseshoes were readily available. Informal competitions were common at family reunions and country fairs. The first horseshoe club on record was founded in Meadville, Pa. in 1892. Soon after, in 1900, a club was formed in Long Beach, Calif.; it had 600 members.

The first world horseshoe tournament was held in 1909 in Bronson, Kan.

It attracted many players from all over the Midwest. Frank Jackson of Kellerton, Ind., who was probably the best player in the country at that time, won the competition.

FIRST MAN TO MANUFACTURE HORSESHOES ESPECIALLY FOR THE GAME

Fred Brust of Columbus, Ohio became the first man to manufacture horseshoes especially for the game of horseshoes in the 1920s. Brust had won the 1919 world title in horseshoes.

HURLING

ORIGINS

Hurling is an ancient Irish game. It was first played centuries before St. Patrick's time. Hurling often looks dangerous to those who are not familiar with the game, but because players have usually played it since childhood, there are actually few injuries.

In Ireland the game was traditionally played between teams representing two different parishes; the boundary between the parishes served as the starting point for the game. The team that succeeded in taking the ball a specified distance into its own territory was the winner.

In 1884, when the Gaelic Athletic Association was founded in Ireland, rules for hurling were formalized. Goal posts were introduced and the number of players was limited to 17 (several years later the number was reduced to 15).

The competition for the All-Ireland hurling championship has been held yearly since 1887 except for 1888, when the Irish teams were touring the United States.

Irish immigrants brought the game to the United States, where they played it informally long before the Gaelic Athletic Association was formed in New York City in 1914. Hurling, as well as Gaelic football, was particularly popular in the major cities along the eastern seaboard, in Chicago and in San Francisco. It continues to be played in some parts of the United States.

CRICKET

ORIGINS

It is something of an accident that cricket is not the national game of the United States, since it was the national game of the mother country when the colonies were founded. Instead, cricket served, to a considerable extent, as the basis of a new game called baseball. While cricket has always been played in the United States, it never achieved the same popularity it has in England, where it remains the national game to this day.

Claims that cricket grew out of the French game of croquet are generally rejected. While the exact origins and heritage of cricket have never been determined, it is known the game was played widely in England in the 14th century. Historians believe, in fact, that cricket has probably been played since the 12th or 13th centuries.

In the 15th century King Edward IV banned cricket because it was taking too much time away from archery practice. Although it was still illegal, open cricket play ultimately resumed, and in the 18th century an English court declared the game legal, while expressing concern about the common practice of wagering on cricket games.

Modern cricket can trace its heritage to a 1788 meeting of the Marylebone Cricket Club in London, where cricket rules were first standardized. Since then the Marylebone Cricket Club has served as the general arbiter of cricket throughout the world.

The first recorded cricket match played in America took place in 1751 in New York. A New York team beat a London team by a score of 166-130. Cricket remained fairly popular in the United States until the second half of the 19th century, which saw the advent of baseball. Early baseball players wore uniforms similar to those worn by cricket players. The first manager of the first professional baseball team, Harry Wright of the Cincinnati Red Stockings, had been a professional cricket player.

Today, however, only a handful of states have a sufficient number of cricket players for organized competition.

FIRST INTERNATIONAL CRICKET MATCH HELD IN THE UNITED STATES

The first international cricket match in the United States was held on Oct. 3, 1859 in Hoboken, N.J. between an All-England team and a team from St. George's Cricket Club of New York. The English team won, to no one's surprise.

CURLING

ORIGINS

Curling has been described by non-players as lawn bowling on ice. It was invented in Scotland, probably one cold winter when work had come to a standstill because of the weather and there was nothing else to do. Someone threw a stone on the ice of a frozen river and it slid along quickly and smoothly. Others began to imitate, and a new sport was born. The first written mention of curling did not appear until after 1600, although according to tradition James IV of Scotland (1475-1513) ordered a silver curling stone as a prize for which curlers were to compete annually.

The Scots eventually introduced curling to the New World. Soldiers in a Scottish regiment stationed in Quebec City around 1760 are known to have played curling. The first curling club in the Americas was formed in Quebec in 1821. The first recorded games of curling in the United States took place during the winter of 1831-32 in Detroit, where the Orchard Lake Club played the game using weighted blocks of hickory wood. The first international curling competition was held in 1865 between teams representing the United States and Canada in Buffalo. The Canadian team won.

MOUNTAIN CLIMBING

FIRST RECORDED MOUNTAIN CLIMB

In 1492 Charles VIII of France ordered his chamberlain, Dompjulian de Beaupre, captain of Montelimar and Sou, to climb a mountain near Grenoble that was then called Mt. Inaccessible. The chamberlain succeeded and led more than 10 other people, including several priests, to the top. The party found only a herd of chamois at the top, where they remained for three days. The mountain was not scaled again for some 350 years.

FIRST CLIMB OF THE MATTERHORN

Edward Whymper first tried to climb the Matterhorn in 1861, but it was not until his eighth attempt, in 1865, that he reached the top. During the descent four members of Whymper's party fell to their deaths: one Englishman fell, and took the others with him when the rope broke. Rumors spread that Whymper and the other guides had cut the rope to save themselves, but nothing of the sort was ever proven.

FIRST CLIMB OF MT. EVEREST

Edmund Percival Hillary and Tenzing Norgay became the first men ever to reach the summit of the world's tallest mountain, the 29,028-foot Mt. Everest, on May 29, 1953. The first woman to climb Mt. Everest was Junko Tabei of Japan, who reached the top on May 17, 1975 after a one-month climb.

CROQUET

ORIGINS

Croquet is a descendant of pall-mall, a game which was transported to England from Italy by way of France in the 17th century, during the reign of Charles II. Pall-mall involved driving a ball (*palla*) with a mallet (*maglio*) through raised iron rings or hoops along an alley. The London street where pall-mall was played came to be called Pall Mall in honor of the game; the name survives even if the game does not.

In 1868 an Englishman named Walter James Whitmore organized the first formal croquet competition, which was held at Moreton on Marsh, England. Whitmore won the competition himself, and thus became the world's first croquet open champion.

In 1870 the All England Croquet Club bought four acres of grassy land at Wimbledon and laid out croquet courts. A few years later, however, the game of lawn tennis had so surpassed croquet in popularity that the club decided to allow one of its courts to be used for the new game of tennis. The club then became the All-England Croquet and Lawn Tennis Club; by five years later it was devoted entirely to tennis.

The National Croquet League was formed in the United States in 1880. George Washington Johnson of the Lemon Hill Club was its first president.

Organized croquet continues to be played in various forms, but the game is most popular at garden parties and family reunions.

FIRST OUTDOOR GAME PLAYED BY WOMEN

During the Civil War croquet was imported to the United States from England and became something of a craze. According to sports historian John Durant, croquet was probably both the first outdoor game played by women and the first game in which men and women played together on an equal basis.

The first women's championship was held in England in 1869. One Mrs. Joad won the competition.

FIRST CROQUET CLUB IN THE UNITED STATES

The first croquet club in the United States, the Park Place Croquet Club of Brooklyn, N.Y., was formed in 1864 with 25 members. Like most people at the time, the club's members played croquet as a pastime, not as a game of skill.

LACROSSE

ORIGINS

Lacrosse is one of the few games whose roots are entirely in North American soil. One day in 1705 Canadian Algonquin Indians were playing a game called *baggataway*; a French cleric named Pierre de Charlevoix watched. De Charlevoix called the webbed stick the Indians used in playing the game *la crosse* because it reminded him of a bishop's crosier. Eventually the French settlers in Canada took up the Indian's game, but called it lacrosse rather than *baggataway*.

The Indians may well have been playing *baggataway* for centuries before the French discovered their game. The Indians' game plan called for injuring as many of the opposing players as possible with "accidental" swings of the stick. Once several of the opposing players had been injured and put out of action, it was obviously much easier to win.

The game continued to increase in popularity in Canada through the middle of the 19th century. The Canadian parliament eventually declared lacrosse the national game.

It was only natural that the game should spread into the United States from its northern neighbor. A number of lacrosse clubs were formed in the New York-Pennsylvania area in the 1870s. New York University formed the first American college lacrosse team in 1877, with Harvard following in 1881 and Princeton in 1882. Harvard, Columbia and Princeton formed the Intercollegiate Lacrosse Association in 1882; New York University and Yale became members the next year. Harvard was the first intercollegiate champion, in the 1881-1882 season.

The Wilson Wingate Trophy honoring the national collegiate championship lacrosse team was established in 1936. The University of Maryland was the first winner of the Wingate Trophy.

JAI ALAI

ORIGINS

In Basque *jai alai* means "a jolly feast." It is one of the fastest and most vigorous sports in existence. Jai alai is the national sport of the Basque people, who often play it at celebrations; hence its name.

Jai alai probably originated among the Basques and then spread to the rest of Spain, southern France and, eventually, much of the rest of the world. A few sports historians, however, believe that the game was invented by the Mayas and Aztecs of Central America and was carried back to Spain by the

Spanish explorers. Jai alai was introduced to the United States during the 1904 World's Fair in St. Louis.

Originally jai alai players used their bare hands to throw and catch the ball, but the ball traveled with such speed that it was painful to catch. So a booster device, used both to protect the hands and to permit throwing the ball at even greater speeds, was introduced. After several experiments the wicker basket, the cesta, was introduced; it changed the character of the game. Instead of batting the ball, the players could use the cesta to throw and catch it.

Betting has often been associated with jai alai. Bets are made as the game progresses; the odds continuously change along with the score.

BIATHLON

ORIGINS

Biathlon is a combination of skiing and rifle shooting that originated in the Scandinavian countries as a survival skill. It was often necessary for a man to be able to ski and shoot well at the same time in order to catch game to eat. Biathlon was also a military skill; Finnish troops trained in biathlon were remarkably successful against superior Soviet troops during the Russo-Finnish War before World War II.

Biathlon competitions have long been popular in Europe, but have only taken place in the United States in an organized form since the 1950s. In 1960 competition was added to the Olympic games. Klas Lestander of Sweden won the gold medal that year. Since that time the standard biathlon event has required each competitor to ski 20 kilometers, stopping four times during the race to fire shots into a target. Each competitor's score is based upon the elapsed time of the ski run, with time deducted for each missed shot.

POLO

ORIGINS

The word polo is a mispronounciation of "pulu," a Tibetan word meaning "ball." This name for the English version of hockey on horseback probably originated when British army officers watched a display of fancy riding in India in the early 1860s which included a game that required players to hit a ball with a stick while riding at a gallop. The ball used by the Indians was probably called a pulu; hence the name of the game. The British took up the game, added goal posts and lines, and called the game polo. It was then taken back to England by troops who had been stationed in India. By 1873 the first code of rules had been published by the Hurlingham Club in London, the headquarters for polo in the British Empire.

Polo was introduced into the United States by James Gordon Bennett in 1876. He imported ponies from Texas and staged the first match in the United States at Dickel's Riding Academy on Fifth Avenue in New York.

FIRST WESTCHESTER CUP MATCH

Americans had been playing polo only since the late 1870s, so in 1886 the British didn't believe that Americans could play the very British sport very well. Griswold Lorillard, the American tobacco magnate, was visiting the Hurlingham clubhouse in Fulham, near London; he mentioned to the assembled British that some Americans played polo rather well. The British, who could not resist such a chance to demonstrate their superiority in the sport, agreed to a match between the Hurlingham club and the Westchester Polo Club, one of America's best clubs.

The match took place in Newport, R.I. on Wednesday, Aug. 25, 1886. Thomas Hitchcock was the captain of the American team; John Watson, of the British. After taking an early lead the Americans lost the first game 10-4. They also lost the second game in the best-of-three competition the next day by a score of 14-2. Hurlingham took home the $1000 cup awarded to the winner, which has since come to be known as the Westchester Cup. British and American teams continued to compete for the Westchester Cup on an irregular basis through 1939.

FIRST 10-GOAL RATED POLO PLAYER IN THE UNITED STATES

Foxhall P. Keene was the first 10-goal rated polo player in the United States. Up to the present only about 40 polo players have ever received a 10-goal rating, or handicap. He won the 10-goal rating 14 times between 1891 and 1920. Keene was a member of the U.S. polo teams that competed in the Westchester Cup matches against Great Britain in 1886 and 1902.

FIRST U.S. POLO TEAM TO WIN THE WESTCHESTER CUP

The first American polo team to win the Westchester Cup was composed of Devereux Milburn, Harry Payne Whitney, Monty Waterbury and Larry Waterbury, who beat the British at Hurlingham in 1909. The Americans used a hard-hitting, rough-riding style devised mainly by Milburn—who is himself considered the first polo player who could hit as well with his backhand as with his forehand—which the British criticized as being too rough. The Americans' tactics have, however, since been adopted by polo teams everywhere the game is played.

18/OTHER FIRSTS

INVENTION OF THE YO-YO

The ancient Greeks had Yo-Yos; so did 17th-century French nobles, although they didn't call them by that name ("Yo-Yo" is, in fact, a trademark). Yo-Yos have seen intermittent popularity through the ages, periodically encouraged by the introduction of a slightly different style or a different name.

American toy maker Thomas Duncan brought Yo-Yos to their first great popularity in the United States in 1929. Duncan called them Yo-Yos because young Filipinos, whom Duncan had seen playing with similar toys, shouted "yo-yo," which translates into English as "come-come."

Demand for the Yo-Yos fluctuates over the years. But in 1961, a banner year, Duncan sold 15 million Yo-Yos.

FIRST RECORDED GAME IN THE ENGLISH AMERICAN COLONIES

The first recorded game in the English American colonies was a game of "bowles"—an early form of bowling—played in the streets of Jamestown, Virginia, which was witnessed and recorded by Sir Thomas Dale in May 1611. Sir Thomas was not at all pleased to see the settlers playing because he had been sent by ship from England to rescue the supposedly starving group. But they were playing bowles so intently when he arrived that they did not even notice his presence.

FIRST SILVER TROPHY DONATED IN NORTH AMERICA

On March 25, 1667 a silver trophy was awarded to Capt. Sylvester Salisbury, a British army officer, for a horse race run on Hansted Plains (later Hempstead), Long Island. The award, presented by the first British governor of New York, Richard Nicolls, was a porringer of solid silver bearing the initials P.V.B. The trophy is believed to be the oldest piece of silver in existence that was created in what is now the United States. The piece may have been made by silversmith Peter Van Brough, which would explain the initials. It is now part of the Mabel Brady Gowan Collection at Yale University. (See also Chapter 5, "Racing," **Origins**, in the section on "Horse Racing.")

FIRST FILM OF A SPORTING EVENT

Thomas Edison made the first film of a sporting event, a fight between Mike Leonard and Jack Cushing which took place in Edison's West Orange, N.J. laboratory on June 14, 1894. Edison had the men fight in a ring 12 feet square so that the stationary camera could catch all the action. The film's scenario called for the two to go a sufficient number of rounds to make the film interesting enough to be profitable, and then for Leonard to knock out Cushing.

The film was shown at a Kinetoscope parlor some two months later. The admission charge was ten cents per round.

FIRST AMERICAN WOMAN TO WIN THE WORLD TROPHY

In 1898 a tennis player named Juliette P. Atkinson became the first American to win the World Trophy, an athletic trophy which is awarded yearly by the Citizens Savings Athletic Foundation (originally the Helms Athletic

Foundation), located in metropolitan Los Angeles, for six different areas of the world: Africa, Asia, Australasia, Europe, North America and South America and the Caribbean.

FIRST TIME THE NATIONAL ANTHEM WAS PLAYED BEFORE AN ATHLETIC EVENT

The custom of playing the National Anthem before sporting events in the United States began in 1918. During the opening game of that year's World Series, with Boston, of the American League, playing at Chicago, of the National League, as the fans stood up for the seventh-inning stretch, the band suddenly began playing "The Star-Spangled Banner." The fans began to sing along. The anthem was also played during the seventh-inning stretch in the following two games in Chicago. It became the custom afterwards to play the National Anthem on the opening day of the baseball season, at World Series games and on occasional special days when there happened to be a band on hand.

The playing of the National Anthem before all major league baseball games and other sporting events did not catch on, however, until World War II.

FIRST COMMERCIAL ENDORSEMENT BY AN ATHLETE

No professional athlete's career would be complete these days without at least a few product endorsements. Today professional athletes from all sports can be seen in newspapers and magazines and on radio and television, testifying to the worth of such products as automobiles, cameras, fur coats, breakfast cereals, various brands of gasoline, even coffee makers. An amateur who wins gold medals in the Olympic Games can turn his or her medals into a veritable gold mine through product endorsements.

A players' agent and manager in the 1920s, C.C. Pyle, can probably be credited with popularizing endorsements by athletes, if not with originating the idea. Pyle, whose initials stood, some thought, for "Cash and Carry," managed football legend Red Grange during the 1920s. Pyle had Grange endorsing such products as hats, sweaters and shoes, a few dolls and a soft drink. Grange, of course, got a fee—and Pyle, a percentage. Pyle even arranged for Grange to endorse a cigarette, but a problem arose: Grange didn't smoke. Legend has it that Pyle said Grange would have been the perfect football player if only he could have learned how to inhale.

FIRST ALL-AMERICAN IN BOTH FOOTBALL AND BASKETBALL

Only five athletes ever have been named All-Americans in both football and basketball. Benny Oosterbann of the University of Michigan was the first. He was named an All-American in football in 1925 and 1927 and in basketball in 1927 and 1928.

THE JAMES E. SULLIVAN MEMORIAL TROPHY

ORIGINS

The James E. Sullivan Memorial Trophy was established by the Amateur Athletic Union in 1930 for the amateur athlete who, by his or her performance, example and good influence, did the most to advance the cause of good sportsmanship during each year. The winner is chosen by sports authorities nationwide; the winner does not have to participate in a sport under AAU control. The trophy was named for James E. Sullivan of New York. Sullivan became secretary-treasurer of the AAU soon after its formation; he was elected its president in 1906, and served three consecutive terms. In 1909 he was once again elected secretary-treasurer; he served in that capacity until his death in 1914.

The Sullivan Trophy was awarded for the first time in 1930 to golf legend Robert T. Jones, Jr., known more familiarly as Bobby Jones. Jones won his first golf title at the age of 9 in 1911; he went on to dominate the world golf scene for 20 years. To climax his career, in 1930 Jones won golf's grand slam: the British Amateur, the British Open, the USGA Open and the USGA Amateur. That feat had never been accomplished before and never has since. Jones, who was 28 in 1930, also won both Walker Cup matches that year.

FIRST WOMAN TO WIN THE SULLIVAN AWARD

One of the greatest female swimmers of all time, Ann Curtis, became the first woman to win the James E. Sullivan Memorial Trophy at the age of 18 in 1944. Curtis had won eight national titles in two years of competition and had captured highest total point honors in the three national meets in which she had competed. At the 1944 National Outdoor Swimming Championships for Women, Curtis won every freestyle event: the 100-meter, 400-meter, 800-meter and 1500-meter races. In 1944 Curtis, from San Francisco, Calif., held 18 American swimming records; she had set world records for the 800-meter and 880-yard events.

FIRST BLACK TO WIN THE SULLIVAN AWARD

Malvin G. Whitfield, a two-time Olympic gold medal winner, became the first black to win the James E. Sullivan Memorial Trophy in 1954. Whitfield, a middle-distance runner, won the gold medal in the 800-meter run at both the 1948 Olympic Games in London and the 1952 games in Helsinki. He won both races with times of one minute, 49.2 seconds, setting an Olympic record. Whitfield also held the world record for the 880-yard run with a time of one minute, 48.6 seconds. Prior to winning the Sullivan award, Whitfield had also won eight U.S. indoor and outdoor championships at distances ranging from 400 meters to 1000 yards.

FIRST BLACK WOMAN TO WIN THE SULLIVAN AWARD

In 1961 Wilma Rudolph was awarded the James E. Sullivan Award as the year's top amateur athlete. She was the first black woman to win the award. Rudolph had been one of the stars of the 1960 Olympics, winning gold medals in three track and field events: the 100-meter race, the 200-meter race and the 400-meter relay.

FIRST USE OF METRIC SYSTEM BY THE AMATEUR ATHLETIC UNION FOR OUTDOOR MEETS

English-speaking countries have traditionally used yards, feet and inches for measurements in athletic events, while other countries and the Olympics have used the metric system. In 1931 the AAU began using the metric system for measuring distances in outdoor meets, but continued to use yards in measuring indoor events. In 1932 the Intercollegiate AAAA also began to use the metric system, but the National Collegiate Athletic Association continued to use yards, feet and inches.

FIRST ATHLETE TO BECOME A BROADCASTER

Nearly every radio and television broadcast of an athletic event today, ranging from billiards to the World Series, features a retired athlete who once was a participant in that particular sport. The former athlete may be either the play-by-play man or the "color man" who, the broadcasters hope, will provide a degree of insight into the event being broadcast.

The first athlete to become a broadcaster was Jack Graney, a journeyman outfielder whose career spanned 14 years and 1400 games, all with the Cleveland Indians. Graney, a lifetime .250 hitter, began broadcasting Indian games in 1932 and continued through the Indians' pennant-winning season in 1954. Graney died in 1978 at the age of 91.

FIRST SPORTSWRITER TO WIN A PULITZER PRIZE

William H. Taylor was the first sportswriter to win a Pulitzer Prize, for his coverage of the America's Cup races in 1934 while he was the yachting editor of the New York *Herald-Tribune*.

FIRST SPORTS SAINT

Probably the first patron saint of a sport was a woman named Lidwina, who was named the patron saint of skating by the Catholic Church in 1944. According to legend, in 1396 Lidwina, a young Scandinavian girl, went ice skating with friends, fell and broke a rib. While recovering Lidwina caught a disease which lasted the rest of her life. She began, however, to perform miracles and to have religious visions.

ORIGINS OF THE FRISBEE

According to legend the Frisbee originated at Yale University in New Haven, Conn., just after World War II, when students there started throwing empty pie plates from the nearby Frisbie Bakery back and forth. A shout of "Frisbee" was frequently heard, the story goes, if someone stepped into the path of a spinning pie plate.

Angeles building inspector named Morrison saw some children playing it in the early 1950s. Morrison came up with the idea of making the plates out of plastic rather than using pie tins. He convinced the Wham-O manufacturing company to market a plastic version. The first version was called the Pluto Platter; later it became the Wham-O Flying Saucer with the patented ridge pattern.

By whatever name, the game took off in popularity; it has, however, usually been called Frisbee (although "Frisbee," like "Yo-Yo," is a trademark).

ORIGINS OF THE PAN AMERICAN GAMES

The Pan American Games were first proposed prior to World War II. They were intended to foster better relations among the countries of the Western Hemisphere and to provide additional international competition for amateur athletes from these countries between Olympiads. The Argentine Olympic Committee, taking the initiative, called a meeting of all countries in the Western Hemisphere at Buenos Aires in 1940. With 16 of the 21 member countries of the Pan American Union in attendance, the decision was made to hold the first Pan American games in 1942. World War II, however, intervened, and the games were not held. The next scheduled games, in 1946, were also cancelled because the world situation remained unstable after the war. A 1950 date was later tentatively agreed upon, but it, too, was rejected in order to avoid a potential conflict with other established athletic competitions. During the 1948 Olympic Games in London, a second meeting of the Pan American Congress was held. Those in attendance decided to hold the first Pan American Games February 25-March 8, 1951 in Buenos Aires. The Argentine Olympic Committee was assigned the responsibility of organizing the games.

Some 100,000 people attended the opening day ceremonies as a Greek athlete, carrying a torch lighted at Mount Olympus, transferred the flame to the Pan American torch. After the Argentine team repeated the Olympic Oath, on behalf of all the participating athletes, Argentine Pres. Juan D. Peron declared the games opened and the Olympic flag was raised over the stadium.

Since 1951 the Pan American Games have been held every fourth year, in the odd-numbered years immediately preceding the Olympic years. The games have been held in the United States only once: They were held in Chicago in 1959.

FIRST WOMAN BULL FIGHTER
FROM THE UNITED STATES

The first woman bull fighter from the United States was Patricia Mc-Cormick, who made her professional debut on Jan. 20, 1952 at Ciudad Juarez, Mexico.

FIRST REVERSAL OF AN ANNOUNCED
DECISION IN A MAJOR RACE
BECAUSE OF A PHOTOGRAPH

In 1952 in the New York Athletic Club Games in Madison Square Garden, the Baxter Mile race ended in what appeared a dead heat between Don Gehrmann and Fred Wilt. Gehrmann was first declared the winner, but analysis of a photograph taken of the finish resulted in Wilt's being declared the winner 40 minutes later. As a result of that race and decision the Amateur Athletic Union ruled that if a photographic device is properly used at the finish of a race, the chief judge can decide to withhold the announcement of the winner until after the photograph has been carefully examined.

FIRST $100,000 PER YEAR SALARY

Sports salaries, some of which now approach—or surpass—the $1,000,000 per year mark, did not reach the six-figure bracket (i.e., $100,000) until 1953. Joe DiMaggio of the New York Yankees became baseball's first $100,000 a year man, and probably the first in professional sports, in 1949, his 11th season with the Yanks.

Other athletes who were the first to reach the $100,000 per year mark in their sports were Johnny Unitas in football, Wilt Chamberlain in basketball and Bobby Orr in hockey.

FIRST STATE TO HAVE
AN OFFICIAL STATE SPORT

In 1962 jousting was established as Maryland's state sport when a bill passed by the state legislature was signed into law by Gov. J. Millard Tawes. Championship jousts are held in Baltimore in early October each year.

BIBLIOGRAPHY

Andrews, Ron, ed. *1979-80 National Hockey League Guide*. n.p., 1979.

Associated Press, The. *The Official Associated Press Sports Almanac*. New York: Alpine Book Co., Inc., 1978.

Berkow, Ira. *Beyond the Dream*. New York: Atheneum, 1975.

Brown, Gene, ed. *The New York Times Encyclopedia of Sports*. New York: Arno Press, 1979.

Burton, Robin. *Sailing the Great Races*. Secaucus, N.J.: Chartwell Books, Inc., 1979.

Campbell, Gail. *Marathon: The World of the Long Distance Athlete*. New York: Sterling Publishing Co., Inc., 1977.

Clerici, Gianni. *The Ultimate Tennis Book*. Translated by Richard J. Wiezell, Ph.D. Chicago: Follett Publishing Co., 1975.

Flower, Raymond. *The History of Skiing and Other Winter Sports*. New York: Methuen Inc., 1976.

Gipe, George, *The Great American Sports Book*. Garden City, N.Y.: Doubleday & Co., Inc., 1978.

Hickok, Ralph. *Who Was Who in American Sports*. New York: Hawthorn Books, 1971.

Hollander, Zander and Bock, Hal, eds. *The Complete Encyclopedia of Ice Hockey*. Rev. ed. Englewood Cliffs, N.J.: Prentice-Hall, Inc., 1974.

Hollander, Zander, ed. *The Modern Encyclopedia of Basketball*. 2d rev. ed. Garden City, N.Y.: Doubleday & Co., Inc., 1979.

Killanin, Lord and Rodda, John, eds. *The Olympic Games 1980: Moscow & Lake Placid*. New York: Macmillan Publishing Co., Inc., 1979.

Krout, John A. *Annals of American Sport*. The Pageant of America, edited by Ralph Henry Gabriel, vol. 15. New Haven: Yale University Press, 1929.

McCormack, Mark H. *The Wonderful World of Professional Golf*. New York: Atheneum, 1973.

McWhirter, Norris. *Guinness Book of Women's Sports Records*. New York: Sterling Publishing Co., Inc., 1979.

McWhirter, Norris. *Guinness Sports Record Book, 1978-1979*. 6th ed. New York: Sterling Publishing Co., Inc., 1978.

Menke, Frank. *All-Sports Record Book*. New York: A.S. Barnes & Co., Inc., 1950.

Menke, Frank. *The Encyclopedia of Sports*. 6th rev. ed. Revisions by Suzanne Treat. Garden City, N.Y.: Doubleday & Co., Inc., 1977.

Michener, James A. *Sports in America*. New York: Random House, Inc., 1976.

Phillips, Louis and Markoe, Karen Ian. *Women in Sports: Records, Stars, Feats, & Facts*. New York: Harcourt Brace Jovanovich, Inc., 1979.

Pratt, John Lowell and Benagh, Jim. *The Official Encyclopedia of Sports*. New York: F. Watts, Inc., 1964.

Reichler, Joseph L., ed. *The Baseball Encyclopedia*. 4th ed., revised and expanded. New York: Macmillan Publishing Co., Inc., 1979.

Rote, Kyle, Jr., with Kane, Basil. *Kyle Rote, Jr.'s Complete Book of Soccer*. New York: Simon & Schuster, 1978.

Schaap, Dick. *An Illustrated History of the Olympics*. 3d enlarged ed. New York: Alfred A. Knopf, Inc., 1975.

Silverman, Al. *More Sports Titans of the 20th Century*. New York: G.P. Putnam's Sons, 1969.

Sporting News, The. *The Sporting News 1978 Official Baseball Record Book*. St. Louis: Sporting News Publishing Co., 1978.

Sports Illustrated. *Yesterday in Sports*. New York: A.S. Barnes & Co., Inc., 1956.

Suehsdorf, Adie. *The Great American Baseball Scrapbook*. New York: Random House, Inc., 1978.

Treat, Roger. *The Encyclopedia of Football*. 16th rev. ed. Edited by Pete Palmer. Garden City, N.Y.: Doubleday & Co., Inc., 1979.

Turkin, Hy and Thompson, S.C. *The Official Encyclopedia of Baseball*. 10th rev. ed. Revisions by Pete Palmer. New York: A.S. Barnes & Co., Inc., 1979.

Twombly, Wells. *200 Years of Sport in America*. New York: McGraw-Hill Book Co., 1976.

Umminger, Walter. *Supermen, Heroes, and Gods*. Translated and adapted by James Clark. New York: McGraw-Hill Book Co., 1963.

Vecsey, George. *The Way It Was: Great Sports Events from the Past*. New York: McGraw-Hill Book Co., 1976.

Yee, Min S. *The Sports Book*. New York: Holt, Rinehart & Winston, 1975.

INDEX

J

S

SABRES (Buffalo ice hockey team)—66
SAILER, Anton—213
St. ANDREWS Golf Club—98
St. CYR, Maj. Henri—213, 214
St. FRANCIS College (Loretto, Pa.)—58
St. GEORGE'S Cricket Club—226
St. LEGER, Col.—73
St. LOUIS, Mo.—60; *See also BROWNS, CARDINALS, REDS*
SALAUN, Henri—119
SALISBURY, Capt. Sylvester—73, 234
SAMPSON (race horse)—73
SAMUELSON, Frank—127
SAMUELSON, Ralph W.—138
SANDS, Charles—99
SAPERSTEIN, Abe—56
SAPORTAS, F. C.—155
SARNOFF, David—172
SARRON, Petey—173
SAUCIER, Frank—27
SAUER, M.—137
SAUNDERS, Charles—111
SAUNDERS, Nell—168
SAWCHUK, Terry—70
SAWICKI, M.—161
SAXON, Arthur—196
SCHAFER, Karl—145
SCHMIDT, Jozef—215
SCHNEIDER Trophy—187
SCHOLLANDER, Don—125, 217
SCHULTE, Frank—16
SCHUMANN, Karl—164
SCHUYLER, M. Roosevelt—133
SCOTT, Blanche—186
SCOTT, Norman N.—144
SCOTT Frost (race horse)—77
SCULLING—208
SEALS (Oakland ice hockey team)—70
SEARS, Eleanora—119
SEARS, Richard D.—110
SEATTLE Slew (race horse)—82
SELVY, Frank—60
SENATORS (Ottawa ice hockey team)—66
SENATORS (Washington, D.C. baseball team)—14-15, 17, 22, 27
SESSIONS, Sally—104
SHAKRAI, Sergei—146
SHEA, Frank J.—156
SHELBY, Ohio—40
SHIELDS, Don—57
SHOEMAKER, Willie—78

SHORE, Eddie—68
SHOT Put—153-154
SHROTH, Frances C.—208
SHUTTLEWORTH, Pamela—107
SIEBERT, Albert "Babe"—68
SIEVERS, Roy—26
SIMBURG, Wyomia Tyus—*see TYUS, Wyomia*
SIMON, Dick—95
SIMPSON, O. J.—52
SIR Barton (race horse)—78
SIR Henry (race horse)—75
SISLER, George—16
SITES, Sharon—133
SKEET Shooting—162-163
SKIING—141-143, 211-213, 216, 220, 222
SKRDLANT, Zdenek—134
SKY DIVING—184-185
SLOCUM, Joshua—132
SLOSSON, George—196
SLOWE, Lucy—112
SMITH, Bill—70-71
SMITH, Billy—169
SMITH, Ed—44
SMITH, Elmer—18
SMITH, Horton—102
SMITH, James—192
SMITH, Karin—158
SMITH, Marilynn—104
SMITH, Owen P.—83
SMITH, Robyn—75
SMITH, Steve—157
SMITH, Zoe G.—117
SMITH College (Northampton, Mass.)—64
SNELL, Peter—217
SNODGRASS, Harvey—113
SOCCER—176-182
SOMERSETS (Boston baseball team)—8
SOUTH Carolina University (Columbia)—39
SOUTHERN Association—21
SOUTHWEST Conference—54
SPAGHETTI Bowl—47
SPALDING, A. G.—22
SPARTANS (Portsmouth football team)—44
SPEAKER, Tris—23
SPEED Skating—145
SPELTERINA, Maria—139
SPIDERS (Cleveland baseball team)—11
SPITZ, Mark—221
SPORK, Shirley—104

TULSA (Okla.), University of—48
TYLER, Albert C.—203
TYNG, James—4
TYUS, Wyomia—157, 219

U

UBER, H. S.—117
UELSES, John—154
UNGARD, Ed—24
UNION League—8
UNIQUES (Chicago baseball team)—7
UNITAS, Johnny—50, 240
UNITED Bowmen of Philadelphia—160
UNITED Soccer Association—181, 182
UNITED States Field Hockey Association—
64
UNITED States Football Association—178
UNITED States Golf Association—99-100,
103
UNITED States Professional Lawn Tennis
Association—113
UNITED States Soccer Federation—178
UNITED States Soccer Football Association
—182
UTAH State University (Logan)—57

V

Van BROUGH, Peter—73, 234
Van BUREN, Adelina—96
Van BUREN, Augusta—96
VANCE, Dazzy—16, 21
VANDERBILT, William K.—89-90
VANDERBILT Cup Race—89-90
VanderMEER, Johnny—23
Van PRAGG, Lionel—97
VARDON, Harry—103
VARE, Glenna Collett—105
VARNER, Margaret—117
VASSAR College (Poughkeepsie, N.Y.)
—67-68
VAUGHN, Hippo—17
VAUS, C. Bowyer—134
VEECK, Bill—13, 27
VENTURI, Ken—105
VEZINA, George—66
VEZINA Trophy—66
VILLANOVA University (Philadelphia,
Pa.)—57
VOGEL Jr., Bill—137
VOLLSTEDT, Rolla—94
VOSS, Carl—67

W

WADDELL, Rube—39
WADDY-Rossow, Debra—61
WAGNER, Honus—14, 23
WAITE, Charles G.—4
WAKE Forest University (Winston-Salem,
N.C.)—39, 57
WALCOTT, Joe—169
WALCOTT, "Jersey" Joe—174
WALKER, George H.—101
WALKER, John—152
WALKER, Moses Fleetwood—10, 12
WALKER, Welday Wilberforce—12
WALKING and Running—149-153, 210,
217, 219, 221
WALLACE, Nunce—168
WALSH, J. W.—109
WALSH, Stella—157
WALZ, Allen "Skip"—46
WAMBSGANSS, William—18-19
WARD, Arch—21, 173
WARD, Holcombe—111
WARHOP, Jack—17
WARNER, Ed—59
WARNER, Pop—41
WASHINGTON, D.C.—6, 11; see also
REDSKINS, SENATORS
WASHINGTON (Pa.) and Jefferson
University—40, 45
WASHINGTON State University
(Pullman)—38
WATERBURY, Larry—231
WATERBURY, Monty—231
WATERFIELD, Bob—49
WATER Polo—135
WATER Skiing—138
WATSON, John—231
WATSON, Maud—110
WATSON, Ray—156
WAYNE State College (Detroit, Mich.)
—46
WEAVER, George "Buck"—18
WEBB, Matthew—123
WEIGHT Lifting—196-197
WEIR, Ike—168
WEISSMULLER, Johnny—124
WELD, Theresa—144
WELLESLEY (Mass.) College—64
WESLEY, Maj. John—127
WESTCHESTER Cup—231
WESTCHESTER Field Hockey Club—
63-64